REMNANT AND REPUBLIC

Adventist Themes for Personal and Social Ethics

REMNANT AND REPUBLIC

Adventist Themes for Personal and Social Ethics

Edited by Charles W. Teel, Jr.

Introduction by Martin E. Marty

Loma Linda University
CENTER FOR CHRISTIAN BIOETHICS

Remnant and Republic: Adventist Themes for Personal and Social Ethics
Copyright 1995 by Loma Linda University Center for Christian Bioethics

Center for Christian Bioethics
Loma Linda University
Loma Linda, CA 92350
TEL: (909) 824-4956
FAX: (909) 825-4856

Cover design: Kelly Herr-Roadruck
Typesetting and Page Design: Amy Timmons
Associate Editors: Gary Chartier, Gayle Foster, Phil Nist, Amy Timmons
Copy Editors: Kathy Ching, Nancy Yuen

Printed in the United States of America

Library of Congress Cataloging-in-Publication Data

Remnant and Republic: Adventist Themes for Personal and Social Ethics
Edited by Charles W. Teel, Jr.
Includes bibliographical references and index.
ISBN 1-881127-02-8:
      1. Adventism—Theology 2. Adventism—Ethics
      3. Adventism—History
I. Teel, Charles W. Jr. (Charles William)

To the memory of

ANA CARLSON STAHL

and

FERDINAND "FERNANDO" STAHL

visionaries who embodied an Adventism that called for
personal ethics and social ethics to be "of one piece of cloth"
and whose presence enlivened both remnant and republic.

Contents

Preface

In times to come when your children will ask their parents "What mean these stones?" tell them....Jos 4:6

Our children are asking of their Adventist heritage, "What mean these stones?" How does our faith heritage make a difference in lived life—in individual experience, and shared corporate experience? in the life of the remnant people and the life of the republic?

Viable communities of faith are communities of remembrance and communities of hope. These groups live "between the times" and are viable precisely because they are grounded in a past which energizes their shared present and informs their shared future. They make a difference.

Acts 2 informs us that the post-resurrection Christian community included old men and women who dreamed dreams of the past as well as daughters and sons who prophesied visions of the future. This bridging of past and future demands an openness to the now. It requires that a heritage be examined in light of the present. It evokes a yeasty and creative tension as symbols and themes from a shared past are re-viewed and in turn infuse new meanings and purposes into common life. Accordingly, such faith communities are always pilgrim peoples *en route*—as befits followers of One who proclaimed himself "the way."

This openness to things present which graced the collective consciousness of the upper room community was not lost on those youthful daughters and sons who founded that community of faith which came to be known as Seventh-day Adventist. Names they assigned their periodicals fairly trumpeted a commitment to reviewing and renewing the past in light of the present: *Present Truth, Signs of the Times, These Times*, and *Review and Herald*.

Communities which fail to procreate soon cease to be: the Shakers are no more. And communities which fail to make a difference fade away. Thus, the generation grown old must pass on a heritage which informs and enlivens the experience of daughters and sons in times present.

The lecture series which produced this anthology is one evidence that there are those in the Seventh-day Adventist faith community who continue to mine their heritage in seeking meaning which impacts life in both personal and public ways. Professors in the discipline of ethics all, the scholars who contributed these chapters are without exception products of (and teachers in) the Seventh-day Adventist school system, a far-flung educational network which grounded them in an Adventism about which they care deeply. They share symbols and themes and narratives which are as profoundly integral to their identities as their mothers' milk. They view the traditional Adventist "landmarks" of remnant, creation, covenant, sanctuary, Sabbath, law, salvation, wholeness, millennium, and Second Coming as indispensable to their family story.

Yet these contributors do not merely repeat the family story as it has been handed down to them. Hailing from a discipline which explicitly demands conscious reflection at both the personal and social levels, they probe ways in which these overarching themes hold implications not only for personal experience but for community building. They want to see these themes making a difference—not only in the realm of personal piety, but also in the arena of public policy; not only in the life of the remnant, but also in the life of the republic.

Accordingly, these Adventist ethicists affirm their Adventism in a way which challenges presuppositions which define either the First Advent or the Second Advent as demanding an apolitical or amoral stance vis-a-vis economics, race, war, gender, or other similar issues. These scholars call First Advent believers to be reminded of the manner in which the Incarnation is the focus of a divine presence and activity that pervades all of life. And these authors invite Second Advent believers to consider that those eternal symbols which offer us hope—the tree of life whose leaves bring healing to the nations, the unlocked city which unites all peoples, the heaven void of temple and shrine and church because God is there—point precisely to the justice, peace, and righteousness which the remnant faithful are called to incarnate as they become the salt and light of God's Kingdom. Now.

In short, these ethicists call their Adventist faith community to consider that for those who wait faithfully, personal and social ethics are "of one piece of cloth."

That ranking churchman, scholar, author, and religious commentator Martin Marty agreed to review these chapters, to make the final presentation at the lecture series, and to grace this volume with the Introduction, signals that fellow travelers are indeed interested in the manner in which the Adventist community struggles to come of age in celebrating its heritage.

The confidence which he places in the contributors who set about the task of asking how landmark themes from the Adventist heritage can inform their present is an expression of collegiality which is truly valued. To Martin Marty and these contributors/presenters/respondents (individually cited at the conclusion of this volume), a genuine thanks is tendered.

It is likewise important to proffer thanks to the Center for Christian Bioethics at Loma Linda University and its co-director David Larson for funding the lecture series and publishing this book of essays. Equally sincere thanks goes to associate editors Gary Chartier, Gayle Foster, Phil Nist, and Amy Timmons, whose intellectual gifts, literary talents, and technical skills readied this volume for publication.

All who participated in creating this volume envision these pages as contributing to the on-going discussion of what it means to be a faith community very much *en route*—a faith community whose children will care enough to ask, "What mean these stones?" Through such continued exchange and example we hope to demonstrate that the Adventist heritage makes a difference no less in the life of the remnant than in the life of the republic—and in God's world of which it is a part.

CHARLES W. TEEL, JR.
Riverside, California
August, 1994

INTRODUCTION

Martin E. Marty

If the scholars in this book are at all representative of frontier Adventist thought; if the themes chosen and the texts and incidents supporting them are faithful examples; if the interpretations are at all sound, *then* the case has been made. There are threads and strands, weavings and quilt pieces, in some cases few and frail and in others almost forgotten, out of which one can make the proposal that Adventist thought at its best is "of one piece:" personal and social ethics connect, like warp and woof.

Indeed, a non-Adventist reader coming upon these interpretations is reasonably tempted to say that the case has been so well made that an "Introduction" allows for some projection into future explorations. For me, the proposal would be on these lines: in this volume, Adventists have mined their heritage to unearth the basics of an ethos that effectively melds personal and social concern. Now, it's time to move further. Next on the agenda might be the question, How does Adventist personal-social ethical thought relate to life in a *republic* and how to life in the larger *church*?

After all, if Adventism saw and sees itself as a "remnant," it is instinctively relational. That is, one is always a remnant of something else that was to have been, that once was, or, in Biblical thought, that might be restored or reborn. A remnant was a part of a whole. It was not created for itself, nor does it exist in isolation. I wish to reflect on these essays in the light of Adventism's larger context today and then offer some relational thinking.

The Enterprise: Historical Reflection

What choices does one have when dealing with the past of a people?

The first choice is to leave. Many Adventists step out of the tradition, out of reaction, rejection, bad experiences, incidents having to do with disappointment, loss of faith, apathy, or intellectual difficulties. Most of these become a part of some other faith movement, or linger between faith and nonfaith, but in most cases quietly disappear. Some, on the other hand, do what Max Scheler has observed of apostates: they spend their whole career taking revenge on their own spiritual past. In contrast to these responses, the scholars represented in this volume have chosen instead an affirmative task.

Second, one can ignore a tradition and its resources. Most people do. Amnesia afflicts adherants of many religious or other movements, and they simply and serenely do an injustice to the past and a disservice to themselves in the present by ignoring resources. These resources might have helped provide identity, meaning, and direction; but they ignore them. These authors did not.

Or one can deal un- or semi-consciously with the past. Most members of a people, a church, *think* they are dealing with a tradition just by remembering, believing what their parents told them about how things were. C. S. Lewis has said that if you do not know history you will inevitably be victims of recent bad history. The past gets caricatured. The recent past is often not the most creative base for the future: a community must, rather, return to its roots as is the case with these scholars.

Fourth, there is the way of nostalgia, of regret for the passing of time, of desire to have lived in the "good old days." But you cannot live there and, if you knew them, you would not have wanted to. Nostalgia is the decor, not the substance of life; it is the rust of memory. It is trivial. Move on, as all our writers did.

Fifth, one can deal with a mythic past, leaving it unexamined. That did not happen here, because while the Adventist past includes expressions of the sort in which truth is told through story, through myth, these scholars know that they serve the story best by analyzing it, by setting out to retrieve what might serve the people.

When scholars of this sort address a heritage—in this case, "Adventist themes"—they may have several purposes in mind. We historians can be content, if we like, with simply exploring the past as past. Literary artists can study the forms: revelations, parables, letters, myths, sermons—these all speak to us in different ways, and literary analysis helps us understand the ways. But in the life of a people, we are interested in texts from the past chiefly to gain a sense of what is ahead of us on the horizon, how we might entertain different ways of thinking, being, and acting. I sense that in the present essays.

At the same time, such essays in the hands of honest scholars involve criticism and interpretation. Paul Ricoeur, in another context, has said that we can believe "before" criticism, the way children do. But we cannot nowadays grow up unsheltered; we will find that our texts are among other texts; that ours is a tradition among the traditions; that our texts and traditions will willy-nilly be subject to analysis and criticism.

Still, choices remain. One can believe "in spite of criticism and interpretation," as fundamentalists do. That works for some, whether it is the path of truth or not. Or one can believe through interpretation, through criticism, by an adult suspension of disbelief, an awareness of perspectives, an eagerness to "try the tradition on" in new ways.

This all means that for thoughtful people in a pluralist society, where we are aware of options, we come to know that all readings of texts and traditions involve our bringing something to them. Thus when I as an "outsider" read these Adventist texts, written by people many would label "outsiders" to the mainstream culture, I do so differently than when I read Lutheran texts of my tradition, or use Lutheran interpretations to read Augustinian, Pauline, or for that matter Millerite and Whitean texts.

When one engages in such reading, as these insiders have done, one serves one's people by enacting what Karl Rahner calls "selective retrieval." You cannot bring the whole past back. You would burden a people by trying to lay it all forth, even if you could. The past haunts as much as it helps save. Rather, you pick themes and engage in interpretations which bring to light elements which might serve the peoples' present and future needs.

In that case, as many students of symbolism tell us, you do not lightly reject something from the tradition just because it does not speak to the present moment. It may be inert for a while, but it may become "ert" again. Thus once-triumphalist Roman Catholicism had to jettison many symbols of "tall tower, total Christendom" thinking at Vatican II. They selectively retrieved symbols such as "pilgrim church" or "people of God" to define their present and guide their future.

Of course, there are limits to this process of restoring and reviving symbols. One does not encourage the Genghis Khan or Joseph Göbbels traditions to be revisited and revivified. It is hard to think of something potentially salvific in such a venture. And a tradition can be so far gone that we cannot retrieve much; one thinks of ancient Sumer or the Hittites. We seek to deal with living traditions that show potentials for saving and healing.

As I read these essays it occurred to me to say what ought to be obvious. Much about the past is irretrievable. Much of it is embarrassing. But these scholars do not approach the embarrassing in a spirit of condescension. We know that we too are limited by our time, our place, our vision; that we will also embarrass those who follow us, and embarrass ourselves, if we should live so long. We deal with the tradition ambivalently, but not with simple superiority.

Why Retrieval is Complex and Necessary

The question posed by this symposium may be translated: *Is there something of value in the Adventist remnant heritage, and does that something of value include the notion that personal and social ethics are to be seen as "one piece of cloth"?* I assume that the questions are born of at least three impulses: a) to be biblically faithful; b) to face contemporary need at a time when a divorce between personal and social ethics may be limiting or destructive; c) to draw on Adventist resources in a world that needs resources of all sorts. The essays say that somewhere in Millerite or Whitean writings or in the movements they energized there are at least some such translatable resources. We now have to ask how the personal and the social came to be divorced.

Notice, first, that the Adventist tradition as we know it grew from evangelical Protestant soil in the nineteenth century. There and then personal ethics had become prime. Evangelicals at that time were better at dealing with personal vice and virtue than with social and structural evil and transformation. So it was natural that unless Adventists set themselves against the culture also in this respect, they would "fit in" with personal ethics.

What we have to notice is that the isolated personalistic way is a deviation from biblical traditions. The Hebrew Scriptures that we call the Old Testament know of no such severances. One belongs to the "congregation of Yahweh" and is saved with "a people." The destiny of an individual connects with the fate of the whole people and vice versa. Early Christianity had more room for the individual but still she was part of a new people of God, the new Israel, the Body of Christ, the communion of saints. Mediæval Christianity may or may not have had models for Adventism; the Adventist response to it was mainly rejective, because Adventists equated mediæval with Roman Catholic and thus saw it as problematic or even demonic. Yet for a thousand years and more Christianity's social dimension did remain prime.

What happened? Modernity happened. Whatever else modernization means, it means specialization, differentiation, or what I call a "chopping up" and a "chopping apart." Modernity severs what had once been connected: church from state, ethnicity from religion, work from residence, fact from value, politics from economics. We like many of these choppings apart, but we also have to learn to live then with new circumstances. Thus religion becomes in modern America a "private affair." There are competing systems of meaning available to people in one place: thus, premillennialists, postmillennialists, and amillennialists vie. Clergy specialize. Denominations form. Adventism was born on this differentiated scene.

When people (ironically called "modernist," though they thought they were acting against this modern development) appeared to counter it, they formed *social* Christianity, a *social* Gospel, *social* interpretations of the faith. They argued that they were reaching further back into biblical and early Christian thought than were the "privatists" or "personalists" around them. This is not the point to see how accurate their retrieval was, but only to notice that they were seen as exceptional for wanting to bring personal and social back together.

Today any effort to bring the two together is problematic. What polity would Adventists use? They do not seek a theocracy; their eschatology is against that, as is their common sense. They oppose church establishment, and have a longstanding reputation as church-state "separationists." They would not know what to do with hegemony, since they do not seek or expect to be a majority, no matter how strenuous their evangelizing efforts. They do not like to rely on secular legislation to carry out churchly purposes. They do not take up the sword like fundamentalist militants some places in the world. They live in the midst of pluralism, and have to make their way in the midst of it. But if some fusion of personal and social ethics is a part of a biblical charter and in their historic precedence, the demands of truth and the search for wholeness force them to begin by acknowledging the melding of the two aspects of ethics in the Adventist heritage.

But They Are in a Republic

Our pluralist society comes in the form of a republic. In a moment I will use many metaphors to show how a republic is a representative of many components, in this case the Adventist movement being one of them. Bracket for now the issue of how long the republic is going to be around before the Second Coming. Obviously, Adventists address that question all the time, but they also obviously care about the republic.

A republic is not a collection of random, isolated persons. Here is my little gallery of definers and definitions: Aristotle says it is a coming together of aggregates. Johannes Althusius speaks of a "community of communities" which are symbiotically related. Edmund Burke speaks of "little platoons" that are inns or way stations between the individual and the large society. Madison said they were *plures*, the many, as in "E pluribus Unum"; they were "factions, interests, and sects" which, together, helped assure freedom. Tocqueville spoke of "voluntary associations" and Justice Frankfurter of the "agencies of mind and spirit" which together help provide the cohesion for a free society.

Being all these things does not exhaust the charter for Adventism or any other church. The churches want to "save" souls and heal bodies and provide eternal meanings and hope. Their life in a republic does not save souls or make sad hearts glad. But it is enacted in the sight of the same God who saves; this God orders their life. So as they see what they can be and do among non-Adventists—those not of the remnant, but in the republic— they do well to revisit these themes. Here they will only get a paragraph or two each, by way of offering readers an overview.

The Themes Revisited

1. *Remnant.* A remnant exists as part of a larger piece, to which it keeps ties of memory and hope. Charles Teel's introductory chapter showns how the Adventist conception of the remnant has been a whole philosophy of history. There are Marxist, progressive, and any number of other philosophies of history, ways of speaking of beginnings and ends, of mission and meaning and purpose. History is not then meaningless, purposeless. Adventism does not say that the world will progress. It does say that its

people have a calling to be faithful; they must "occupy till I come." They began by participating in a few social causes; a number of leaders worked for abolition; many worked in temperance causes. They showed that the remnant had a relation to a larger body.

Today they explore what the idea of having "come out" and being separate means for the future. From this coming out they acquired identity, but there was the danger of dividing the world too sharply, on Manichæan lines. Today the concept of Adventist calling will help the members find their place in the larger whole and in so doing see a need to be explicit about connecting personal and social ethics.

2. *Creation*. The essay by Jack Provonsha wisely evades or transcends nineteenth-century style arguments about creation and evolution and gets to a larger, more basic point. I would say that the concern is: who controls history? And the answer is: the one who creates it and all things. Here is a call for what H. R. Niebuhr called "radical monotheism" and with it a social ethic, for we cannot live as stewards of creation without engaging in common, social action: to save the environment, the creation that God made and we did not.

3. *Covenant*. Michael Pearson has it almost easy, one might say, for he can show that covenantal thinking, basic in Adventism, is automatically social. Of course one is personally responsible and obedient within the covenant, but a covenant is made between God and people. An ethic of responsibility, of one piece of cloth, necessarily results. Of course a remnant people does not expect the whole society to be faithful to the covenant, but it works to promote such faithfulness.

4. *Sanctuary*. For us "outsiders," David Larson has the most difficult task. To non-Adventist Christians the couple of Bible passages on which Adventism's sanctuary teaching is based can be easily overshot, overlooked. They would mean something different in our exegesis than in Adventism's, which was coping with the "Great Disappointment," interpreting an earthly non-happening by reference to what they believe was a heavenly happening. So I cannot get inside it except to follow Larson's clues about metaphorical and analogical thinking and to welcome his statements about "literal" or "nonliteral" thinking about a sanctuary object in Heaven, also among Adventists. But I find value in his call for holiness, the "don't pollute the sanctuary" theme.

5. *Sabbath*. Miroslav Kis deals with one of the themes that most non-

Adventists know about a "Seventh-day" people: the keeping of the Sabbath. I would say that Adventism's gift here is to re-teach the society what Abraham Joshua Heschel called the "hallowing of time." Not all times are like all others; there are weighted, freighted times, with stipulations. Here one welcomes Heschel's and Adventists' view of the "social" Sabbath, with its personal-ethical call to "notice" family, neighbors, strangers, society. Kis has begun to work out an ethic of obedience to replace older Adventist legalisms, and bystanders will cheer the effort.

6. *Law.* The non-member is not subject to Law as interpreted by Adventism, but looks in and on because Adventists believe they are interpreting biblical laws which make a claim on all Christians. James Walters rightly urges that we not engage in "blueprinting" and wants to work on both motive and social aspects of law. Law, again, is a social expression: God engenders divine law, but human mirrors or extensions of it are formed by citizens, peoples, governments, constitution writers.

7. *Salvation.* Charles Scriven stresses solidarity with Jesus Christ and shows how concepts of social healing and wholeness are at least compatible with the more familiar Adventist personal efforts at saving. We have been cautioned against reading Pauline letters as being nothing but charters for getting out of the world. They are addressed to people who have already experienced "salvation" but who have trouble with their social and communal life.

8. *Wholeness.* Obviously, given its historic "health message," Adventism has a patent on aspects of this theme, as Ginger Harwood can easily point out in an essay on the "ecology of existence." What becomes ever more clear in a world where someone else's cigarette smoke kills me, where my smokestacks kill others, where all can misuse sea and sky or misallocate medical care is that old Adventist concerns can be updated to serve the larger republic, where we are still far from wholeness—and cannot offer it just through personal ethical response, however valuable that personal version is.

9. *Second Advent.* Throughout these essays the radical theocentrism of the Adventist vision is strong. How to connect Adventist appropriations with those of others in republic and church is part of the program of the future. Meanwhile, there is homework: how will this community collate and appropriate these findings? How will they be taught in the congregations and classrooms of the movement? The goal cannot be just to produce

denominational statements on political issues. That activity is not very satisfying anywhere. The issue of how Adventists will connect with each other in fusing personal and social ethics will keep them busy, while people like me want to see the impact of such connecting on the rest of us.

10. *Millennium*. Gerald Winslow speaks of another Adventist theme that "the whole world" knows about if it knows Adventism at all: millennium. Here again we come to a whole philosophy of history. While Adventists have plenty of premillennial kin, they do not represent all Christian views of the end. But they do make a contribution by stressing so seriously that there *is* an end, that the Lord of history has endtimes in his hands. It is important to see how millennium-minded people deal with mean times. There is room for a social ethic even if the time is short.

This Introduction, then, turns out to be a prospect of a very full agenda. The Center for Christian Bioethics at Loma Linda University should never be accused of leaving Adventists with nothing to do, or something about which to be bored. The charter is full of difficulties, but it is also full of excitement and promise.

Chapter One

REMNANT

CHARLES W. TEEL, JR.

Look! Here is the bridegroom! Come out to meet him.[1]

Fallen, fallen is Babylon the great!...Come out of her my people.[2]

I saw another beast;...it had two horns like a lamb and it spoke like a dragon. [3]

Then the dragon was angry with the woman, and went off to make war on the rest
of her children, those who keep the commandments of God and hold the
testimony of Jesus.[4]

Worship God! For the testimony of Jesus is the spirit of prophecy.[5]

Just as Adam named the animals in the Edenic garden, so nineteenth-
century Adventist expositors rushed to name those beasts which prowl the
Patmos zoo of St. John the Divine. Deciphering the beasts and dragons and
timetables of the Apocalypse enabled a Millerite Adventist community to
date the eschaton, to survive the agony of the 1844 Millerite Disappointment, and to find meaning and mission in the discovery of themselves as the
remnant of 12.

One hundred years later Miller's children's children "humbly" assert
the remnant status of the Seventh-day Adventist Church with a finality akin
to that of a Millerite evangelist prophesying the world's end:

> From the very first, Seventh-day Adventists...have humbly believed their
> movement to be the one here designated as the "remnant" [in Rev
> 12:17].[6]

> When a person looks for...identifying marks of God's true people, he finds
> that there is only one Christian movement in all the world that fits ...and
> that is the Seventh-day Adventist people.[7]

> The Seventh-day Adventist Church is unique....It is a supraorganization,
> apart from, and above, all other organizations.[8]

> God has committed to the Seventh-day Adventist Church the last task to

1

save the world. We have God's package deal...the gospel from beginning to end.[9]

It is the purpose of this study to examine the concept of remnant in Adventist life and thought, to sketch a broad-stroke overview of ways in which Seventh-day Adventists and their forebears related to the social context of the republic, and to suggest implications that the remnant motif may hold for personal and social ethics. As this chapter is the first of a series dealing with the remnant and the republic, key elements of nineteenth-century Adventist history will be reviewed by way of offering a context within which to reference not only the remnant motif, but also other themes to follow.

The Millerite Adventists

Behold the Bridegroom cometh! For William Miller, self-educated farmer from upstate New York, the remnant consisted of "the last of the church who keep the commandments of God and have the testimony of Jesus Christ"[10]—phrases that Miller broadly interpreted as referring to the gospel. This faithful band would meet the Lord when He returned to earth to save His church "about the year 1843." Armed only with a Bible, a concordance, and a wooden literalism that allowed the prophetic and apocalyptic works of Scripture to interpret themselves when compared line upon line and precept upon precept and number upon number, Miller did not identify the remnant with an organized body—nor did he intend to form such. "We have no purpose . . . to get ourselves a name by starting another sect," the Millerites affirmed at the First General Conference of Advent Believers in 1840. "We neither condemn, nor rudely assail, others of a faith different from our own."[11] The remnant "last of the church" were those in the church universal who responded to the inclusive call to meet the Bridegroom.

The personal ethic espoused by this self-proclaimed last generation of the faithful is familiar to students of nineteenth-century American religious history: debts were to be paid, sobriety was to be practiced, and witness to the Advent Near was to be offered in and through all aspects of life. Only more recently have investigators come to examine the social ethics involvements and evolvements of the Millerite band.

2

That the Millerites rated a billing on the roster of social reformers—or, at minimum, social reform enthusiasts—is suggested by Henry Steel Commager's account of heady Boston at mid-century:

> For the reformers, at least, Boston was the Hub of the Universe. They could preach pantheism in the pulpit, transcendentalism in the schoolroom, socialism in the marketplace, abolition in Fanuil Hall; they could agitate the most extravagant causes and you would have to listen to them. And they consorted with the worst of men, and of women too. Whither they went they trailed behind them clouds of high flying enthusiasts— spiritualists, phrenologists, Swedenborgians, Millerites, vegetarians, Grahamites, prohibitionists, feminists, non-resisters, Thomosians, Comeouters of every shape and hue.[12]

No less a reformist vehicle than William Lloyd Garrison's *Liberator* carried notice of Miller's Boston meetings and hailed him as a "thorough" social reformer: "Mr. Miller, being a thorough abolitionist, temperance man etc., will no doubt give much truth in the course of his lectures, that will be of a salutary character—aside from his computations of the end of the world."[13]

Miller was assisted early on by a trio of leaders who had cut their teeth on reform activism. Chief Millerite publicist Joshua V. Himes, a Christian Connection minister who brought Miller to the cities, was well established among reformist circles in Boston as being "among the most radical of the radicals."[14] Charles Fitch, creator of the famous 1842 chart used effectively to communicate Miller's calculations of the end time, had earlier published the volume *Slaveholding Weighed in the Balance of Truth and its Comparative Guilt.*[15] And Josiah Litch, the earliest Miller ministerial recruit, sprang from anti-slavery ranks and temperance agitators.[16]

This triumvirate of key Millerite lieutenants is but the beginning of the list of Millerite social reformers. Millerite editor and lecturer Henry Jones, who carried the cause of temperance throughout the North, was banned from churches for his abolitionist stance.[17] Millerite convention leader Henry Dana Ward was not only an ardent New York City abolitionist but also a temperance organizer introduced to social activism by the anti-Masonic movement of the 'twenties.[18] Baptist Millerite churchman Elon Galusha, son of the governor of Vermont, was chair of a county anti-slavery society and chaired an 1841 interdenominational convention that called for resolutions against slave-holding churches.[19] The Millerite newspaper, *Midnight Cry*, was edited by Nathaniel Stoddard, a reformer involved in the issues of temperance, anti-slavery, and education who served as acting editor of the *Emancipator,* an anti-slavery paper.[20] Millerite minister George Storrs preached his abolitionist activism not only to anti-slavery types but also to restive Methodist bishops who did not share his enthusiasm for reforming either church or world.[21] And seasoned Millerite preacher and conference organizer Joseph Bates earned the dual distinctions of carrying his abolitionist activism into hostile Southern territory and captaining the crew of a "dry" merchant ship that plied the seven seas.[22]

That a Millerite eschatological hope could exist side-by-side with a reformist social ethic is demonstrated in the life and work of Joshua V. Himes. An examination of his involvements demonstrates that he was indisputably the most active of the Millerites in marketing the movement, while at the same time a most ardent champion of social reform. After bringing Miller to Boston in 1839, Himes functioned as Millerism's chief organizer and publicist. He purchased the "biggest tent in the country" for Miller's meetings, recruited and scheduled other evangelists for speaking tours, organized campmeetings, and convened numerous Second Advent conferences. Further, he edited two Advent journals—*The Midnight Cry* in New York and *The Signs of the Times* in Boston—and helped found others in Philadelphia, Cincinnati, Cleveland, Rochester, and Montreal.[23]

Himes' involvement in promoting temperance, Christian unionism, abolition, and non-resistance continued through the very years he helped engineer Millerism's rise to movement status—right up to the initially calculated Jubilee Year of 1843. Chardon Street Chapel, which Himes established in 1837 as Boston's Second Christian Church, rocked with such an assortment of reform activities that Garrison's *Liberator* hailed the chapel as "a building which is destined to become famous in the City of Boston, and for which we entertain more respect and affection than for any other in the city."[24]

Garrison's respect was deserved. During the years of Himes' ministry, Chardon Street Chapel was up to its steeple in reform movement agendas. The Chapel was the venue for annual meetings of the Non-Resistance Society (which embraced such radical causes as women's rights, among others, and numbered among its members Henry C. Write, Lucretia Mott, Samuel J. May, Edmund Quincy, and Adiun Ballou), with Himes registered as a charter Society member who served repeated terms on its executive committee. Garrison's New England Anti-Slavery Conventions were held at Chardon Street Chapel and Himes continued to be re-elected as one of the counselors of the Massachusetts Anti-Slavery Society (along with such activists as Wendell Phillips, Ellis Gray Lording, Oliver Johnson, Amasa Walker, Edmund Quincy and David Lee Child). Further, the Friends of Universal Reform gathered at the Chapel and issued a call for a wide-ranging series of Chardon Street Conventions.[25] Ralph Waldo Emerson, writing in *The Dial*, offered the following description of these exchanges:

> If the assembly was disorderly, it was picturesque. Madmen, madwomen, men with beards, Dunkers, Muggletonians, Come-outers, Groaners, Agrarians, Seventh-Day Baptists, Quakers, Abolitionists, Calvinists, Unitarians, and Philosophers—all came successively to the top, and seized their moment, if not their hour, wherein to chide, or to pray, or preach, or protest. The faces were a study. The most daring innovators and the champions-until-death of the old cause sat side by side.[26]

In light of Himes' capacity to balance reform commitments to the republic and earnest endeavors proclaiming the Advent Near, one biographer notes: "Christ's words to His followers—'occupy till I come'—were ever on his lips."[27]

Although Garrison more than once publicly commended the Chardon Street Chapel pastor as "an early and true friend of the cause," Himes removed himself from the abolitionist leadership slate for the year 1843. In chronicling Himes' resignation from the abolitionist movement, Garrison's children appeared to be expressing some resignation of their own: "Great was the popular fermentation over Millerism which drew off many abolitionists from the ranks, including Charles Fitch and J. V. Himes."[28] That Himes waited right up to the year of the expected eschaton to move from a multi-issue to a single-issue movement focus suggests that he viewed reform objectives as fully consistent with tendering the Millerite invitation to welcome the Bridegroom: the Bridegroom, in turn, would be the ultimate reformer.

Come out of her my people! The "popular fermentation" over Millerism certainly increased as the once broad-based movement that had moved freely among various religious bodies and social reform movements took on the baggage of an organization.[29] In turn, as the date-setters and come-outers gained ascendancy, the remnant "last of the church" with the inclusive cry "Behold the bridegroom cometh," became the remnant "last church" with the exclusive cry "Come out of her, my people." Charles Fitch's 1843 sermon of the same title[30] rallied those who would call the remnant not only out of Roman Catholicism and the sects of Protestantism, but also out of all other human institutions and governments.[31] What had begun as an inclusive movement grew embattled—indeed embittered. The beast of Revelation that most Protestants interpreted as Catholicism had sprouted horns. The wanton Babylonian woman had birthed daughters. And only the separated Millerite remnant remained to usher in the Coming.

Miller did not condone this fracturing. "I have not ordained anyone to separate from the churches to which they may have belonged unless their brethren cast them out," he wrote as late as January 1844. "I have never designed to make a new sect, or to give you a nickname."[32] Only in an uncharacteristic moment did he appear to align himself with the language of Fitch's Call. But with this new separatist cry the movement gained momentum of its own, a momentum Miller "feared." Shrinking from those giving "another cry, 'Come out of her, my people,'" Miller confided his concern: "I fear the enemy has a hand in this, to direct our attitude from the true issue, the midnight cry, 'Behold the Bridegroom cometh.'"[33]

The inclusive remnant had become an exclusive remnant, a remnant which had come out of religious bodies as well as the world and its social institutions. The Millerite Adventists experienced the dubious distinction of coming out of all of the republic's social institutions merely to await that good kingdom whose builder and maker was God. And they were disappointed.

The Sabbatarian Adventists

Where does a Millerite go once the symbols that shape a cosmology have been shattered? The options reported by a believer writing in the aftermath of 1844 suggest that New England territorial loyalty survived the Disappointment intact and provide an unintended lighter note that contrasts with the pathos of the many surviving accounts: some believers in the Advent Near, observes this New England brother, struggle on in hope, others have turned to strong drink, and others have gone to California![34]

6

One segment of the disappointed Millerites which elected to struggle on in hope rather than with strong drink or California affirmed Miller's emphasis on the Advent while admitting his error in chronology. They would become the Advent Christians. Another segment, those who would later become the Seventh-day Adventists, affirmed both Miller's Advent imminence and his chronology but infused new meaning into the year 1844: that year inaugurated a final era of divine judgment.

The visions of Portland, Maine, teenager Ellen Harmon in 1845 and 1846 reinforced this new interpretation of the significance of the 1844 event and brought solace and comfort to the disappointed faithful—variously referred to as the "remnant," the "little remnant," and the "scattered remnant."[35] Later published under the title *To the Remnant Scattered Abroad* these visions drew upon the remnant motif as an inspiration to struggle on in the hope of the Advent.[36] The subsequent marriage of Ellen Harmon to Millerite preacher and movement organizer James White in 1846 forged a union which would comfort the faithful and in turn establish them as a rooted remnant community.

The commandments of God. Not surprisingly, these Sabbatarian Adventists mined the Apocalypse blessing of Revelation 12 that had informed Miller's definition of remnant: "Here is the patience of the saints; here are they that keep the commandments of God and the faith of Jesus." Millerite Himes could speak of the "commandments" of God interchangeably with the "commands" of God.[37] But Millerite Adventist *cum* Sabbatarian Adventist Bates clearly read the "commandments" of God as the Ten Commandments of the Mosaic Decalogue—and especially the command of the seventh-day Sabbath.[38] Accordingly, a remnant of Sabbath-keeping Adventists emerged that had found its place in history. All bodies that had preached the imminent Advent had pronounced the first angel's message of Revelation 14 ("Judgment has come!"); the Millerites had sounded the second angel's message in 1844 ("Come out!"); and they, the Sabbath-keeping Adventists, were now to proclaim to the world the message of the third and final angel ("Keep the commandments!").[39]

While so vast a responsibility would have overwhelmed the uninitiated, the parochial presuppositions of the remnant flock pared the task down to size. The population eligible to receive the remnant message were those on whom the door of salvation had not shut in 1844—Millerites who had prepared to receive the bridegroom and who had "come out."[40] Buoyed by

7

this discovery of meaning and mission, this band of believers pooled their reserves, founded journals, proclaimed the Sabbath truth, and set exegetes at work to push the remnant motif further and to name those apocalyptic beasts that remained unidentified.

The testimony/faith of Jesus. Discerning the meaning of this second characteristic of the remnant apocalyptic blessing involved a route so tortuous as to confound any but the most patient saints. In 1847 Joseph Bates identified the testimony/faith of Jesus broadly as the New Testament gospel.[41] James White, however, emphatically declared what he believed to be "present truth" in the matter: just as the "commandments of God" grounded the fledgling movement's commitment to the seventh-day Sabbath, the expression "testimony of Jesus" referred to its second distinctive, the doctrine of the Shut Door. White's certainty with regard to finding Adventism's two distinctives—"as plain as the prophetic pencil could write it;"[42] "never was there a people whose opposition was so plainly marked out in the Word as ours" [43]—led Bates and others to follow White's lead.

The Shut Door was pried open at mid-century as individuals outside the Millerite fold sought entrance to fellowship. In 1850, James White's *Present Truth* pulled back to the Millerite position identifying the testimony/faith of Jesus as the teachings of the Gospel.[44] Leaders and readers followed suit and endorsed the new light that experience had forced upon them.

Another year passed and yet another position surfaced: James White drew on Joel 2:32 to note that the remnant of that verse experienced the last-day outpouring of spiritual gifts.[45] Two years later he identified the "spirit of prophecy" as one of the characteristics of the remnant church.[46] It was now but a short step to equating the "testimony/faith of Jesus" with the "gift of prophecy" and, by clear implication, with the ministry of Ellen White— exegesis undertaken by James White in a 1855 article.[47] White's subsequent definition of the remnant of Revelation as commandment-keeping Adventists who claim the "spirit of prophecy" exhibited in the "testimonies" of Ellen White[48] remained as Seventh-day Adventist exegesis and doctrine for over a century.[49]

The lamb/dragon beast. Reviewing the naming—and depicting—of the mutant lamb/dragon creature of Revelation 13 which had horns like a lamb and spoke as a dragon offers a window for discerning the relation between the remnant and the republic. Young biblical exegete J. N. Andrews took to the pages of the *Advent Review and Sabbath Herald* in 1851 to name this curious creature. In the course of two series of articles consisting of fully forty-three columns of fine print, this beast is roped, tied, and squarely branded as none other than the United States of America.[50]

It was precisely in the identification of this beast that the Sabbatarian Adventists had opportunity to declare their stance on such social policy issues as slavery. The lamb-like horns of this beast suggest the "mildness" of this power. These two "uncrowned" horns signify "its Republican civil power and its Protestant ecclesiastical power," twin virtues that Andrews extolls with some passion. Yet while the republic professes to be lamb-like, its practice is dragon-like. The republic professes republicanism; it practices slavery. "If all men are born free and equal, how do we hold three million slaves in bondage?" thunders Andrews.[51]

"Father" Joseph Bates, sometime sea captain and veteran Millerite preacher who would later co-found the Seventh-day Adventist Church with James and Ellen White, had anticipated this disillusionment with the republic a few years earlier when commenting on another portion of the Apocalypse. He had fired off a broadside protesting what he saw as slavery-motivated expansionism by the United States in waging an undeclared war on Mexico: "The third woe has come upon this nation, this boasted land of liberty; this heaven-daring, soul-destroying, slaveholding, neighbor-murdering country."[52] Within a matter of weeks after Andrews published his identification of the two-horned beast, Bates and James White rushed into print with enthusiastic endorsements.[53]

The pre-civil war interpretation of this beast was summed up by Uriah Smith, editor and prodigious author who later wrote what served for years as the church's standard commentary on the books of Daniel and Revelation: "The lamb feature is a fit emblem of the profession and the incipient acts of this government. But it now speaks like a dragon—a fit emblem of the practice of this hypocritical nation." Taking a page from Andrews, he continued: "Look at the Declaration of Independence and the Constitution; and then look at Slavery, look at the religious intolerance, the corruption and oppression existing throughout the land."[54] In the same vein, esteemed Adventist leader John Loughborough offered a caustic revision for the Declaration of Independence: It should say that all men are free and equal "except 3,500,000."[55]

The dragonic nature of the republic was made indelibly clear in the enactment and enforcement of the Fugitive Slave Acts. Ellen White, emerging as the movement's charismatic voice, classified the Fugitive Slave Act as a "bad" law that was not to be obeyed.[56] Furnishing extensive editorial comment sympathetic to the anti-slavery movement, the *Review* reported William Lloyd Garrison's activities, chastised the Kansas-Nebraska Act, and chided Congress for its "gag-rule" and the South for its violations of First Amendment freedoms.[57]

These believers did not view the slavery struggle as merely a struggle between Democrats and Whigs. The stakes were higher. Slavery, "a sin of the darkest dye,"[58] represented the cosmic controversy between Heavenly Jerusalem and Earthly Babylon. Under the title, "The Sins of Babylon," Ellen White castigated the sin of slavery and declared that "God's anger will not cease until he has rewarded Babylon double."[59]

By drawing on the apocalyptic imagery of universal history, these Adventists could speak the language of the radical reformers. Yet their apocalyptic perspective separated the Adventists from the reformers. Precisely because this controversy was cosmic in scope, these Adventists left it to angels and winds and vials and plagues unleashed by God—and not to reform movements—to reward Babylon double. Adventists need not even vote.

This boycott of the ballot box illustrates not only the extent to which the Sabbatarian remnant defined themselves as outsiders to the social processes of the republic, but also the extent to which apocalypticism and Adventism's identification of the lamb/dragon beast informed this collective self-definition. Under the title "How Shall I Vote?" and with an eye toward the 1856 elections, *Review* contributor R. F. Cottrell opens by stating his apocalyptic presuppositions: "The government of the United States, I have no doubt, is the one symbolized in prophecy, but a beast with horns like a lamb." The dragonic nature of this beast has become clear in that "the lamb-like Protestantism of America is making an image to the Catholic beast as decreed by prophecy." How shall I vote? "I cannot aid in a work that God hates, certainly. On the other hand, if I vote against this work, I shall vote against the fulfillment of Prophecy." Can I vote against slavery? Because bondsmen will exist until the end, one cannot free the slave: "I cannot, therefore, vote against slavery: neither can I vote for it." Can I vote against cruel, persecuting Catholics? "Persecution is coming; and since I must meet it, what difference does it make from whom it comes?" Can I vote at all? "I cannot vote for a bad man, for that is against my principles; and I could not wish to elevate a good man to office, for it would ruin him." The article's concluding lament resolutely affirms come-outerism in language that carries a plaintive come-outer ring:

> Babylon is fallen. Come out of her my people.
> Ephraim is joined to his idols; let him alone.[60]

In this context, historian of American religions Jonathan Butler observes: "Quite consistently the Radical Republicanism of Adventists remained a paper radicalism that evoked more verbiage than action."[61] Thus the same Uriah Smith who created a woodcut of the lamb/dragon beast, complete with forked-tongue, razor-sharp teeth, pointed horns, and a whip-like tail could author an editorial on politics that urged passivity in the face of the 1856 elections. Adventists favored temperance, Protestantism, Republicanism, and abolitionism, yet they eschewed the reform movements and the political process. Because the lamb/dragon beast now spoke as a dragon, the eschaton must surely be imminent. Irrespective of how they voted, nothing could "hasten or retard" the divine timetable.[62] Butler concludes: "They adhered to a prophetic determinism that would neutralize any political effort of their own and leave the great juggernaut of political history in God's firm hand."[63]

In one sense this prophetic determinism heightened when war came. Although Adventists sought ways to avoid combat, they sang Julia Ward Howe's "Battle Hymn" with gusto from the sidelines. But the "coming of the Lord" heralded by these believers differed altogether from that of which the Union troops sang. Slavery, an irrefutable "sign of the times," would be rectified not by the marching of truth toward an earthly millennium, but by the Lord's coming in judgment in the clouds of heaven; not by the Battle of Appotamatox but by the Battle of Armageddon.[64] Wrote Ellen White: "God alone can wrench the slave from the hand of his desperate oppressor."[65]

The Sabbatarian Adventist remnant thus echoed the rhetoric of the republic's radical reformers, but they waited on God to usher in the reforms. They espoused a radical social ethic, but they left it to Jesus' return to enact the same. And they were frustrated.

Seventh-day Adventists
in the Nineteenth Century

Church organization. As months became years and years became decades, the Sabbatarian remnant band cautiously prepared to put down roots and settle in for the long haul. They—the come-outers of the come-outers who had eschewed all human structures—now organized a religious institution. Co-founders James White, Ellen White, and Joseph Bates pushed the scattered flock of Sabbath-keeping Adventists to "take a name" and organize, James having astutely substituted the euphemism "gospel order" for the term "organization" in an effort to appease fellow come-outers who equated all social structures with Babylon.[66] Further, he called for a management style of servant leadership as an antidote to keep the young remnant organization from evolving into a "great iron wheel,"[67] a metaphor used to describe the mechanistic nature of Babylonian institutions.

James White was to the Sabbatarian Adventists what Himes had been to the Millerite Adventists. Yet White had some advantages: his spouse was the movement's prophet; his second co-founder, Bates, had served as Himes' able co-worker during the heyday of Millerism; and James had the further advantage of not working under an imminent deadline. By the time of James White's death in 1881, Seventh-day Adventists had established medical, educational, and publishing institutions at home and abroad that were to give a permanence to Adventist expression for the next full century. By 1901 the Adventist membership of 75,000 supported sixteen colleges and high schools, a medical school, twenty-seven hospitals and sanitaria, thirteen publishing houses, and thirty-one other miscellaneous institutions.[68] On the basis of these endeavors Edwin Gaustad, following Winthrop Hudson, has observed that while "Seventh-day Adventists were expecting a kingdom of God from the heavens, they worked diligently for one on earth."[69]

This incredible success in institution-building, however, took its toll. As institutions multiplied during the last decades of the century, organizational machinery became autocratic and self-serving, causing Ellen White to bemoan that the forebodings of those who had opposed organization had in fact "come about."[70] The founders' vision of servant leadership had given way to "the great iron wheel." Ellen White's strong rebukes made it clear that even ecclesiastical institutions formed by a dedicated remnant band can participate in collective sin: "man ruling power," "dictatorial authority," "kingly power," "propensity to rule," galling yoke," and "a species of slavery"[71] are epithets she hurled against a self-serving leadership during the last two decades of the nineteenth century. By the time of the 1901 General Conference session, it became clear that at least one social institution of the republic was fair game for reform activity by the righteous remnant: namely, the Seventh-day Adventist Church.[72]

Reform movements. When the remnant organized in the 1860s, it was necessary to establish that organization *per se* did not constitute Babylon. And if the organization of church structures—both ecclesiastical and benevolent—did not constitute Babylon, might it be appropriate for the remnant to work through the social and political structures of the republic?

The answer was a qualified affirmative: participation was possible in areas such as temperance and religious liberty, areas of direct concern to the corporate church. With few exceptions—such as Edson White's Mississippi River work aboard *The Morning Star* on behalf of the freed slaves as financed, in part, by mother Ellen White's offerings—the faithful chose not to follow the lead of those who supported the course of Reconstruction following the Civil War.[73] They did form alliances with the Anti-Saloon League and the Women's Christian Temperance Union to wage war on demon rum.[74] And their 1888 fight against the Blair Bill to promote Sunday worship displayed a zeal that would have done the American Civil Liberties Union proud. Deemphasizing their teetotaling sympathies in favor of religious liberty principles, Adventists now found themselves aligned against the Women's Christian Temperance Union and the major Protestant churches and on the side of the liquor interests, Jews, and Seventh-Day Baptists. They lobbied Congress, received good press and circulated petitions to garner 300,000 signatures which contributed to the defeat of Blair's proposal. Some years later a lobbyist for Sunday legislation singled out the work of the California Adventists for a compliment of sorts, lamenting that 26,000 Adventists had done more petitioning than 26,000,000 "Christians."[75]

Just as the Ellen White of the 1890s deplored the sins of institutionalism that characterized church structures, in the same period she criticized those whose narrow definitions had earlier kept them from backing the republic's efforts to reconstruct the social and economic structures of the South. Acknowledging that some "persevering efforts have been put forth by individuals and societies" to restructure the economic and educational lot of the freed slaves, she specifically rebuked both "government" and "Christian churches" for their lack of sustained commitment to Reconstruction, emphatically asserting that "the Seventh-day Adventist Church has failed to act its part." While she extolled the work of "some Seventh-day Adventists" on behalf of Reconstruction, she issued a stern reprimand for the lack of action on the part of the general membership and—in particular—their "ministering brethren."[76] In short, the Ellen White of the 1890s recognized that sin can be manifest in structures and that such structures/communities/entities as government, Christian churches, the Seventh-day Adventist Church, church members, and ministers are called to mediate salvation and healing in the face of such structural sin.

Perhaps it was this renewed critique of the dragonic qualities of slavery that inspired selected Adventist writers at the turn of the century to draw upon the two-horned beast imagery and to decry the republic's "national apostasy" from republicanism to imperialism as evidenced in United States dealings with Cuba and the Philippines.[77] Yet such challenges to the established order on behalf of such dispossessed populations appear to be the exception. Rather, the tendency was for the Seventh-day Adventist remnant to work through the structures of the republic to achieve goods for itself—notably in the area of religious liberty, where its own interests were threatened. With regard to the republic, these Adventists tended to look out for themselves. And they were isolated.

Seventh-day Adventists
in the Twentieth Century

The pattern of exclusive remnant definition and selective, indeed self-interested, involvement in the social structures of the republic continued virtually unchanged for the first half of the twentieth century. Developments involving three distinct populations within the church community at mid-century offered opportunity for a review of remnant definition and social involvement in the life of the republic as the Adventist subculture began to relate in new ways to the larger world. First, Adventist ecclesiastical administrators gingerly re-assessed and re-defined the nature and scope of the remnant as the result of ecumenical dialogue initiated by evangelical leaders. Second, academics exposed both to broader Christian fellowship and to tools of Biblical scholarship called for a more inclusive remnant definition. Third, graduate students and other segments of the church membership challenged Adventism's social commitments as such issues as race, war, and women's rights demanded individual and corporate responses both within the church and society at large.

Remnant definition. The 1957 volume *Seventh-day Adventists Answer Questions on Doctrine* resulted from Adventist-evangelical exchanges and included a chapter provocatively titled "Who Constitute the 'Remnant Church'?" *Questions* discreetly avoids reference to the fact that the final point of the baptismal vow answered the query in a concise and unqualified single sentence: "I believe that the Seventh-day Adventist Church constitutes God's remnant people." In contrast, this chapter weaves a remnant definition which is decidedly less direct:

> While we believe that the Seventh-day Adventist Church is the visible organization through which God is proclaiming this last special message to the world, we remember the principle that Christ enunciated when he said, "Other sheep I have, which are not of this fold" (Jn 10:16). Seventh-day Adventists firmly believe that God has a precious remnant, a multitude of earnest, sincere believers, in every church, not excepting the Roman Catholic communion, who are living up to all the light God has given them. The great Shepherd of the sheep recognizes them as His own, and He is calling them into one great fold and one great fellowship in preparation for his return.[78]

The chapter stops short of explicitly identifying this ultimate eschatological fold as the Seventh-day Adventist Church by noting that the end time context requires a "special message" and that God has "raised up a movement—known as the Seventh-day Adventist church—for the express purpose of making it, in a special way, the depository and exponent of this message." Thus it is that the remnant of Revelation 12:17, who keep the commandments of God and have the testimony of Jesus, are identified as the Seventh-day Adventist Church: "To us it is the logical conclusion of our system of prophetic interpretation."[79]

A survey of selected contemporary Adventist remnant studies suggests that Adventism is no longer informed by a single "system of prophetic interpretation." Nor does it appear clear to all that the traditional interpretations brought to the remnant motif necessarily stand as "logical conclusions."

By far the most extensive review of the remnant theme by an Adventist scholar is Gerhard Hasel's *The Remnant: The History and Theology of the Remnant from Genesis to Isaiah*, published in 1972.[80] Although it is not Hasel's stated intent to apply his findings directly to the contemporary Adventist remnant experience, he raises key points that are instructive for such an endeavor: the remnant theme is *existential* in that it has its origin in the problem of human existence and humankind's struggle in the face of uncertainty and the possibility of destruction (Near Eastern flood stories); *salvific* in that it declares the aim of God to be that of salvation and not destruction (Noachian flood story); *elective* in that it points to God's gracious choices (Genesis cycles); *ethical* in that election is conditional upon an ethical response that enthrones justice in society's social structures (Amos); and *eschatological* in that it is ever possible for new remnants to emerge (Amos/Isaiah).

Directly following Hasel's Old Testament survey, Daniel Smith's 1974 Pacific Union College honors thesis investigated the theme from a New Testament perspective: "A Study in the New Testament of the Remnant with Reference to the Seventh-day Adventist Position." Recognizing that he was breaking new ground in print, Smith phrased his statement of purpose cautiously: to seek "a more precise interpretation (tentative) of the term 'remnant' in Revelation 12:17."[81] Following some eighty pages devoted primarily to syntactical, grammatical, lexical, analogical, and exegetical analyses of the passage in question, Smith concludes that while the Seventh-day Adventist church is called to be a "remnanting" church that proclaims a "remnanting" message, no institutional body can legitimately claim to *constitute* the remnant of Revelation 12:17—a company whose membership will be known only at end time.

Two papers presented at Loma Linda University's Division of Religion retreat in 1975 challenged an apocalyptic interpretation that limits such symbols as remnant and Babylon to single historical entities and called for a recognition that a remnant faithful is present in all chapters of human history—as is Babylon. Jack Provonsha's paper, later published as "The Church as a Prophetic Minority," was occasioned by "an increasing personal uneasiness" over the use of the terms "remnant church," "God's church," "God's people," and "God's package deal," employed at the 1975 General Conference session which he had recently attended. Rather, Provonsha defined the remnant as the "church prophetic," which reflects God's "specially called" people in every age, called to function as "prophets" to his larger people. They represent centers of growth and sensitivity in the progression of the truth as it unfolds to men. They are always the bearers of the "present truth" for every age and thus enjoy, not God's special favor, for God is no respecter of persons, but the high privilege of being where at the moment the action is. They have no corner on God's concern and insofar as they are "true prophets" their faces are turned in love toward their brethren everywhere.[82]

I delivered a second paper, "The Call to be a Prophetic Remnant," which was later drawn upon in framing the participatory worship service published as "The Apocalypse as Liturgy." This presentation contended that such Apocalypse symbols as "remnant" and "Babylon" must first be understood in light of the experience of the early Christian Church vis-a-vis the Roman Empire: the faithful "last of the church" in Asia Minor were encouraged to hold fast against the Babylonian political power which was forcing false religious worship and the slave-trading economic power whose cargo ships dealt in human cargo: the "souls of men." Secondarily, these terms stand as overarching portents which signify just and unjust structures and movements in every age:

> Whatever symbols elude us in our interpretation of the Revelation, one basic apocalyptic theme is clear: a remnant community of the saved is called to bear a prophetic witness against—indeed to overcome—those oppressive Babylonian institutions characterized by the beasts and dragons; structures that are impersonal, persecuting, manipulative, domineering, and autocratic.[83]

This paper argued that a prophetic remnant will exhibit qualities in its communal life which are polar opposites to those of Babylon. Nor will a prophetic remnant be content merely to fight Babylonian beasts and dragons of centuries past—beasts which may now be toothless or no longer baring their fangs. Rather, by definition, a prophetic remnant is always called to stand against those forces that oppose God's truth and justice in the present.

Accordingly, the liturgy arising out of this paper drew exclusively upon the text of the Apocalypse, with sketches by gradeschoolers of apocalyptic symbols along with photos of remnants and Babylonian forces from all ages covering the sanctuary walls. The service was introduced by an hour-long program entitled "Stories of Contemporary Beasts and Remnants" with storytellers standing amidst seven giant golden candlesticks—signifying experiences of remnant believers throughout history. Remnant/beast narratives included accounts of Sabbath-keeping Adventist pioneers who spoke out in apocalyptic language against the Babylonian beast of slavery; Lutheran pastor Dietrich Bonhoeffer, who elected to leave a secure teaching post at New York's esteemed Union Theological Seminary and return to Germany to join the underground church in protesting Hitler's Third Reich; sainted Catholic priest Maximillian Kolbe, who offered his life in substitution for a fellow concentration camp prisoner during World War II—and whose story was related by one who observed this selfless action while interned in that death camp; Rosa Parks, who defied the Jim Crow laws of Montgomery, Alabama, and whose arrest sparked the year-long bus boycott which launched Martin Luther King's civil disobedience crusade; and "True and Free Adventist" Russian dissident Vladimir Shelkov, hailed as a venerable spiritual leader by acclaimed Russian refusnik Alexander Ginzburg who was nurtured by Shelkov's abiding hope and courage as they jointly endured stark Soviet imprisonment because of their respective remnant testimonies.

More recently, three additional authors have examined the remnant theme through the social ethics lens. Charles Scriven contributed to the dialogue in an emphatically-titled article, "The Real Truth about the Remnant,"[84] which argued forcefully that the remnant theme retains "socio-political" significance whether found in the Old Testament prophets, the Gospels, the Epistles, or the Apocalypse. Loma Linda University religion graduate student Stephan Mitchell wrote a master's thesis which surveyed diverse theological understandings of key remnant biblical passages, and argued that remnant eschatology and ecclesiology must cohere first and foremost at the level of ethical imperatives: the remnant are those faithful who work cumulatively throughout history—not merely culminatively at the end of history—to "do justice, love mercy, and walk humbly with God."[85] And *Spectrum* editor Roy Branson's work in "apocalyptic ethics" has boldly asserted that the claim to remnant status demands a radical obedience grounded in a social ethic no less than a personal ethic, an ethic that cannot ignore the social realities of principalities and powers as integral to salvation history.[86] Yet a second article by me, "Growing Up with the Beasts: A Rite of Passage," details a spiritual pilgrimage in celebration of the Apocalypse call to "remnantness" as a joint call to spiritual awareness and social consciousness: those ultimate eschatological realities of righteousness and justice for which the remnant hopes will be precisely those realities for which the remnant waits and works faithfully in the warp and woof of this present order.[87]

To what extent is this expanded definition of remnant being embraced by the church population beyond academia? A survey was taken of one hundred pastors from the Pacific Union Conference in October of 1987 and results clearly suggest that a redefinition of remnant is in process. Drawing upon a cross section of pastors representing diverse age categories and ethnic populations, respondents were offered three understandings of the term "remnant" and asked to indicate which definition *least* reflected their personal understanding of the term:

A. I believe that SDA believers will be among those who one day will emerge as God's remnant people.
B. I believe that the SDA church is called to be a part of God's remnant people.
C. I believe that the SDA church constitutes God's remnant people.

That the respondents picked "C" by a thumping two-to-one margin as *least* representative of their personal understanding of the remnant motif—the phrase is quoted directly from the recent baptismal vow—suggests that the church's remnant identity is being redefined in the real world of the parish no less than in the ivory tower of academia.[88] This survey finding also offers a classic illustration of the dynamic way in which perceptions of truth develop: even when a community's ecclesiological self-understanding is so central as to merit a declarative affirmation in the baptismal vow, pastors—among others—clearly advance "glosses" by way of refining, redefining, and rejecting such stated "truth" by way of keeping up with "present truth."

Structural involvement. Methods of assaying the relationship between twentieth-century Adventists and the republic include conducting content analyses of church periodicals and identifying issues about which church leaders have asked the faithful to write their congressional representatives. At best, when church members are invited to participate in public policy issues, such involvement tends to be motivated by a parochial concern for the collective life of the remnant rather than by an inclusive concern for the shared life of the republic. At worst, church members are warned against any church involvement in public policy issues.

Typifying this narrow and self-interested approach to the social order is an article in the *Pacific Union Recorder* by the Pacific Union Religious Liberty Department Director calling church members to write their congressional representatives in opposition to the confirmation of two Supreme Court nominees whose views were alleged to represent a threat to church-state separation.[89] Although much concern was being expressed at the time throughout the republic on how the appointment of these candidates might negatively impact the human rights of the nation's diverse minority groupings (counterparts of those racial minorities, religious minorities, and colonized minorities whose rights were championed by the earliest nineteenth-century Adventists), the concern voiced in this article was limited to the religious rights of Adventists—a narrow parochialism subsequently challenged by the readership.[90]

Little in the content of the *Review and Herald* of the 1960s indicated that the nation was experiencing what Robert N. Bellah refers to as the "third time of national trial" (the first two such trials being the Revolutionary War and Civil War periods).[91] This third time of national trial was fanned by the same winds that had fed the anti-slavery movement just one century earlier: social justice concerns related to race and war. Yet whereas the 1860-65 *Advent Review and Sabbath Herald* issues carried nearly 150 articles on race and war, the 1960-65 *Review and Herald* is virtually silent on these matters[92]—a deafening stillness which is echoed in the *Youth's Instructor* of the same period.[93]

Indeed, an 1864 editorial by J. N. Andrews openly attacked readers of the *Review* who thought they could sit out the slavery debate by irresponsibly relegating this moral/religious/ethical issue to an out-of-bounds realm labelled "Politics."[94] In contrast, a 1965 *Review* editorial title inveighed strongly against "Churches Meddling in Politics." The 1960s context involved not a civil war over slavery but a decade-long drive to make good on the promise of emancipation in terms of employment, housing, schooling and the ballot box. The black preacher from Alabama and the brown migrant worker from California—among others—who led this drive grounded their call to action on some of the same biblical themes which surely informed the Andrews editorial: God's righteousness and justice call a prophetic people to speak out on behalf of the marginalized poor, the widow, orphan, and resident alien. Yet the 1965 editorial asserted:

> Seventh-day Adventists are of the firm conviction that political questions not directly involving religion or matters of conscience are strictly out of bounds for churches and church agencies. The increasing tendency of the major religious bodies in the United States to influence public policy with respect to them, prostitutes their moral authority to affairs that Christ significantly omitted from the gospel commission. The apostles were instructed to teach and to baptize, not to discuss politics or to lobby in Congress, lest they blunt their witness to the truth of heaven by becoming involved in controversial matters of an earthly nature. [95]

This 1965 editorial only implicitly references the race issue, and its phrasing is meticulously qualified. But generalizing as it does in ruling public policy discussions as *ipso facto* out of bounds for church groups—and appearing as it does in the very season that churches and individuals are invited to right the injustices of centuries past—this editorial could only bring comfort to individuals harboring those very attitudes which Andrews condemned. Whereas Andrews' editorial struck out against believers who would dismiss slavery as a "political" issue rather than a moral or spiritual one, the later editorial called religious groups "not to discuss politics." Where Andrews argued in the church paper that religion cannot side-step the issue of race even as it carries social/political freight, this later editorial contended that involvement by religious groups in public policy issues "prostitutes their moral authority." Where Uriah Smith called on Congress and President to pursue a "less conservative" stance[96] and Andrews else-where labeled Congress as perpetrators of an "act of infamy" upon the passage of the Fugitive Slave Act[97] and Ellen White called for civil disobedience of the Fugitive Slave legislation in language which bears striking similarity to definitions advanced by Martin Luther King,[98] the 1960s *Review and Herald* editorializes against blunting a "witness to the truth of heaven by becoming involved in controversial matters of an earthly nature."

In light of these comparative positions on matters regarding the remnant relating to the republic, it might readily be argued that even a "paper radicalism" is better than no radicalism at all. A community of faith which isolates itself from public policy issues can never be described as prophetic. It might be described as irrelevant.

21

Remnant and Ethics
Retrospect and Prospect

Will the call to be a part of God's prophetic remnant continue to carry meaning for our children? Or will the symbol fade into history? What will be the end of the inclusive remnant movement whose once-radical stance confronted the public order in the face of social and economic injustices while at the same time announcing that God's kingdom was about to break into human history? Will descendants of those rugged Millerite Adventist forebears be satisfied with being no more than an accommodating church—a religious institution whose thin veneer of religiosity barely masks the fact that its corporate life differs in but very minor ways from institutional enterprises informed solely by the values of contemporary culture? Will they eschew formal fellowship with a religious community they feel no longer makes a difference in their personal and/or collective experience? Or will they be attracted to a contemporary remnant which confronts institutions no less than individuals with the prophetic call to do justice, to love mercy, and to walk humbly with God in ways which impact public polity no less than personal piety?

Sociologist of religion J. Milton Yinger has hypothesized that those religious movements which chiefly emphasize the individual nature of sin and salvation (personal ethics) tend to accommodate to the cultural *status quo* and settle into a bland denominationalism. Conversely, those religious movements which challenge broader institutional sins and call for God's righteousness and justice to impact the social order (social ethics) tend to accommodate less readily to the larger society and in turn articulate more thoroughly an alternate value system, develop a higher group identification and morale, and become established religious movements which stand in opposition to the value system of contemporary culture.[99]

Retrospect. A prophetic remnant, by definition, is called to stand against much of the value system of contemporary culture where such does not square with the prophetic admonition of doing justly, extending mercy, and walking humbly. This historical overview of Adventism has suggested four periods of Adventist history which have offered various interim ethical models—ways of living "between the times" in anticipation of the Advent.

Millerite Adventist inclusivism: The remnant "last of the church" eschewed the sectarian label of "last church" in favor of an inclusive remnant call. Remnant leaders classified as among the "most radical of the radicals" advanced a social ethic which continued to call for reform of the republic's structures while proclaiming the positive message of the Bridegroom's return as constituting the ultimate reform. And they were energized.

Millerite Adventist come-outerism: Those who were once radical reformers were influenced by the date setters to turn their backs on the republic's institutions and to issue the negative and exclusive call to "come out" of these. This position negated a social ethic and resulted in an interim ethic which called adherents merely to await that kingdom whose builder and maker would be God. And they were disappointed.

Sabbatarian Adventist radicalism: These come-outers of the come-outers, even though they were locked away on the safe side of the Shut Door, nevertheless perceived God's law as calling not only for a strict personal ethic but also for a radical social ethic. Informed by the perceived immediacy of the eschaton, these interim ethic adherents who ran with the rhetoric of the radical reformers left it to God to run with the reforms. And they were frustrated.

Seventh-day Adventist institutionalism: That self-proclaimed remnant which had once viewed church organization as a mark of Babylon organized as a religious body and in short order created the beginnings of a vast chain of medical, educational, and publishing institutions that circled the globe. While a service ethic motivated many individuals at a personal level, an interim social ethic encouraged participation in the socio-political processes of the republic in selective and primarily self-serving ways—a self-interested social ethic concerned chiefly with building up the remnant institution. And they were isolated.

Students of the remnant theme in the contemporary Seventh-day Adventism cited above are calling the church they love to seriously wrestle with the implications of such remnant-related terms as "prophetic remnant," "socio-political imperatives," and "apocalyptic ethics." These investigators suggest that they are learning from and standing upon the shoulders of remnant pioneers, preachers, and prophets who have gone before.

Millerite Adventist inclusivism has suggested that a radical social ethic combined with an imminent eschatological hope is at once possible to set forth and difficult to sustain.

Millerite Adventist come-outerism has shown that an exclusivism which abandons the world and its institutions in favor of an imminent eschaton ends in disappointment.

Sabbatarian Adventist radicalism has demonstrated that a radical social ethic apart from action ends in frustration.

Seventh-day Adventist institutionalism suggests that a self-interested social ethic ends in isolationism and irrelevance—an isolationism and irrelevance which can result in exclusivism and triumphalism and leaves little room for self-criticism.

Contemporary Adventists who argue against an exclusivist remnant ethic and for an Adventist theology of remnant which calls their church to a more inclusive and radical social ethic find some support in the Ellen White of the 1890s. We have noted that this seasoned Ellen White deplores with equal passion twin evils that have beset both the remnant and the republic: institutionalism and injustice. She names institutional sins of society and church alike, and calls the faithful remnant to join with others in addressing these social sins that inhere in structures.

Prospect. How do we assess the impact of these contrasting definitions of remnant and the accompanying social ethic? What remnant definition and ethic might inform Adventism in the future? How might the remnant motif survive the dawn of the twenty-first century? What counsel might we take from our past as we gear up for the future?

The relationship between the remnant and the republic has cautiously expanded since mid-century. The plaque on the church headquarters door which once read "Religious Liberty Department" has now been changed to read, "Department of Public Affairs and Religious Liberty." The church has named a congressional liaison/lobbyist to monitor public policy discussion and proposed legislation that would impact the church's many institutions, including far-flung educational, medical, and publishing endeavors. This same office also cautiously builds coalitions with other entities in the republic which share selected concerns. Active congressional lobbying and public policy debate is also fostered by the lay-led Washington Institute, whose efforts in bringing together the Coalition on Smoking OR Health and its ecumenical support group, The Inter-Religious Coalition on Smoking

OR Health are especially notable. Just as the national public debate on "health reform" has taken a once-personal ethical issue and elevated the discussion to a social ethics agenda, so the Institute is calling our society to recognize that tobacco use negatively impacts not only individuals but also our shared life as citizens of the republic.

Not unexpectedly, academia provides a context for fostering discussion and action which may move the church toward social ethics concerns *vis-a-vis* the republic. Campus forums have addressed such topics as nuclear arms, the "Religious Right," religion and revolution in the "Third World," foreign policy and human rights, as well as such "ethics at the edges of life" issues as abortion, euthanasia, transplant organ allocation, and health care reform. Student associations from the denomination's North American colleges and universities are following the lead of other groups calling for remnant structures to abandon a century-long pattern of patriarchy and to be truly gender inclusive. Some campuses actively support Amnesty International's work on behalf of prisoners of conscience, and at least one university has co-sponsored campus events with Physicians for Social Responsibility. In addition, one Adventist university has mounted an ecumenical and international campaign to create ten thousand quilts for AIDS babies and other displaced children worldwide—providing opportunity for thousands of individuals to respond personally to the AIDS crisis while also facilitating a heightened public awareness of this global issue. Such republic-related issues have been reported in, and at times generated as a result of, exchanges encouraged by the journal *Spectrum*—itself a venture launched by a graduate student community that came of age in the 1960s and called its generation to face more squarely the question of how a remnant community might responsively interface with the republic and the world at large.

Several developments within the church are facilitating discovery and discussion which foster the living out of a social ethic from an explicitly global perspective. Adventist-sponsored public health teams have served as consultants in facilitating the creation of health care delivery systems which are truly structural in nature. The Adventist Development and Relief Agency (ADRA) International has not only expanded development and relief activities to include nearly two hundred countries of the world, but also has expanded volunteer and internship opportunities which enable the church's young people to directly face—and participate in—human rights and limited resources realities that are global and structural in scope. Adventist centers—the Far Eastern Division's Buddhist Center in Bangkok, the Newbold College-based General Conference Global Center for Islamic Studies, Atlantic Union College's Weidner Center for Cultivation of the Altruistic Spirit, Loma Linda University's Center for Christian Bioethics, and La Sierra University's Hancock Center for Youth Ministry and the Stahl Center for World Service—are fostering a dialogue which impacts structures beyond ecclesiastical and geographical borders. And while addressing global involvement, it should be noted that Adventist young people (and others not so young) played active roles in the sweeping structural reform contexts which accompanied the breakdown of the former Soviet Union.

Thus, segments of contemporary Seventh-day Adventism are groping for ways to affirm their prophetic remnant heritage at both personal and social levels. This approach calls for remnant faith communities which are inclusive rather than exclusive; communities which are called to function in a cumulative manner within history rather than being limited to a culminative context at the end of history; and communities which invite institutions and individuals alike to respond to God's gracious call in ways which mediate God's justice and righteousness through both the personal and social realms.

If the thesis advanced earlier regarding religious communities and personal/social ethics is even remotely accurate, I propose that our community of faith will be embraced by its twenty-first century children only as we can pass on those stories from our heritage that call for personal ethics and social ethics to be "of one piece." Our children will not be convinced that they should embrace a remnant heritage on the basis of argumentation which rises or falls on biblical exegesis, objective or subjective genetive language forms, or historical footnotes. Nor will their spiritual and intellectual energies be enlivened by linking biblical texts to "prove" Adventism's remnant status. Rather, they will be attracted to a "cloud of witnesses": a faithful remnant community which is responding to God's gracious acts by truly seeking to incarnate God's justice and righteousness in the lived life of the remnant, the republic, and the world.

Stories which may evoke such a response will include accounts of Joshua Himes' reform movement involvements; John Kellogg's Underground Railroad exploits; John Byington's convention floor fight to advance a strongly-worded anti-slavery resolution; Uriah Smith's censure of what he perceived as a too-cautious President Lincoln for "following his present

26

conservative, not to say, suicidal, policy"; J. N. Andrews' badgering of *Review* readers who would naively contend that their religion can be kept discretely separate from their politics; Sojourner Truth's tie with Adventism while living out her feminist and abolitionist roots; Joseph Bates' castigation of the United States as "this heaven-daring, soul-destroying, slave-holding, neighbor-murdering country" when the U.S. effectively annexed the now-Southwest from Mexico; O. A. Johnson's likening of the U.S. presence in the Philippines to that of the imperialism of Rome; and Ellen White's call to civil disobedience of the Fugitive Slave Acts in phrases that closely parallel those of Martin Luther King.

These stories delineating early Adventism's concern for social justice will be told along with stories of William Miller's calculations on the eschaton, Hiram Edson's pathos in mourning the Disappointment, and Joseph Bates's discovery of the Sabbath teaching. There will also be accounts of wholeness, water cures, health reform, and bloomers—as well as stories of J. N. Andrews setting sail for Europe, Fernando and Ana Stahl establishing schools in the Peruvian Andes, and of H. M. S. Richards preparing to take to the airways from a converted chicken coop to proclaim the Advent hope. These narratives will in turn lead to stories of Dietrich Bonhoeffer, Mohandas Ghandi, Martin Luther King, Mother Theresa, Desmond Tutu, Oscar Romero and other remnant witnesses who have peopled history and of whom the world is not worthy.

The call to exhibit the spirit of prophecy—a truly prophetic spirit—by way of faithfully testifying to Jesus is a call mediated to humankind every generation anew. The prophetic remnant is a faithful remnant, a community of faith that seeks present truth, recognizes the signs of the times, hears God's call for justice and righteousness in these times, and risks acting upon what it hears. Accordingly, the prophetic remnant articulates and incarnates the empowering and hope-full news that God's truth and justice will triumph, that the woman outlasts the dragon, the baby wins over the beasts, and the remnant overcomes Babylon.

A people does not fulfill a "remnanting" function merely because the biblical text may have suggested to forefathers and foremothers that their community was God's remnant—any more than a people can claim to be prophetic on the basis that it once had a prophet. Nor does a faith community merit remnant designation merely on the basis that ecclesiastical leaders or biblical exegetes proclaim such to be the case. For the remnant designation is neither a designation to be claimed or proclaimed. It is, rather, a gracious calling to be humbly listened for and radically lived out.

The children of any would-be remnant community deserve—and will pledge commitment to—nothing less.

Endnotes

This chapter draws upon research generated while the author was a participant in a National Endowment for the Humanities Seminar at Harvard University during the summer of 1984. The initial publication resulting from this investigation was "Bridegroom or Babylon, Dragon or Lamb: Nineteenth-Century Adventists and the American Mainstream," *Adventist Heritage* 2.1 (Spring, 1986): 13-25.

[1] Mt 25:6

[2] Rev 18:2

[3] Rev 13:11

[4] Rev 12:17

[5] Rev 19:10

[6] *Seventh-day Adventist Bible Commentary*, 7 vols. (Washington, DC: Review and Herald, 1957) 7: 815.

[7] J. L. Shuler, "Rediscovering the Faith of Jesus," *Advent Review and Sabbath Herald* 135.21 (May 8, 1958): 8.

[8] Kenneth H. Wood, "The Role of Seventh-day Adventists in End Time," *North American Bible Conference*, by Biblical Research Committee of the General Conference of Seventh-day Adventists (Washington, DC: Review and Herald, 1974) 1.

[9] W. Duncan Eva, qtd. in J. D. Douglas, "Adventists in Vienna: God's Package Deal," *Christianity Today* 27.6 (August 29, 1975): 42.

[10] William Miller, *Evidence from Scripture and History of the Second Coming of Christ About the Year 1843, Exhibited in a Course of Lectures* (Troy, NY: Kemble, 1836) 175. The overview on the rise of the Millerites is Ronald L. Numbers and Jonathan M. Butler, ed., *The Disappointed: Millerism and Millenarianism in the Nineteenth Century* (Bloomington, IN: Indiana University Press, 1987).

[11] Henry Dana Ward, "Circular," Report of the General Conference 20, qtd. in P. Gerard Damsteegt, *Foundations of the Seventh-day Adventist Message and Mission* (Grand Rapids: Eerdmans, 1977) 48.

[12] Henry Steele Commager, *Theodore Parker: Yankee Crusader* (Boston, MA: Little, 1936) 152-3.

[13] "Millerite Lectures," *Liberator* 5.7 (Feb. 14, 1840): 27.

[14] Joseph Tracy, "Anti-Sabbath Convention," *Liberator* 5.49 (Dec. 4, 1840):

194; cp. David T. Arthur, "Joshua V. Himes and the Cause of Adventism" (MA Thesis, University of Chicago, 1950) 6-46; David L. Rowe, "Thunder and Trumpets: The Millerite Movement and Apocalyptic Thought in Upstate New York, 1800-1845" (PhD Dissertation, University of Virginia, 1974) 97; Francis D. Nichol, *The Midnight Cry: A Defense of the Character and Conduct of William Miller and the Millerites, Who Mistakenly Believed that the Second Coming of Christ Would Take Place in the Year 1844* (Takoma Park, MD: Review and Herald, 1944) 174-6.

[15] Charles Fitch, *Slaveholding Weighed in the Balance of Truth and Its Comparative Guilt* (Boston, MA: Knapp, 1837) 121.

[16] Litch, Josiah, *Seventh-day Adventist Encyclopedia* (Takoma Park, MD: Review and Herald, 1976) 791; Nichol, 185-8.

[17] Nichol, 177-80; Rowe, 97.

[18] David Bernard, *Light on Masonry: A Collection of All the Most Important Documents on the Subject of Speculative Free Masonry* (Utica, NY: Williams, 1829), cited in Rowe 97-8.

[19] Rowe, 115; *Rochester Daily Democrat*, Aug. 11, 1834 and July 8, 1838; Eliezer Wright, Jr., to Gerritt Smith, July 16, 1836 (Gerritt Smith Papers, Syracuse University), qtd. in Rowe 323n72; Whitney Cross, *The Burned-Over District: The Social and Intellectual History of Enthusiastic Religion in Western New York*, 1800-50 (Ithaca, NY: Cornell University Press, 1950) 223-4.

[20] Nichol, 191-2.

[21] Ibid.; Isaac Welcome, *History of the Second Advent Message and Mission Doctrine and People* (Yarmouth, ME: Welcome, 1879) 272.

[22] Joseph Bates, *The Autobiography of Elder Joseph Bates* (Battle Creek, MI: Steam Press, 1868) 204ff, 241ff; Nichol 180-4; "Bates, Joseph," *SDA Encyclopedia*, 132-4.

[23] Arthur, "Himes"; "Joshua Vaughan," *SDA Encyclopedia* 585; Winthrop S. Hudson, *Religion in America* (New York: Scribner, 1981) 196.

[24] "Chardon-Street Chapel," *Liberator* 7.20 (May 20, 1842): 79.

[25] Arthur, "Himes"; 36ff; Joshua V. Himes, "Refuge of the Scoffers," *Signs of the Times* [Millerite] 1.9 (Aug. 1, 1840): 72.

[26] Ralph Waldo Emerson, "Chardon Street and Bible Conventions," *The Dial* 3.1 (July, 1842): 101.

[27] Arthur, "Himes"; 39.

[28] Wendell Phillips Garrison and Francis Jackson Garrison, *William Lloyd Garrison: The Story of His Life As Told to His Children*, 4 vols. (New York: Century, 1885-9) 3: 94.

[29] David T. Arthur, "Millerism," *The Rise of Adventism: Religion and Society in Mid-Nineteenth-Century America*, ed. Edwin S. Gaustad (New York: Harper & Row, 1974) 154ff; Ernest R. Sandeen, *Roots of Fundamentalism: British and American Millenarianism, 1800-1930* (Chicago: University of Chicago Press, 1970) 53-4.

[30] Charles Fitch, *Come Out of Her, My People!* (Rochester, NY: Shepard, 1843).

[31] Rowe, 222-3.

[32] Himes, "Opposition in the M.E. Church—Zion's Heralds vs. 'Millerisms,'" *Signs of the Times* [Millerite] 6.2 (Jan. 31, 1844): 196.

[33] William Miller, letter to Elon Galusha, April 5, 1844 (Orrin Roe Jenks Collection of Adventist Materials, Aurora College, Aurora, Illinois), qtd. in David T. Arthur, "Come Out of Babylon: A Study of Millerite Separatism and Denominationalism, 1840-1865" (PhD Dissertation, University of Rochester, 1970) 75; cp. Nichol, 167.

[34] M. P. Chaplin, "Letters to the Editor," *Advent Review and Sabbath Herald* 3.21 (Mar. 3, 1853): 167.

[35] Damsteegt, 147.

[36] For the original account of these early visions see "Letter from Sister Harmon," *The Day Star* 9.7-8 (Jan 24, 1846): 31-2.

[37] Joshua V. Himes, *Views of the Prophecies and Prophetic Chronology Selected from Manuscripts of Wm. Miller; with a Memoir of His Life* (Boston: Dow, 1941) 138, qtd. in Stephan Paul Mitchell, "We are the Remnant: A Historical, Biblical, and Theological Analysis of Seventh-day Adventist Ecclesiological Self-Understanding" (MA Thesis, Loma Linda University, 1988) 7. Mitchell's work informs this section on the faith/testimony of Jesus.

[38] Joseph Bates, *Second Advent Way Marks and High Hopes, or a Connected View of the Fulfillment of Prophecy, by God's Peculiar People from the Year 1840-1847* (New Bedford, MA: Lindsey, 1847).

[39] This period is especially described in James White, Ellen G. White, and Joseph Bates, *A Word to the Little Flock* (Brunswick, ME: np, 1847); cp. Damsteegt 140-6.

[40] Discussion of "the shut door" may be found in such works as "Open and Shut Door," *SDA Encyclopedia*, 1034-7; Ingemar Linden, *1844 and the Shut Door Problem* (Stockholm: University of Uppsala Pres, 1982); Damsteegt, 149-64; Rolf J. Poehler, "And the Door Was Shut" (unpublished paper presented at the Seventh-day Adventist Theological Seminary, 1978); Arthur L. White, "Ellen G. White and the Shut Door Question" (unpublished paper prepared for the Ellen G. White Estate, 1971); Robert W. Olson, ed., "The Shut Door Documents: Statements Relating to the 'Shut Door,' the Door of Mercy, and the Salvation of Souls by Ellen G. White and Other Early Adventists Arranged in a Chronological Setting from 1844 to 1851" (unpublished compilation with occasional commentary by Olson, prepared for the Ellen G. White Estate, 1982); and Dalton D. Baldwin, "The Shut Door" (unpublished paper prepared for the Loma Linda University Division of Religion, nd).

[41] Bates, *Second Advent*, 71-2.

[42] James White, letter to Brother and Sister Hastings, 1848, rptd., in part, as "Letter to Brother Hastings," Olson "Door" 20-1.

[43] James White, letter to Brother Bowles, Nov. 8, 1849.

[44] James White, "The Third Angel's Message," *Present Truth* 1.9 (Apr. 1850): 66-7; James White, A Brief Exposition of the Angels of Rev 14 (np [1850]) 27.

[45] James White, "The Gifts of the Gospel Church," *Advent Review and Sabbath Herald* 7.1 (Apr. 21, 1851): 69-70.

[46] James White, "The Signs of the Times," *Advent Review and Sabbath Herald* 4.7 (Aug. 11, 1853): 50-1, 54-5; 4.8 (Aug 24, 1853): 57-9, 62-3; 4.9 (Sept.4, 1853): 65-7, 70-1; 4.10 (Sept. 13, 1853): 73-6.

[47] James White, "The Testimony of Jesus," *Advent Review and Sabbath Herald* 7.12 (Dec. 18, 1855): 92-3.

[48] James White, *The Perpetuity of Spiritual Gifts* (Battle Creek, MI: SDA Publishing, nd) 15-9; James White, "The Gifts—Their Object," *Advent Review and Sabbath Herald* 7.22 (Feb. 28, 1856): 172-3.

[49] Seasoned academic, administrator, and editor Richard B. Lewis was the first Adventist official to critique in print Adventism's equation of the Apocalypse's term "the spirit of prophecy" with Ellen White. See "Spirit of Prophecy," *Spectrum* 2.4 (Autumn 1970): 69-72. A summary of this article is offered in Donald R. McAdams, "Shifting Views of Inspiration in the 1970s," *Spectrum* 10.4 (Mar. 1980): 28. "[Lewis] pointed out that to use the expression 'Spirit of Prophecy' to refer to Ellen White or her writing was neither precise use of language nor unquestionably sound exegesis of Revelation 14:12 and Revelation 12:17."

[50] J. N. Andrews, "Thoughts on Revelation XIII and XIV," *Advent Review and Sabbath Herald* 1.11 (May 19, 1851): 81-6; expanded in "The Three Angels of Rev. XIV, 6-12," 6.25 (Mar. 20, 1855): 193-6; 6.27 (April 3, 1855): 209-12; 6.28 (May 1, 1885): 217-8; issued in book form as *The Three Messages of Revelation XIV, 6-12; Particularly the Third Angel's Message, and Two-Horned Beast* (Battle Creek, MI: Review and Herald, 1892). John N. Loughborough contributed to this discussion in a series of four articles entitled "The Two-Horned Beast of Rev. XIII, a Symbol of the United States," *Advent Review and Sabbath Herald* 5.8 (June 25, 1857): 57-60; 5.9 (July 2, 1857): 65-8; 5.10 (July 9, 1857): 73-6; 5.11 (July 16,1857): 81-3.

[51] J. N. Andrews, "Thoughts on Revelation XIII and XIV," *Advent Review and Sabbath Herald* 1.11 (May 19, 1851): 83-6.

[52] Bates, *Second Advent*, 47-8.

[53] Joseph Bates, "The Beast With Seven Heads," *Advent Review and Sabbath Herald* 2.1 (August 5, 1851): 3-4; James White, "The Angels of Rev. XIV—No.1," *Advent Review and Sabbath Herald* 2.2 (August 19, 1851): 12.

[54] J. N. Andrews, "Prophecy," *Advent Review and Sabbath Herald* 16.1–2 (May 29, 1860): 1-7.

[55] J. N. Loughborough, "The Two-Horned Beast," *Advent Review and Sabbath*

Herald 5.9 (March 21, 1854): 66.

[56] Ellen G. White, *Testimonies for the Church*, 9 vols. (Mountain View, CA: Pacific Press, [1948, 1859]) 1: 201-2.

[57] Uriah Smith, "The Two-Horned Beast," *Advent Review and Sabbath Herald* 9.19 (Mar. 12, 1857): 148; "Traitors in Power," 19.10 (Feb. 4, 1862): 77-8; James White, "The Seven Times of Lev. XXIV," *Advent Review and Sabbath Herald* 23.9 (Jan. 26, 1864): 68.

[58] White, *Testimonies*, 1: 359.

[59] Ellen G. White, *Early Writings* (Washington, DC: Review and Herald, 1882 [1858]) 275-6.

[60] R. F. Cottrell, "How Should I Vote?" *Advent Review and Sabbath Herald* 7.26 (Oct. 30, 1856): 205.

[61] Jonathan Butler, "Adventism and the American Experience," Gaustad, *Rise* 187. As perhaps the most distinguished cultural interpreter of Adventist history, Butler footnotes Roy Branson, "Ellen G. White—Racist or Champion of Equality?" *Review and Herald* 147.15 (April 9, 1970): 2-3; "Slavery and Prophecy," 147.16 (April 16, 1970): 7-9; and "The Crisis of the Nineties," 147.17 (April 23, 1970): 4-6; as well as Ronald D. Graybill, "America the Magic Dragon," *Insight* 2.48 (Nov. 30, 1971): 6-12. I gratefully acknowledge Butler's provision of a framework for this section of my chapter.

[62] Uriah Smith, "Politics," *Advent Review and Sabbath Herald* 8.19 (Sept. 11, 1856): 152. Temperance appears to be an exception, with some Adventists electing to vote on that issue.

[63] Butler, 187.

[64] James White, "The Nation," *Advent Review and Sabbath Herald* 20.11 (Aug. 12, 1862): 84.

[65] White, *Testimonies*, 1: 266

[66] James White, "Gospel Order," *Advent Review and Sabbath Herald* 4.22 (Dec. 6, 1853): 173; 4.23 (Dec. 13, 1853): 180; 4.24 (Dec. 20, 1953): 188-90; 4.25 (Dec. 27, 1853): 196-7.

[67] Raymond F. Cottrell, "Making Us A Name," *Advent Review and Sabbath Herald* 16.18 (Mar. 22, 1860): 140; James White, "Organization," *Advent Review and Sabbath Herald* 16.15 (June 19, 1860): 36. The organization debate is illustrated in these two articles, both of which employ the "great iron wheel" metaphor. White's reference to a servant leadership model is found in "Organization and Discipline," *Advent Review and Sabbath Herald* 57.1 (Jan. 4, 1881): 8.

[68] Howard B. Weeks, *Adventist Evangelism in the Twentieth Century* (Washington, DC: Review and Herald, 1969) 14.

[69] Edwin S. Gaustad, *Historical Atlas of Religion in America* (New York: Harper & Row, 1966) 115.

[70] Ellen G. White, Ms. 11, 1895, 22.

[71] Ellen G. White, Ms. 43, 1895; letter to J. A. Burden, Nov. 2, 1906; letter to Brethren [A. G. Daniells, J. A. Irwin, W. W. Prescott], Oct. 1, 1907; Ms. 6, 1891.

[72] For discussion of the structural reforms enacted as a result of the 1901 General Conference session see A. V. Olson, *Thirteen Crisis Years: 1888-1901* (Washington, DC: Review and Herald, 1981) and Gilbert A. Jorgensen, "An Investigation of the Administrative Reorganization of the General Conference of Seventh-day Adventists as Planned and Carried Out in the General Conferences of 1901 and 1903" (MA Thesis, SDA Theological Seminary, 1949).

[73] Ellen White's involvement in the work for freed slaves is addressed in Ron Graybill, *E. G. White and Church Race Relations* (Washington, DC: Review and Herald, 1970); and *Mission to Black America: The True Story of Edson White and the Riverboat Morning Star* (Mountain View, CA: Pacific Press, 1971).

[74] For a survey of temperance activities during this period, see Yvonne D. Anderson, "The Bible, the Bottle, and the Ballot: Seventh-day Adventists and Political Activism, 1850–1900," *Adventist Heritage* 7.2 (Fall, 1982): 38-52.

[75] B. Basette, letter to Charles D. Stone, July 26, 1906, cited in D. A. Ochs, "A Study of Religious Legislation in California" (MA Thesis, University of the Pacific, 1934) 55, qtd. in Eric D. Syme, *A History of SDA Church-State Relations in the United States* (Mountain View, CA: Pacific Press, 1973) 28.

[76] White, Testimonies, 9: 205.

[77] Doug Morgan, "Apocalyptic Anti-Imperialists," *Spectrum* 22.5 (January, 1993): 20-7. Morgan cites such sources as various A. T. Jones articles from *The American Sentinel* and Percy T. Magan, *The Peril of the Republic* (Chicago, IL: Revell, 1899): 121. Morgan might also have cited O. A. Johnson, *Bible Textbook* (Washington, DC: Review and Herald, 1900) 161.

[78] R. A. Anderson, *et al.*, *Seventh-day Adventists Answer Questions on Doctrine: An Explanation of Certain Major Aspects of Seventh-day Adventist Belief* (Washington, DC: Review and Herald, 1957) 192.

[79] Ibid.,195.

[80] Gerhard Hasel, *The Remnant: The History and Theology of the Remnant from Genesis to Isaiah* (Berrien Springs, MI: Andrews University Press, 1980).

[81] Daniel Smith, "A Study in the New Testament of the Remnant with Reference to the Seventh-day Adventist Position" (Senior Honors Thesis, Pacific Union College, 1974).

[82] Jack W. Provonsha, "The Church as a Prophetic Minority" (unpublished essay, 1975) 13, published as "The Church as a Prophetic Minority," *Spectrum* 14.1 (Wint. 1981): 18-23.

[83] Charles W. Teel, Jr., "The Call to be a Prophetic Remnant" (unpublished essay, 1975) 7, published in part as "The Apocalypse as Liturgy," *Spectrum* 16.3 (Sum.

1983): 33-43.

[84] Charles Scriven, "The Real Truth About the Remnant," *Spectrum* 17.1 (Oct. 1986): 6-13.

[85] Mitchell.

[86] Roy Branson, "Trumpet Blasts and Hosannas: A Once and Future Adventism," *Spectrum* 18.3 (Dec. 1987): 29-35; "The Demand for New Ethical Vision," *Bioethics Today—A New Vision*, ed. James W. Walters (Loma Linda/Riverside, CA: Loma Linda University Press, 1988) 13-27.

[87] Charles Teel, Jr., "Growing Up with the Beasts: A Rite of Passage," *Spectrum* 21.3 (May 1993): 25-34.

[88] This survey was conducted on October 30, 1989, at the John Osborn Lecture Series, an annual symposium coordinated by the La Sierra University School of Religion and the Pacific Union Conference and held in Riverside, California.

[89] John V. Stevens, Sr. "Supreme Court Balance Threatened?" *Pacific Union Recorder* 86.17 (Sept. 1, 1986): 6.

[90] "Supreme Court Nominations," letter, *Pacific Union Recorder* 86.20 (Oct. 20, 1986): 3.

[91] Robert N. Bellah, *The Broken Covenant: American Civil Religion in Time of Trial* (New York: Seabury, 1975).

[92] Students in my Religion and Society course at what is now La Sierra University's School of Religion conducted this content analysis in the spring of 1985.

[93] Sidney Allen, "The Christian and Modern Culture," *Perspective* 2.2 (1967): 7-13.

[94] J. N. Andrews, "Slavery," *Advent Review and Sabbath Herald* 24.22 (Oct. 25, 1864): 172.

[95] Raymond F. Cottrell, "Churches Meddling in Politics," *Review and Herald* 142.30 (July 19, 1965): 12.

[96] Uriah Smith, editorial comment before "Letter to the President," *Advent Review and Sabbath Herald* 20.17 (Sept. 23, 1862): 30.

[97] Andrews, "The Two-Horned Beast," 203.

[98] See *Testimonies* 1:201-2 for Ellen White's call to civil disobedience of the Fugitive Slave Acts. It is interesting to compare how closely her discussion of civil disobedience parallels that of Martin Luther King, Jr., in his "Letter from a

Birmingham Jail," *Christian Century* 80.24 (June 12, 1963): 767-73.

In no sense do I advocate evading the law as would the rabid segregationist. That would lead to anarchy.

There are two types of laws: just and unjust.

A just law is a man-made code that squares with the moral law or law of God.

One who breaks with an unjust law must do so openly, lovingly and with a willingness to accept the penalty.

Martin Luther King, Jr.
"Letter from a Birmingham Jail"
We have...laws to govern the people. Were it not for these laws the condition of the world be worse than it is now.

Some laws are good, others are bad.

When the laws of men conflict with the laws of God, we are to obey the latter.

The law of our land requiring us to deliver a slave to his master, we are not to obey; and we must abide the consequences of violating this law.

Ellen G. White
Testimonies, Volume 2

[99] J. Milton Yinger, *Religion, Society, and the Individual* (New York: Macmillan, 1957) 267.

Chapter Two

CREATION

JACK W. PROVONSHA

In the beginning ...God created the heavens and the earth.[1]
For in six days the LORD made heaven and earth, the sea, and all that is in them.[2]
Fear God and give him glory, for the hour of his judgment has come; and worship
   him who made heaven and earth, the sea and the springs of water.[3]

Of the topics addressed in a series of essays examining Adventist beliefs
and their significance for personal and social ethics it is hard to imagine one
more foundational to Adventist thought than the doctrine of Creation, or
one more easily side-tracked into areas having little to do with the central
theme of the series—ethics. The mere mention of creation in an Adventist
setting may be an open invitation to rejoin ancient and recent battles over
the correct interpretation of the Genesis account on the one hand, or, for the
few among us who comprehend the new physics, the cosmological implications of Heisenberg's indeterminacy principle on the other.[4]

In this paper I shall avoid both the strict literalism of the fundamentalist
approach to creation and the complexities of quantum mechanics cosmology. Rather, what I shall attempt is to take the biblical foundations on which
our understanding of the Creator and the creation are based and consider
what such beliefs imply for personal and social ethics. Those who wish to
join other battles will have to find for themselves a different jousting field.

The Lord Is One

What are the biblical texts really saying? Let us consider first the
statement that "the LORD made heaven and earth, the sea, and all that is in
them." If we take that statement seriously and conjoin it with the Judaic
Sh'ma, "Hear O Israel, the LORD our God, the LORD is One,"[5] we have the
basis for what H. Richard Niebuhr calls "radical monotheism,"[6] radical in

37

the sense of "roots," monotheistic to its roots or foundations. On this basis the theme of creation is above all profoundly monotheistic. There is for Adventist faith a unity at the heart of the matter. We live in a *uni*verse, not a *multi*verse.

Ellen White sensed this when she wrote that though in the view of some "there is a marked distinction between the natural and the supernatural" and the "natural is ascribed to ordinary causes, unconnected with the power of God," such a position is best described as "false science." "God does not annul His laws," she emphasizes, "but He is continually working through them as His instruments. They are not self-working. God is perpetually at work in nature."[7] This sense of creative, sustaining unity at the heart of things has multiple ramifications that informs virtually every facet of human existence. For example, it not only bridges over the gulf between natural and supernatural, but also softens the distinction between secular and sacred. Thus, Ellen White observes:

> All right inventions and improvements have their source in Him who is wonderful in counsel and excellent in working. The skillful touch of the physician's hand, his power over nerve and muscle, his knowledge of the delicate organism of the body, is the wisdom of divine power, to be used in behalf of the suffering. The skill with which the carpenter uses the hammer, the strength with which the blacksmith makes the anvil ring, comes from God. He has entrusted men with talents, and He expects them to look to Him for counsel. Whatever we do, in whatever department of the work we are placed, He desires to control our minds that we may do perfect work. Religion and business are not two separate things; they are one....Divine and human agencies are to combine in temporal as well as in spiritual pursuits, in mechanical and agricultural labors, in mercantile and scientific enterprises.[8]

Similarly, Paul suggested to the Corinthians the possibility of "sanctifying the secular" when he exhorted, "So, whether you eat or drink, or whatever you do, do everything for the glory of God."[9]

This means that wherever or whenever one acts in a manner to assist, support, or cooperate with the divine creation, one works with and for God. Ambrose Paré, renowned barber-surgeon of three centuries ago, was correct when he said, "I dress the wounds, God heals them," as is the scientist who "thinks God's thoughts after Him."

"Dressing the Wounds"

Those wounds that we dress and God heals should include those in our natural environment. No more effective motivation could be imagined for achieving the enduring sense of stewardship our world is going to need over the long haul for rescuing its skies, lakes, rivers, land and growing things than an awareness that "the earth is the Lord's."[10] Sky, lakes, rivers, streams, land, and growing things—all are God's. To worship the Creator is to respect the creation; to abuse the creation is an affront to the Creator.

This also extends to life itself. Albert Schweitzer's reverence for life is entirely understandable to those who worship the Creator—all life, but especially those forms of life that it is not necessary to destroy out of regard for life at higher levels. Those who may be entrusted to look after life on this planet are those who have come to value the Creator's handiwork at every level. As naturalist Edwin Way Teale once put it, "It is those who have compassion for all of life who will best safeguard the life of man. Those who become aroused only when man is endangered become aroused too late."[11] Thus the Adventist emphasis on a diet that largely excludes using for food those forms of life with which human beings can identify has more than mere dietary significance.

Monotheistic thinking about creation provides the basis for an environmental ethic in which the tension between the "subdue it" motif of Genesis 1:28 and the command to "till it and keep it" of 2:15 is overcome. The goodness of what is created is presumed prior to the coming of humanity. Humanity's role is that of caretaker, one of maintenance and preservation, and after the Fall, one of restoration, rather than one of modification and innovation. Let genetic engineers beware. It is one thing to discover novel ways of increasing the supply of scarce biologicals for the correction of deficiencies in nature, insulin, growth hormone, interferon, and the like, even the replacement one day of defective genes such as those underlying Huntington's chorea; it is quite another to conjure up unknown and possibly dangerous new life forms or, even worse, dream of giving evolution a boost toward some superman of the future. (Whose superman? According to what ideal? The last supermen we had were blond Aryans hurling panzer units around Europe and stoking cremation ovens in places like Dachau and Auschwitz.) It is an act of high blasphemy for human creatures to attempt to usurp the role of their Creator.

According to the biblical doctrine of creation it would be utter dereliction to continue on the present course. As Loren Eisley has said:

> It is with the coming of man that a vast hole seems to open in nature, a vast black whirlpool spinning faster and faster, consuming flesh, stones, soil, minerals, sucking down the lightning, wrenching power from the atom, until the ancient sounds of nature drowned in the cacophony of something which is no longer nature, something instead which is loose and knocking at the world's heart, something demonic and no longer planned—escaped, it may be—spewed out of nature, contending in a final giant's game against its master.[12]

The trouble is, we know what to do about most of the environmental problems that beset us; what we lack is the will. How do we teach people to care—supremely? Never has the call to "Worship Him who made the heavens, the earth, the seas and the springs of water" (Rev 14:7) seemed more poignant. "The earth is the Lord's" (Ps 24:1).

The Sacred and the Secular

The creation includes more, of course, than the starry heavens, the sky, birds and flowers, and physiology, even more than the life of our fellow creatures. God also created humanity's social structures and interactions—the domain of social ethical concern. To cooperate with and support the natural order at the level of the family and community is also to assist in the work of creation. Parents properly rearing their children are doing the work of God—and so are those who endeavor to make their communities safer, healthier, cleaner, better places in which to live. (Let the infertility expert take care, however. It is doing "creation-work" to assist in bringing families into being, but not if one uses means that place in jeopardy the family as a social institution. Surrogate mothers or fathers can be ways of producing offspring, but as recent events suggest, the technique has great potential for producing familial confusion. "Whose baby is this?" is a question that implies "anti-creation-work" at the *social* level.)

According to the radical monotheistic premise no activity is intrinsically secular. There are no such sharp antinomies as intrinsically secular versus intrinsically sacred. There are, for example, no profane versus sacred callings or vocations as such, provided they are consonant with the Creator's intentions. There are only profane or sacred people in them, people who do or do not recognize the unity and essential goodness of everything God has made or is making. On these terms the laboratory can be as holy as the chancel and the market-place as sacred as the sanctuary; there is holiness in housework and good government, in being a mother or a mayor, or in constructing a fine piece of furniture.

Surely this is the sense of Paul's reference to the spiritual gifts in 1 Corinthians 12. In the words of Thomas Chalmers: "If it be the characteristic of a worldly man that he desecrates what is holy, it should be of the Christian to consecrate what is secular and to recognize a present and presiding divinity in all things."[13] There are, however, some places, objects, times, and vocations that call attention to this truth more than others. These may play a symbolic, reinforcing role. A sanctuary can come to stand for the universal Presence of God, a book can come to symbolize the Word of God, the Sabbath can call attention to the sacredness of all time, and we ordain ministers and priests to remind us of the sacredness of all callings.

The radical monotheism of the biblical creation rejects another ancient antinomy that was to have fateful consequences for the social order, that of spirit and matter. As John A. T. Robinson reminds us, a man "does not *have* a body, he *is* a body. He is flesh-animated-by-soul, the whole conceived as a psychophysical unity."[14] The unity of the human person is a microcosmic reflection of the ultimate unity of creation.

Such a wholistic view has been a dominant theme in Adventist thought from the beginning. Mainly, at first, it projected a belief in conditional immortality. In the course of time, however, the consequences of the idea went far beyond convictions about the state of human persons in death. The following from the pen of Ellen White written about the turn of the century demonstrates how wholistic thinking eventually came to be expressed:

The relation that exists between the mind and the body is very intimate. When one is affected, the other sympathizes. The condition of the mind affects the health to a far greater degree than many realize. Many of the diseases from which men suffer are the result of mental depression. Grief, anxiety, discontent, remorse, guilt, distrust, all tend to break down the life forces, and to invite decay and death.[15]

41

> Whatever injures the health, not only lessens physical vigor, but tends to weaken the mental and moral powers. Indulgence in any unhealthful practice makes it more difficult for one to discriminate between right and wrong, and hence more difficult to resist evil. It increases the danger of failure and defeat.[16]

Such wholistic thinking was bound to affect the way the body was viewed by early Adventists. The syncretism of Christian and Platonic notions about the body, the spirit, and the after-life, especially the dualism that had been reshaped by Gnostic and Manichæan negativism regarding matter, had fateful consequences. The material body came to be viewed as a burden, a clog to the soul. St. Dorotheus, one of those desert fathers who took such notions over-seriously, was asked what he was doing out working in the heat of the sun. Did he not know that he might kill his body in this way? He replied, "I mean to kill it, for it is killing me." St. Hildegard, possibly the earliest woman physician, said in the same spirit, "God rarely dwells in a healthy body." Francis Thompson captures the ethos of the period in his essay *Health and Holiness.* "To drive a donkey to death was regarded as cruel, but to do the same to one's own body was thought to be meritorious."[17] Before their deaths, this tyrannical treatment of their "curse-laden" bodies brought pangs of conscience to some of the most zealous of these saints. "I was too hard on Brother Ass," St. Francis confessed when it was too late. It was only then that he invented the beautiful phrase, "Brother Body."

Creation, Health, and Healing

Though sometimes too-vigorous in their pursuit of health, Adventists were not motivated by ascetic reasons. To believers in creation the body was a temple, to be looked after, nurtured, and protected from harmful substances and practices.

Creation thinking lay behind one of the most distinctive marks of the Seventh-day Adventist Church, its emphasis on health and healing. This emphasis has resulted in the establishment of two medical schools, a dental school, schools of public health and allied health, numerous schools of nursing, one of the largest health care systems in the United States, and literally hundreds of medical and health-related institutions around the world.

The kind of health care given in these institutions also reflects creation-conditioned thinking. Adventist health-care personnel think in terms of "the wisdom of the body," natural remedies, whole-person care, and assisting the body's own healing processes. Even the fact that the latest scientific technology, instruments, and therapeutic agents enter into the healing regimen reflects a wholistic conception of the Creator and of divine activity at every level.

There has been an association of religion and healing, of course, since time immemorial. The healing ministry of Jesus and His, "Which is easier, to say 'Your sins are forgiven you,' or to say, 'Stand up and walk'?"[18] established a basic ideal for the Christian church. Centuries after New Testament times this prayer was still being said at the ordination of bishops: "Grant him, O Lord, to loose all bonds of the iniquity of demons, the power to heal all diseases, and quickly to beat down Satan under his feet." What was intended by this, however, was "spiritual" or "faith" healing rather than scientific therapeutics. In fact, Justinian I closed down the medical schools at Athens and Alexandria as invasive of the church's healing prerogatives.

But while some protested "that confidence in drugs and material remedies detracted from the 'pious acknowledgement of God,'" the facts are that the very flowering of science is actually a natural consequence of radical, monotheistic creation thinking.[19] An affirmation of nature as a domain of the Creator's activity is a fruitful soil for scientific investigation and application. It is on this ground that early Adventist thought rejected the manipulative, largely prescientific therapeutic use of often dangerous chemicals in favor of more "natural remedies."

Ellen White had much to say that was critical of drug therapy as it was practiced in the last century—as well she might. But it also followed that resistance against medicinal treatment softened as medical practice became increasingly scientific, based on an understanding of human physiology not available earlier. "Natural remedies" came to be those that were consonant with the body's physiologic processes—even if they were packaged as pills and injectables. The Creator can also be at work in the scientist's laboratory!

Ideas Have Consequences

Ideas usually have consequences. For example, how a group views reality will frequently reflect itself in the institutions it creates and vice versa. Adventists have been slow to grasp some of the consequences of monotheistic thinking, for a variety of reasons, including sectarian other-worldliness. But the implications of commitment to Creation are being seen with increasing clarity of vision. This is partly due to the relative independence education has brought to many Adventists. It is an important development because it offers that possibility of self-renewal, without which every social institution ultimately arrives at social entropy. Wound up clocks inevitably run down at the end unless they are periodically re-wound.

Dualistic thinking, especially when the material was downgraded under the influence of the Gnostics and Manichæans, historically conditioned social structures, notably the church. One result was a dualistic separation of clergy and laity. Institutionalized, this duality came to reflect a role-value distinction analogous to that given to soul and body. Spirit was good, flesh was evil, hence the "spirituals" became valued in ways that "seculars" were not. Eventually this resulted in a clerical power-elite pretty well running things while the primary role of the lay masses was simple obedience.[20]

Radical monotheism rejects such antimonies. There are *functional* differences within social structures that reflect the larger reality, but no categorical value-level distinctions. God dwells on both floors!

The organizational wholism that this suggests is enormously important to the history of an institution. That self-renewing, entropy-resisting potential that is so crucial to the continued vitality of a movement or organization depends on a free flow of influence from below to the top as well as from the top down. Indeed, renewal usually wells up from below. Rarely is it engineered by those at the pinnacles of power. Wholism suggests the interaction of the whole. It knows how to create authority, and also knows how to guide, nurture, and check it.

Creation and the Moral Order

Finally, one of the most important aspects of a radically monotheistic perception of creation has to do with its implications for moral verity. God, who is the creative source of all that is, is also its sustaining ground of being. Because there is ultimately nothing higher, outside of, or beyond God there is no morality beyond God either, that is, to which God need conform. God is thus also the creative ground of all moral being. All valid patterns of moral behavior (ethics) will necessarily reflect the divine creation and can be considered as descriptions of it (in contrast with being arbitrary or merely prescriptive).

Another way of stating this is in reference to the will of God. It is common-place in Bible-based ethical discourse to say that the right and the good are what God wills. But the Creator of everything wills what truly *is*, and the *ought* can properly be derived from it. I realize that this statement can be either a source of confusion or of assurance as one tries to put it into practice, depending upon whether one feels confident about one's access to what truly *is*. It may help a little if I explain that by what *is* I simply mean that to which God has given being, what God has created, namely, for present purposes, the natural personal and social orders *as God has willed them*, the creation, in other words, in accordance with the divine intention.

It is precisely here that we encounter the perpetual "storm over ethics" that dissipates so much of our moral energy. Those created, natural orders are not nearly as obvious or simple as people think—or as all of us might wish. But let us back up a bit.

One of the strengths of a creation-based ethic is the level of seriousness it brings to the ethical enterprise. Our changing ethics lexicon reflects the gradual loss of its base in creation thinking. For example, terms like "maladjusted," "sociopathic," or even "unethical," can never really substitute in power for that old-fashioned word that is on almost nobody's lips these days—*sin*, sin as opposition to or disharmony with the moral creation.[21]

Sin is a theological term; that is, its definition depends upon some kind of conception of God. The two stand or disappear together. Bertrand Russell notes, "Although the sense of sin is easy to recognize and define, the concept of sin is obscure, especially if we attempt to interpret it in nontheological terms."[22] Similarly, Frederic Greeves stresses that the Christian "cannot complete any statement about the nature of sin without reference to God."[23]

It is God's Creatorship that puts a serious face on the ethical enterprise. Without this ground we would have to be content with vitiated motivational relativities like prudence, preference, and taste as the foundations of ethical responsibility.

But there is a "rub" in all this. If we base moral judgment on the creation, on the will of God, the *ought* on God's *is*, we are still left with the practical question, that of what this *is* consists. What has the Creator created? Surely not everything we see around us.

As soon as we include the word sin in moral discussion we also infer qualities like responsibility, culpability, and guilt that in turn presuppose freedom of choice on the part of sinners. This is, of course, manifestly biblical. The Bible goes even further, however, placing the issue in the cosmic arena. There is a Fall. There is opposition to the Creator and the creation affecting nature as well as the natural orders. Paul speaks of "the whole creation...groaning in labor pains."[24] Unfortunately, the cosmic problem of evil is not the assignment before us. I refer to it only to make the point that discovering what we ought to do in any particular instance by merely looking around us is to invite moral disaster. Surely the *ought* is not to be simply derived from *this is*. The facts are that norms cannot simply be read off from any purely human appraisal of the "creation" presently available. And surely we have had enough misery in the world from Nietzsche's attempt to ground the "good" on Charles Darwin's description of nature.

> What is good? Everything that heightens the feeling of power in man, the will to power, power itself. What is bad? Everything that is born of weakness. What is happiness? The feeling that power is growing, that resistance is overcome. Not contentedness but more power; not peace but war, not virtue but fitness....What is more harmful than any vice? Active pity for all the failures and all the weak: Christianity.[25]

Der Antichrist and two world wars should have settled that issue forever. Given the ambiguity of the creation as it is now perceivable by us, human observation alone can never give us the normative certainty we desire.

Without the Creator's assistance we shall never be certain about the right and good. Believers recognize that such assistance comes in a variety of forms and never fully bypasses human participation. One form it has taken is called revelation. Revelation of one sort or another is a key to confidence in doing normative ethics.

Unfortunately, revelation of the divine will, the true *is* of creation, has its own share of problems, including lack of specificity. Often it seems out of date and behind the times. We shall probably never be able to simply read off the answers to complicated bioethical dilemmas from a guide-book that never dreamed of our technological revolution, and we shouldn't expect it.

What we are given, however, are clues and basic principles that help us to discover the essence of the creation-ideal, especially in the Word that was made flesh and dwelt among us. We can also catch glimpses of what the whole creation is intended to be like under the hand of its Creator, glimpses of a time and place in which all persons are brothers and sisters, children of a common Father. This is the highest ethical meaning of a radically monotheistic creation. The unity of all things points to the unity of all persons. Surely this is at least a part of the significance of those Isaiah descriptions of the heavens and the earth made new. Creation is about universal sisterhood and brotherhood one day.

An Orderly Universe

To summarize: the concept of a Creator who creates and sustains everything that is, and who is thus beyond and prior to every creature as well as that upon which every creature depends, is a doctrine portraying a radically monotheistic reality. This is a concept with implications for every facet of existence.

The Creator who is One is the ground of a *uni*verse, that is of a creation in which a fundamental, multidimensional unity everywhere prevails. This perception rejects stark antinomies of natural and supernatural, of secular and sacred, and of material and immaterial as in a separable spirit or soul and material body.

It follows from this that the Creator may be encountered also in the natural realm over which God gave us stewardship. To worship the Creator is to respect and to show protective regard for that creation in all of its dimensions, for the natural environment, especially in all its living forms, including one's own body. It also includes looking after the created social orders, the family, the various levels of community, etc. The primary task of ethics is to develop patterns of behavior that fulfill the demands of that stewardship.

An ethic based on the creation gives to the enterprise a level of seriousness that transcends prudence, preference, or taste. To be unethical, to oppose, to negate or destroy the creation is, in fact, to sin against the Creator. "The earth is the Lord's," and that includes all the creatures in it as well as their created social orders.

The creation motif acknowledges such opposition in the Christian concept of the Fall. But the Fall has so confused the creation according to the biblical understanding of evil that another fact of existence enters the picture. Because of it, it is now not possible simply to read off the Creator's will and intentions in nature or human relationships. In other words, it is not possible at this point in time to derive the Creator's *ought* directly from what now *is*. We need assistance, and that assistance comes in what has been traditionally called revelation. According to the Bible, the Creator has also been at work in the creation guiding and informing as well as sustaining. It is this that lends special force and relevance to a biblically-based ethic.

We are thus given to know by faith that even in this time and place the quest for meaning in ethics is not an empty one. Ours is an orderly universe. There is purpose and the rule of beneficent law in it. There is also a living, personal Creator to assist us as we strive to be true to the divine creational intent.

Endnotes

[1] Ge 1:1.

[2] Ex 20:11.

[3] Rev 14:7.

[4] My sympathies lie at present with the late Andrei Kolmogorov, Soviet mathematician and developer of modern probability theory, who once said, "Mathematics begins where common sense leaves off." Even Einstein responded to Heisenberg's indeterminacy principle, "Herr Gott würfelt nicht"—God does not play dice.

[5] As in Dt 6:4.

[6] H. Richard Niebuhr, *Radical Monotheism and Western Culture* (New York: Harper & Row, 1960).

[7] Ellen White, *Testimonies to the Church*, 9 vols., (Mountain View, CA: Pacific Press, 1871-1912) 8: 259-60.

[8] Ellen White, *Christ's Object Lessons* (Washington, DC: Review and Herald, 1900) 359.

[9] 1Co 10:31.

[10] Ps 24:1.

[11] Edwin Way Teale, source unknown.

[12] Loren Eisley, *The Firmament of Time* (New York: Atheneum, 1962) 123.

[13] Qtd. in Frank S. Mead, ed., *Encyclopedia of Religious Quotations* (Old Tappan, NJ: Revell, 1965) 226.

[14] John A. T. Robinson, *The Body: A Study in Pauline Theology* (Chicago: Allenson, 1952) 14.

[15] Ellen White, *Ministry of Healing* (Mountain View, CA: Pacific Press, 1909) 241.

[16] Ibid., 128.

[17] Qtd. in Josef Goldbrunner, *Holiness is Wholeness* (New York: Pantheon Press, 1955) 20.

[18] Lk 5:23 NIV.

[19] Leslie Weatherhead, *Psychology, Religion, and Healing* (New York: Abingdon Press, 1951) 81.

[20] Karl Holl, "History of the Concept 'Vocation' (*Beruf*)," trans. H. F. Peacock (unpublished, nd) 16, 17. Holl characterizes this development in the later Middle Ages as it affected the professions:

> On this basis, late scholasticism projected an over-all plan for social life within which it sought to relate to one another the calling (*Beruf*) of the monk and secular work. It is found broadly developed first in Berthold of Regensburg. Taking his start from Pseudo-Dionysius and his nine angelic choirs, Berthold sees the human social order divided into nine choirs. At the top stand the three ruling choirs: the pope with the priests; then the spiritual people, *i.e.* the monks; in the third place, secular magistrates, lords and knights. Beneath these come the six lower choirs; from the garment makers down to those who deal with medicine.
>
> A tenth choir was made up of prostitutes, usurers, hucksters, junk dealers, indulgence preachers and the like who were considered to be engaged in occupations in which doing right was impossible. Holl does not emphasize as he might the gulf between the three ruling choirs and

what came below in matters affecting the church.

[21] Karl Menninger, dean of American psychiatrists, notes the move away from sin-language in his last book, *Whatever Became of Sin?* (New York: Hawthorn, 1973) 13.

[22] Qtd. in Frederic Greeves, *Meaning of Sin* (London: Epworth, 1956) 3.

[23] Greeves, 16.

[24] Ro 8:22.

[25] Friedrich Nietzsche, "The Antichrist," *The Portable Nietzsche*, trans. Walter Kaufman (New York: Viking Press, 1954) 570.

Chapter Three

COVENANT

MICHAEL PEARSON

I am...your very great reward.[1]

In the last six months of 1982, Seventh-day Adventists were provided with a set of Sabbath School lessons on the covenant; the two quarters' lessons collectively were described as constituting a "covenant series." One quarter's lessons, by Gerhard Hasel, pursued the covenant theme from creation through Noah, Abraham, Moses, and David to the new covenant with Jesus Christ. The other set, by Gottfried Oosterwal, explored such contemporary moral and social issues as divorce, abortion, racial tension, and the right to work.

Two things struck me as odd about this "covenant series." First, in Hasel's set of lessons, the word "covenant" was liberally sprinkled about in the titles of lessons, sub-headings, and paragraphs, while it rarely appeared in Oosterwal's lessons. Secondly, Oosterwal's lessons on ethical issues were on the agenda for the third quarter, with Hasel's contribution following during the fourth. Thus, consideration of the practical issues *preceded* study of the covenant motif itself.

These lessons suggested a number of things about the Adventist understanding of the covenant. I sensed that the concept of covenant was inextricably bound up with our identity *as a group*, that we wished to demonstrate to ourselves—if to nobody else—that we were the covenant people in the contemporary world. But it nonetheless appeared that this business of identification had little to do with the way we conducted ourselves in the wider world. Evidently, for Adventists, the covenant was—paradoxically— a personal and private matter, intended principally to address the individual's relationship with God. Consequently, Adventists found it difficult to conceive of social responsibility as issuing from the terms of the covenant itself; covenant and social responsibility were thus distinct, even unrelated, in most Adventist minds.

The first impressions created in me by those Sabbath School lessons have, of course, to be tested against a wider range of Adventist thought and action; this is what I shall seek to do here. Its purpose is threefold: to do some preliminary sounding in Adventist thought on the theme of covenant; to assess the merits of those attitudes that we observe; and to explore the ways in which the biblical notion of covenant might inform Adventist behavior now and in the future.

The Concept of Covenant

There are various understandings of what "covenant" means. The political model emphasizes the continuity between God's covenant and the formal contracts which underpinned those alliances that were common in the history of the ancient Near East.[2] These treaties generally adopted the following scheme:

1. A statement of the jurisdiction of the king or kings involved.
2. An outline history of the relationships that existed between the forebears of the signatories.
3. An enumeration of the conditions of the treaty.
4. An account of the benefits accruing to each party from the treaty.
5. An invocation of the appropriate gods as witnesses to the alliance, together with promises of blessings that would reward fidelity to the treaty and threats of curses that would attend upon its non-fulfillment.

It is not surprising to find the idea of covenant extended beyond the political realm to describe a religious reality. The use of such a metaphor was quite common in the ancient Near East and seems to be used to describe Yahweh's relationship to Israel.

Some commentators, however, are unhappy about pressing the parallel between political treaties and God's covenant with Israel too far. The reason is perhaps not too hard to find: this understanding of the covenant may appear to make humanity's part in it little more than a prudential act, a series of calculations based on long-term self-interest. These scholars prefer to emphasize the idea that what we find in the covenant is nothing more than the series of commitments and expectations, privileges and responsibilities, joys and sorrows, that go with belonging to a family. They would cite as evidence the fact that the biblical covenant contains a much higher number of appeals to good motivation than might be expected in formal legislation. Others see *promise* as the dominant theme of the covenant. For them, covenant history is an account of God's desire to be prodigal in the distribution of His benefits and of His frustration at humanity's narrowness of vision.

Traditional Adventist Views

Early comment carried in the *Review and Herald* represented a uniquely Adventist contribution to this attempt to define the nature of covenant. Those who addressed the issue took pains to emphasize that the Ten Commandments, an expression of God's character, existed from eternity, and believers were commanded to obey them. The covenant, on the other hand, was an agreement entered into by Israel with God, made with respect to the Decalogue and subsidiary concerns. This distinction between the Ten Commandments and the Covenant served in early Adventist thinking to guard against the possibility that the Decalogue—and with it the Sabbath, the most important distinguishing characteristic of this group of Christians—might be understood as having been nullified when God replaced the Old Covenant with the New. It is perhaps not without significance that early Adventists were required to sign a "covenant" in which they promised to keep the Sabbath.

One cannot escape the conclusion that Ellen White's perspective on the covenant was broader than that of her fellow-travelers, that she recognized that in considering the covenant theme there was more to do than defend denominational identity. Thus she speaks of the "wide-embracing terms of the covenant" and the responsibility of the Israelites to share the practical benefits of covenant-keeping.[3] When she applied the term to church life, she referred to a range of activities: avoidance of debt,[4] child-care,[5] consumer-spending,[6] diet,[7] use of language,[8] membership in secret societies,[9] healing,[10] and so on. The dominant impression is of a wider understanding of the term than was common among other Adventist writers.

A Contemporary Perspective

Not only were Ellen White's contemporaries sometimes less sensitive to the breadth and depth of the covenant's meaning than she, but their successors have not always exhibited greater appreciation for its varied dimensions. Paradigmatic for Adventist thought on the covenant to date are, I believe, Gerhard Hasel's Sabbath School lessons, to which I return briefly.

Throughout these lessons it is stressed that it was God who took the initiative in pursuing fellowship with man; it was God who preferred to indulge in spontaneous acts of love rather than exact obedience. Hasel is cautious about drawing too close a parallel between the covenant and political treaties because he wants to insist that "the keeping of the covenant is not designed to earn anything."[11] Beginning with Noah, Hasel traces throughout biblical history the theme of a chosen people called to covenant obedience which, he stresses, "was the result and not the condition of being a holy people."[12]

In the first eight lessons certain pervasive and continuing tensions are evident—the tension between enjoyment of the privileges emanating from a special relationship with God and the temptations to exclusivism, self-congratulation, pride, and triumphalism; the tension between genuine response to God's generosity and disciplined but calculated formalism. In lesson nine, one senses that the tension is broken; this lesson is devoted to the Sabbath. The Sabbath, we are told, is "to be observed as an external and visible sign of a relationship with God."[13] It is a "test of loyalty," a "sign of God's covenant community."[14] It "separates God's people from the rest of mankind."[15] Hasel supports his position by quoting Ellen White,[16] but I think he fails to address her own subtle qualifications about who constitute the people of God. Lesson eleven is devoted to a consideration of the sacrificial system and the heavenly sanctuary, and a further lesson to the practical consequences of living in a covenant relationship with God—principally the enjoyment of peace within and a general desire to share the good news.

I cannot escape forming two conclusions: first, that a primary purpose of these lessons was to reassure Adventists of their special status as God's covenant people; second, that the lessons were more concerned with the identification of the covenant community than with a consideration of its responsibilities, which seems strange in light of Hasel's acknowledgement that the covenant-keeping people are "separated unto [God]...for service to the world." As such, these lessons on the covenant appear to be a rather self-centered exercise, though it should be remembered that at the time when they appeared, the church was in considerable doctrinal turmoil.

Separation and Responsibility

The problem I have sought to identify is part of a larger dilemma that Christians from many traditions have long sought to resolve: How does one pursue purity of life while maintaining solidarity with those whose lives are impure? How does a community of faith maintain distinctiveness of identity without becoming isolated from the wider world? How does the church remain a faithful remnant that seeks to protect its moral integrity while attempting to communicate the everlasting gospel to a world in which such integrity seems increasingly meaningless?

The typical Adventist response to this dilemma has been characterized by stress on inner purity. But Adventists have never been able to feel entirely comfortable about adopting *in toto* this fruit of their Anabaptist heritage. The Anabaptists believed that the church was to be a visible community which was to function as a model to the world of how life was to be lived. Their commitment to a self-evident purity begat a stress on rigorous discipline and on rebuke. It produced sanctity sometimes at the price of aloofness, and engendered hostility, sometimes perhaps unnecessarily. In principle, at least, the evangelistic imperative does not allow for such aloofness in Adventism.

Remnant and Covenant

Adventist eschatology must surely be taken into account as we try to understand the continuing tension between separation and responsibility. There is undoubtedly an ambivalence in Adventism between the remnant's anticipation of the Second Advent and the here-and-now focus of its social concern, an ambivalence between the dark and threatening clouds of apocalyptic judgment and the clear, secure image of an Adventist hospital.

55

Adventism's perception of its role in the end time demands above all else that the church be preserved inviolate to perform its vital eschatological function. A principal consequence has been that Adventists have sought an elusive political neutrality. This policy of maintaining a low profile in order to dispel opposition to the church's evangelistic work may work more or less well in liberal democracies, but it has left the church awkwardly placed on occasions when it exists under a form of totalitarian government.[17]

It is paradoxical, however, that while avoiding political involvement as far as possible, there have been times when the church has used the machinery of politics to protect the interests of its own members in relation to such issues as religious liberty, labor union membership, and military service. The church's concern to protect the civil liberties of its members, while entirely understandable, has created difficulties in the eyes of some observers. It seems that the covenant people have unwittingly espoused an ethic of self-interest. Other worthy but non-denominational causes have normally failed to attract Adventist support. Believing ourselves to be separated for service, we have nonetheless found it easier to separate than to serve.

Some Possible New Directions in Covenant Thinking

As we attempt a reassessment of the covenant's meaning for the present, we may well need to look again at the Ten Commandments, the center of the covenant as we have typically understood it. We may have, for instance, to look at the commandment against bearing false witness and ask whether our failure to make our voices heard on certain issues is not tantamount to lying. Might not a "low profile" sometimes be just a cover for low integrity? We keep silence individually, sometimes, in order to retain our influence, or even our jobs, and corporately in order to promote internal unity or to avoid costly engagement in socio-political issues. Such a craven spirit is not in harmony with the covenant.

We may have to inquire whether our failure to champion human rights is the equivalent of breaking the sixth commandment by installments. These may be the human rights of those persecuted under totalitarian regimes in whose plight we show little interest.[18] They may even be the rights of a particular group in our own midst whose members die a little inside every time we deny them the respect and access to opportunity that should be theirs.

The Decalogue further demands that we honor our fathers and mothers. In a society where we tend to esteem people according to their function we need to look at this commandment again. Does the retirement home business represent institutionalized rejection of the fifth commandment? While that might be to overstate the case, we must still ask ourselves whether we can be truly content with a situation in which, because of our compulsive addiction to work and our thoughtless commitment to social mobility, old people are isolated from that which and those whom they love best.

And there is also a political dimension to the question.[19] Would we be so prepared to honor our seniors that we would accept a substantially higher level of taxation in order to make more revenue available for their well-being? Is it in any way an indictment of our society that care of the elderly is passing from social to private agencies? Unwilling freely to accept greater economic responsibility for such groups, we subject them to the whims of market forces.

But the covenant beyond the Decalogue has more to teach us. As I reread the terms of the Sinaitic covenant I am impressed by the sense of corporate responsibility that pervades it. In cases, for instance, in which the death penalty was to be visited upon an offender, *the people of the community* were to join in stoning him or her.[20] The laws governing gleaning and the Jubilee Years further underline the idea that we *are* our brothers' and sisters' keepers.

Unfortunately, this notion of civic responsibility is somewhat diluted in Adventist thinking. To the general Protestant emphasis on individual responsibility, Adventists have added an understanding of judgment that tends to lend great weight and urgency to matters of personal piety and private morality. In Adventist literature, the emphasis on the role of the will in human behavior is strong. The Adventist commitment to a self-sufficient individualism tends to be resistant to the idea of corporate responsibility.

Let me offer an example: some Adventists would wish to take a strong stand in opposition to abortion. They would want to say that anyone having an abortion commits sin, that huge numbers of abortions are among the cardinal sins of the age. They would feel that it was part of the witness of a covenant people to say such a thing. But, if they are right, the covenant demands that we go further. If we wish a woman in our midst who is unwillingly pregnant to proceed to term, then we as a church community must be prepared to provide that support—emotional, social, financial—which will make the difficult option of continuing the pregnancy possible. If we wish simply to state an ideal without helping desperate individuals to reach that ideal, then I believe, the covenant teaches we ourselves are guilty too.

Closely allied to the idea of corporate responsibility is the concept of structural sin. We not only perform discrete sinful acts but incorporate sinful attitudes, values, and responses into the mechanisms by which we habitually regulate our lives. Inside the church we may create administrative systems that concentrate power into the hands of the few and that perpetuate a kind of ecclesiastical "insider trading." Outside the church, we are part of a socio-economic system that, for example, disadvantages Third World peasant farmers in order to provide us with inexpensive bananas. Hasel asks us to ponder the question, "What grief may my sin have caused God today?"[21] It is a legitimate question. But we must also inquire "What grief may our sins—corporate sins of omission as well as commission—have caused God today?"

And here we are close to another prominent covenant theme: the covenant community cannot tolerate within itself extremes of wealth and poverty. We must be alert to the temptations of consumerism, for there is ample sociological evidence to show that Adventists believe that they have a right to their fair share of the national prosperity. Members of the covenant community have to maintain an economic availability to weaker members.[22]

A character who figures relatively frequently in the terms of the covenant is the alien. The stranger in Israel was always to be treated with respect and generosity. In our culture a commitment to this principle might translate into respect for refugees or immigrants. More generally, I think it means treating justly and with respect any whom we perceive to be a threat to us. It may mean struggling with our prejudices against those of different ethnic backgrounds. Equally it may mean cultivating sensitivity toward our superiors or our juniors. I am convinced that in contemporary Adventism, it means extending to women prerogatives hitherto only conferred upon men, not least ordained ministry and responsibility for the future of the church. Resistance to such a move, I think, is often born of a deep and unarticulated fear in the male psyche. The spirit of covenant love casts out such fear.

Again, the covenant constantly warns us against all forms of idolatry. We are well aware of our inclination to make idols of our material possessions and professional aspirations. Another form of idolatry is nationalism. We are sometimes blindly committed to the supremacy of our nation in some field regardless of other social or moral consequences.

Further, it is legitimate to question whether Adventism has absorbed into its ethos any traits which derive from the identity of the United States rather than the covenant people.[23] I wonder, for example, whether Adventism's compulsive concern for unity—which is often simply a concern for uniformity of practice—is in any way an expression of the American anxiety to make one nation out of many.

It is also possible, of course, to idolize even the symbols and fruits of God's covenant blessing. Israel's experience with the bronze serpent provides an instructive case. God provided the serpent so that Israelites who had been victims of potentially fatal snake bites might live. Later, however, in the reign of Hezekiah, the serpent had to be smashed because it had become an object of idolatry. Is there anything within Adventism that was designed to be a blessing but has become a hindrance because we have become idolatrous in our attitudes toward it? Could this apply to our organization, to health reform, to the ministry of Ellen White, to our remnant identity?

And I have hardly scratched the surface of covenant teaching. The covenant theme offers insight into how we should conduct ourselves in the modern world. It teaches ecological concern. The principle of not harvesting fruit from a new tree until its fifth year, together with the Sabbatical year, warns us against overexploitation of the earth. We should be active in protecting our environment even though we may believe that it is destined not to last forever in its present state.

The covenant teaches that work confers dignity on people. Further, our work confers significance on our Sabbath. Can we therefore legitimately speak of the right to work, and what would be the practical consequences of such talk? In my own country, Great Britain, where (until recently) ten percent of the work force faced the debilitating effects of unemployment, it is an important question.

The covenant encourages us to act considerately toward the handicapped. What have we done to promote the interests of the disabled? Is there any point of contact between covenant *shalom* and the peace movement? Does the covenant provide any insight into our treatment of AIDS victims? In short, there are rich veins in the covenant yet to be mined.

Some Guiding Principles

Rather than continuing indefinitely to delineate specific conclusions that ought to follow from our commitment to the covenant, let me suggest some principles that may help to guide our thinking as we continue to explore ways to make our dedication to God real in the present.

We uphold the covenant's integrity and foster its continuing vitality when we avoid the temptation to limit its applicability by appealing to Ellen White. I can well imagine that you shrink, as I do, from the demands of the covenant that I have described because they are so huge. We seek to restrict or contain the demands of the covenant, to make them manageable, achievable. One of the ways in which we have done this is by using the writings of Ellen White to redefine the terms of the covenant. We have used her writings to create a set of demands that, if fulfilled, we have believed, constitute honoring of the covenant. But surely this is inadequate, as I suspect she would be quick to point out were she alive today. Society has moved on and the problems confronting us are not identical with those faced by our Victorian forebears. We must be careful that we do not try to tame a covenant whose terms, as Ellen White reminds us, are all-embracing.[24]

We fulfill the terms of the covenant through availability and vulnerability to God and others. You may feel that I have used the covenant motif to promote Adventist involvement in all kinds of contexts. You would not be far wrong. But this is not in an attempt to be fashionable. It is not activism for activism's sake, not relevance at all costs. As is the case with any intimate relationship, there is no limit to the claim upon our being. The God of the covenant calls us to availability and vulnerability: to God and to God's other children, our brothers and sisters. The kinds of social responsibility I have described are not an optional extra for would-be covenant keepers; they are a natural outgrowth of the covenant.

We make the covenant operative through committed service in small groups. Throughout this essay I have talked about "we," "Adventists," and "the church," and it is time to say exactly what I intend. There is, I believe, no distinction between social and personal ethics. I am not for a moment suggesting that the church should immerse itself in social activism at the expense of evangelistic concern. The institutional church *could* involve itself more without unduly exposing itself, but it clearly cannot take direct responsibility for all the causes to which I have referred. Rather, I should like to see individual Adventists, groups of Adventists, Adventist congregations, feeling more inclined to give themselves to causes for which they are fitted by their situations, interests, and expertise. And those who do thus involve themselves should be made to feel by the rest of us that they are bearing witness, that they are using their spiritual gifts, that they are performing a ministry.

We show our faithfulness to the covenant when, individually and communally, we are open to people "where they are." The covenant is always initiated and restored by a God who relentlessly pursues the best interests of the covenant people. And surely those created in the divine image should similarly take the initiative in extending those blessings. Too often we expect people to come to us, to meet us on our own ground and on our terms. We like to tell them what they need rather than listen to their account of their own needs. In this we are unduly protective of ourselves, of our purity and identity.

We witness to the God of the covenant as we speak prophetically to the moral issues of our time. I fear that we have allowed our concern for doctrinal uniqueness to degenerate into a social unobtrusiveness that is but a short step from irrelevance. It is easy to be so concerned with discerning the signs of the times that we accept no responsibility for changing those times. We prefer to follow the "script" than to speak freely. We could feel greater pride in our church if we could more frequently speak from a position of strength on moral issues. That is, we could take initiatives early rather than grudgingly make concessions under pressure from the state or radical groups in our midst.

Lastly, we affirm the covenant when our discussions of its meaning never eclipse the loving community to which it calls us. I believe that the fighting that takes place in Adventism over the covenant—over law and grace, justification and sanctification, sinfulness and perfectionism—is a great offense. We need to learn to trust each other more fully even when we disagree.

In short, the covenant calls us to *do* the truth, corporately as well as individually. Shall we accept that challenge, or do we have too many vested interests in maintaining the *status quo*?

Endnotes

[1] Ge 15:1.

[2] These continuities have been ably exhibited by Meredith G. Kline in *The Treaty of the Great King* (Grand Rapids: Eerdmans, 1966). Portions of this book have been reprinted in *The Structure of Biblical Authority* (Grand Rapids: Eerdmans, 1971).

[3] Ellen White, *Prophets and Kings* (Mountain View, CA: Pacific Press, 1908) 368.

[4] Ellen White, *Counsels on Stewardship* (Washington, DC: Review and Herald, 1940) 257.

[5] Ellen White, *The Ministry of Healing* (Washington, DC: Review and Herald, 1905) 396.

[6] White, *Counsels on Stewardship*, 74.

[7] Ellen White, *Testimonies for the Church*, 9 vols. (Mountain View, CA: Pacific Press, 1948) 9: 153.

[8] Ibid., 243.

[9] Ellen White, *Evangelism* (Washington, DC: Review and Herald, 1946) 618.

[10] White, *Testimonies* 2: 273.

[11] Gerhard F. Hasel, "The Everlasting Covenant," *Senior Sabbath School Lesson Quarterly* (1982): 20. See also his *Covenant in Blood* (Mountain View, CA: Pacific Press, 1982) 11.

[12] Ibid., 42.

[13] Ibid., 88.

[14] Ibid., 92.

[15] Ibid., 93.

[16] For instance, Ellen White, *Selected Messages*, 3 vols. (Washington, DC: Review and Herald, 1958) 2: 160.

[17] For examples, see the various articles in *Spectrum* 8.3 (March 1977): 2-24.

[18] Including our own members. The story of Romanian Adventist Dorel Catarama and his treatment by the Romanian Adventist hierarchy is detailed in Sidney Reiners, "Catarama's Romanian Ordeal—Where Was the Church?" *Spectrum* 18.1 (Oct. 1987): 26-31.

[19] As to many of the questions a reconsideration of the commandments force us to address.

[20] Lev 20:2.

[21] Hasel, "Covenant," 131.

[22] Joe Mesar offers a challenging proposal for the achievement of this goal in "Income-Sharing in the Local Church," *Spectrum* 16.2 (1985): 24-28.

[23] For discussions of this problem in the broader context of conservative American Protestantism, see Richard Quebedeaux, *The Worldly Evangelicals* (New York: Harper & Row, 1984) and Tom Sine, *The Mustard Seed Conspiracy* (Waco, TX: Word, 1982) 5-83.

[24] Ellen White, *Prophets and Kings*, 368.

Chapter Four

SANCTUARY

David R. Larson

And have them make me a sanctuary,
  so that I may dwell among them.[1]
And the word became flesh and lived among us,
  and we have seen his glory,
  the glory as of a father's only son,
  full of grace and truth.[2]
And I heard a loud voice from the throne saying,
  "See, the home of God is among mortals.
  He will dwell with them as their God;
  they will be his people,
  and God himself will be with them;
  he will wipe away every tear from their eyes"[3]

It is difficult to ponder Seventh-day Adventist interpretations of the earthly and heavenly sanctuaries as portrayed in the Old and New Testaments without mixed feelings. On the one hand, it is easy to take pleasure in the comfort the "sanctuary message" provided those who eventually formed the denomination following the "Great Disappointment" of October 22, 1844.[4] Their "blessed hope" exposed the Millerites to ridicule; however, it also gave their lives meaning and purpose and their associations a closeness that few human groups enjoy. Their common anticipation assured the Millerites, some of whom had once worshipped a distant and almost indifferent God as deists, that God was in their midst, that indeed the Creator did dwell with humanity.

All this ended on October 23, 1844. The Millerites had been wrong and now they knew it. They were heartbroken and embarrassed. Perplexed and dejected, they felt abandoned even by God, the very One who had once seemed so near. The suggestion of Hiram Edson and others that the cleansing of the sanctuary which began on October 22 took place in heaven

65

rather than on earth assured these forerunners of Seventh-day Adventism that something of cosmic importance actually did occur on that date. This doctrinal proposal also renewed among them a continuing sense of God's presence.[5] Those who passed through the Great Disappointment received much solace from the "sanctuary message" and they bequeathed their sense of God's nearness to their descendants. For this, it is easy to be grateful.

On the other hand, thoughtful observers must be saddened by the conflict this doctrine has prompted for virtually a century and a half. Debates between Seventh-day Adventists and other Christians have been painful enough; the disputes within the denomination have been unbelievably agonizing, especially in the twentieth century.[6]

Sanctuary Stresses and Strains

As long ago as 1905 Albion F. Ballenger, a clergyman who had served successfully as a specialist in religious liberty and public evangelism in the United States and Great Britain, was expelled from the Seventh-day Adventist ministry because his views regarding the sanctuary were deemed unacceptable. Among other things, Ballenger doubted that the resurrected Jesus postponed His intercessory ministry until the middle of the nineteenth century. Ballenger pled to be shown wherein his understanding of the Bible was in error and contended in almost pathetic ways that he was a loyal member of the church. Despite his pleas, Ballenger's ministerial colleagues banished him from the calling to which he had devoted his life. He died a brokenhearted man about a decade and a half later.

Two young ministers named L. H. Christian and M. L. Andreasen eavesdropped on Ballenger's 1905 heresy trial at a campmeeting in Washington, D.C., by alternately standing on each other's shoulders in the dark outside an open window.[7] Although their theological sympathies were with Ballenger's accusers, they found him personally engaging in subsequent encounters. Andreasen was especially attracted to Ballenger; nevertheless, he spent much of his long career refuting Ballenger's views. Andreasen detected more quickly than others in the 1950s that some Adventists were perhaps leaning too far backward in their attempts to make the denomination's convictions acceptable to such conservative Protestants as Donald

Grey Barnhouse and Walter Martin. Andreasen, by then quite elderly, wanted Adventist thinkers to "stand tall" and not compromise their commitment to the church's traditional beliefs—and he said so vigorously, sometimes even vociferously.

The result of the conflict that ensued was that on April 6, 1961, about half a century following the dismissal of Ballenger, Andreasen was removed from the ministry for promoting too strongly views which were similar to the ones held by those who had previously expelled Ballenger. Andreasen was more than eighty years old when his credentials were removed. He subsequently became distressed, depressed, and sometimes even delusional. He died on February 19, 1962 from a bleeding ulcer; on March 1 his ministerial credentials were posthumously restored.[8]

This unhappy state of affairs would prompt more than enough sorrow even if these debates and their accompanying pain had died with Ballenger and Andreasen. But they didn't. They have continued, with the wounds becoming deeper and wider as those whose views are more like Andreasen's and those whose views are more like Ballenger's debate each other and other points of view in ways that are sometimes unworthy of followers of the Prince of Peace.

In view of these difficulties, it is not surprising that some contemporary Seventh-day Adventists distance themselves from all current discussions of the "sanctuary message." This is a mature choice to make if the only options are to side with the Andreasen camp or to support the Ballenger forces—since to do either would be to continue the destructive battles.

But there are other options. One of these is to return to the Old and New Testaments, and to reconsider their portraits of the earthly and heavenly sanctuaries to see if these portions of the Bible can speak with power to those in this generation as they did to earlier ones. Seventh-day Adventists who exercise this third option might do well to imagine themselves standing on the theological shoulders of Ballenger and Andreasen, the first to the left and the second to the right. From that more lofty position, with one foot on each giant's shoulder, they can hope to see more clearly what the sanctuary meant to the ancient people of Israel and what it might mean to themselves and to their children.

At times they will lean more heavily on Andreasen's views; on other occasions they will press more firmly on Ballenger's; in still other circumstances they will leap with joy and freedom into theological heights that neither envisioned. They will do so with respect and gratitude to both Andreasen and Ballenger, however, as well as to the many others who did so much at such great sacrifice to make it possible for another generation to discover for itself the presence of God through the "sanctuary message." It is in this spirit that I offer the following reflections.

Sanctuary and Metaphor

The sanctuary motifs of Scripture remind us that religious language, like all human discourse, is metaphorical. Appropriate confidence and caution are therefore in order.

When I was an undergraduate at a Seventh-day Adventist college, it was sometimes popular to distinguish theological liberals from conservatives by asking, "Do you believe there is a literal sanctuary in heaven?"[9] Even then it seemed to me that there was something wrong with that question. My uneasiness about framing the issue in that way has increased over the years.

No Seventh-day Adventist has ever believed that in heaven there is a temple that corresponds exactly to the tabernacle that was pitched in the middle of the camp during ancient Israel's wilderness wanderings.[10] To mention just one relevant consideration, the Israelite sanctuary was covered in part with the skins of certain dead animals. No one would suggest that God dwells in such a structure. This is why in 1887 Uriah Smith declared that the heavenly sanctuary resembled the earthly "as nearly as heavenly things may resemble the earthly...."[11] Smith may have put it the wrong way around—Scripture, after all, suggests that the earthly is patterned after the heavenly, something he knew.[12] He is certainly right, however, to note that there are differences between the two realities which wise persons must bear in mind. Adventists have always rejected the notion of a one-to-one correspondence between the heavenly and earthly sanctuaries. They have also sensed, I believe correctly, that there is some similarity between the two that can be instructive and illuminating if properly understood.

In their struggles over this issue, Adventists in their own way have been participating in the old and complicated debate regarding the logical function and status of religious language. Believers have always wondered how eternal and divine matters can be described in the words of finite and fallible humans. The assumption that religious terms are univocal, in the sense that one can use the same word in reference to two items, one transcendent and one mundane, and mean precisely the same thing, seems unrealistically literal, naïvely so. The opposite view, that religious language is equivocal, leaves us wondering if we can communicate at all because a single term can mean such different things when used regarding the earthly or the heavenly.

Eventually, the conviction that religious language is neither univocal nor equivocal but analogical triumphed in most theological circles. On the analogical view, there is a "point of contact" between the meanings of a term when applied to either matters human or divine, but these meanings are not identical. One uses religious discourse with confidence, therefore, that one is speaking meaningfully but also with caution bred by a keen awareness of the limitations of such expressions.[13]

At least three features of the religious language discussion in the twentieth century are pertinent to this discussion. One of these is the distinction made by Paul Tillich and others between "signs," which arbitrarily refer to things other than themselves, and "symbols," which involve themselves and us in participatory and telling ways in what they describe.[14] In this sense, the earthly sanctuary may be viewed as a symbol of the heavenly. It actually involved the believer in the reality toward which it pointed: reconciliation of humans to God and with each other. The sanctuary and its various services did not merely point toward these possibilities in haphazard ways. It involved the worshipper in God's ongoing work of reconciliation through rituals, holy days, and artifacts that appealed to human senses.

A second feature of the discussion in the twentieth century is that, in some circles, the term "analogical" is being replaced by the term "metaphorical."[15] This is not a mere change in words about the same thing with no further significance. At the very least, the idea that religious language is metaphorical rather than "merely" analogical emphasizes that such discourse appeals to the whole person and to the entire community and not merely to the cognitive abilities of a few academics. Metaphor stands, perhaps, in the same relation to analogy as poetry does to prose: more evocative, more provocative, and more comprehensive in its appeal and no less true for being so. Metaphors can be clustered in "models" for some specific purpose; the gain in coherence, however, usually requires a greater or lesser sacrifice of immediacy. Biblical language regarding the heavenly sanctuary is decidedly metaphorical.

A third feature of the conversation regarding religious language in the twentieth century may be the most important. This is the growing consensus that all human discourse, and not merely religious language, is inescapably figurative or metaphorical. Some Christians attempt to express the metaphors of Scripture in modern, non-metaphorical language—"de-mythologizing," as this translation is often called. The difficulty with this approach, which strikes me as a fascinating but futile cul-de-sac, is not that it recognizes how metaphorical (or, as some would say, "mythical") biblical language is and how foreign to contemporary sensibilities the metaphors of the Bible sometimes are; the problem, rather, is that these translators seem naïvely unaware of the metaphorical ("mythical") nature of their own terms as well as of the limited potency of some of their own figures of speech.

It is not as though we have two kinds of language, literal and metaphorical. All human discourse is figurative. Some metaphors are clearer than others. Some are more precise than others. Some are more successful in promoting individual and communal well-being than others. Some are more consistent with themselves than others. And some cohere more adequately with others. In these and other ways a particular metaphor can be more or less true. There is, however, no purely literal realm of human language in any sphere of endeavor.

Modern readers of the Bible have no reason to be embarrassed by the figurative nature of its depictions of the heavenly sanctuary or of anything else. Neither do they have any reason to treat these metaphors in overly literalistic or wooden ways. Instead, every attempt should be made to allow this language to speak to us in truth and with love.

The Centrality of Worship

The sanctuary motifs of Scripture remind us that an early question historically and an important question ethically is "which deity will you honor with the whole of your life?"

One who reads what the Bible says about the earthly and heavenly sanctuaries can begin with one or the other of several different passages. It is particularly useful, however, to start with some material in the Holiness Code as it is now available to us in Leviticus 17. This selection helps us to understand the origins of the sanctuary as well as the moral and political significance of its development:

The Lord spoke to Moses: Speak to Aaron and his sons and to all the people of Israel and say to them: This is what the Lord has commanded. If anyone of the house of Israel slaughters an ox or a lamb or a goat in the camp, or slaughters it outside the camp, and does not bring it to the entrance of the tent of meeting, to present it as an offering to the Lord before the tabernacle of the Lord, he shall be held guilty of bloodshed; he has shed blood, and he shall be cut off from the people. This is in order that the people of Israel may bring their sacrifices that they offer in the open field, that they may bring them to the Lord to the priest at the entrance of the tent of meeting, and offer them as sacrifices of well-being to the Lord. The priest shall dash the blood against the altar of the Lord at the entrance of the tent of meeting, and turn the fat into smoke as a pleasing odor to the Lord, so that they may no longer offer their sacrifices for goat-demons, to whom they prostitute themselves. This shall be a statute forever to them throughout their generations.

And say to them further: Anyone of the house of Israel or of the aliens who reside among them who offers a burnt offering or sacrifice, and does not bring it to the entrance of the tent of meeting, to sacrifice it to the Lord, shall be cut off from the people.[16]

This passage's portrait of a priest sprinkling the blood of animals upon the tabernacle's altar and of God enjoying the odor of burning fat are not likely to be easily enjoyed by modern readers. The selection is instructive, however, because it reminds us that the people of Israel had forms and objects of worship, including sacrifices, before the sanctuary became a part of their lives. Before the sanctuary was universally accepted by the journeying Israelites, they and the others in their encampments were already sacrificing in a variety of places and ways, each family or clan possessing its own form of worship as well as its own deities. Moses attempted to unite the various clans into one community that worshiped one true God in one sanctioned spot in one approved manner.

We see here the shifts, gradual though they were, from polytheism through henotheism toward monotheism. We also notice that continuing membership in the emerging unified community of Israelites was contingent upon shifting from local sacrifices to common ones. The severe penalties imposed upon those who continued to sacrifice in their own ways and places to their own local deities testify to the importance of these transitions for the new society. These punishments also imply that there was a strong temptation to worship and sacrifice locally.

The people apparently experienced an inner tug-of-war, pulled toward the sanctuary service and toward solidarity with the other Israelites, but tugged as well by the local satyrs in smaller communities where they habitually sacrificed. The passage pictures Moses declaring in different words the message of the first commandment, "You shall have no other gods before me."[17] The question before the people of Israel was not whether they would worship but what, or whom, they would honor with the whole of their lives and with their sacrifices.

The question, "Which deity will you serve?" emerged early in the history of the sanctuary system in Israel. It erupts quickly in the moral experience of modern persons and societies as well. Like those who trekked from Egypt to the Promised Land, we, too, are faced with decisions regarding the local satyrs and provincial communities we tend to serve. And like them, the question for us is not "Will you worship?" but "What, or whom, will become the center of your lives?" This is a theological question. It is also an ethical one. It is actually the most important ethical question an individual or society can ponder.

At this point we confront a biblical assumption about human beings. This assumption is that, in addition to everything else that distinguishes them from other animals, humans are creatures that worship. Biblical religion does not countenance the possibility of comprehensive atheism, if by asserting this possibility one implies that it is conceivable that some persons or groups might worship nothing at all. Thus the Bible rarely wonders aloud if God exists. It assumes that many gods do in fact exist and that these satyrs or centers of value simultaneously tug various persons and various communities in different directions. The satyrs whom we serve may be kind or foolish, righteous or evil, permanent or temporary; however, they will be present and powerful in one form or another.

The first challenge that must be addressed in the modern quest for moral maturity is the same question that emerged so early in the development of the sanctuary system in ancient Israel. It was uttered by Elijah on Mount Carmel centuries later: "How long will you go limping with two different opinions? If the Lord is God, follow him; but if Ba'al, then follow him."[18]

This challenge provides a distinctively theological contribution to political analysis that can be exhibited if we consider the fury of movements such as Nazism. One can study Hitler's movement from historical, psychological, sociological, economic, and geographical perspectives and learn much. One will nevertheless fail to understand Nazism, or any other totalitarian regime, unless one also understands it as personal and communal idolatry. Only then does one understand the intense devotion, the willingness to sacrifice everything to the cause, and the eagerness to destroy every competing system. To miss the sad truth that Nazism made a particular human community the supreme object of its devotion in idolatrous ways is to trivialize the Third Reich even though one's other analyses of the movement may be illuminating.

An interesting comparison of cultural analyses is available to students of Christian ethics in Walter Rauschenbusch's *A Theology for the Social Gospel*[19] and H. Richard Niebuhr's *Radical Monotheism and Western Culture*.[20] Both volumes are worth reading, but I suspect that the judgment of history will be that Niebuhr's critique is the more penetrating. Although Rauschenbusch provides many helpful insights, he mistakenly declares that idolatry is no longer a major temptation for modern men and women. Niebuhr's work, by contrast, proceeds from the premise that idolatry is the single most pervasive and permanent temptation that moderns face. His book invites us to stop offering sacrifices to the provincial satyrs, irrespective of their great attractiveness, and to make the Creator the center of our trust, loyalty, and value. This is a recent echo of a challenge that the Holiness Code portrays Moses as offering at the door of the tabernacle in ancient Israel.

Liturgy and Moral Integrity

The sanctuary motifs of Scripture remind us that in authentic worship liturgy and moral integrity enable and enrich each other.

Intense religious devotion sometimes smothers all interest in personal and social holiness. This can occur in several ways. The most cognitive expression of this tendency occurs when persons become persuaded that the ordinary world of everyday life is so lacking in either value or actuality in comparison with spiritual realities that it makes no sense to improve the tangible affairs of life. A more affective version of this same tendency occurs when people are so overwhelmed by intense moments of religious ecstasy in personal or corporate worship that they become bored with the daily struggle to improve the living conditions of humans and other creatures.

73

The voluntaristic variation of this trend takes place when persons exhaust themselves so completely in liturgical or ceremonial fastidiousness that they have no remaining vision or vigor for improving things. Jesus warned of a perennial problem when he criticized those of his day who tithed "mint, dill, and cummin" while neglecting "the weightier matters of the law: justice and mercy and faith."[21]

Because their various doctrines of creation agree that the ordinary world is real and good though finite and fallible, Judaism, Christianity, and Islam are not particularly inclined toward cognitive circumventions of moral and political endeavor. Even the affective temptation, though it is felt somewhat more strongly than the cognitive one, is not experienced as powerfully by Jews, Christians, and Muslims as the voluntaristic ones.

Persons and communities whose lives have been shaped by the Bible's view of the world as God's creation tend to be energetic and activistic. Too often, however, this ethical vitality and political forcefulness lose their sense of purpose and proportion. The faithful then become faithless by investing great sums in matters of small consequence.

The condemnation of this tendency is severe throughout the whole Bible. Consider God's attitude as depicted by Amos:

> I hate, I despise your festivals,
>   and I take no delight in your solemn assemblies.
> Even though you offer me your burnt offerings and grain offerings,
>   I will not accept them;
> and the offerings of well-being of your fatted animals
>   I will not look upon.
> Take away from me the noise of your songs;
>   I will not listen to the melody of your harps.
> But let justice roll down like waters,
>   and righteousness like an everflowing stream.[22]

The New Testament in its own way warns of the difficulties Amos denounced when, among other things, it declares that in the stressful times of the last days there will be those who will be seen "holding to the outward form of godliness but denying its power."[23]

The Old Testament depictions of the ancient tabernacle remind us that the sanctuary and its services were designed to enhance the quest for personal and social holiness. Consider, for one thing, the tabernacle itself and its furniture. Within the Most Holy Place of the tabernacle twin cherubim gazed downward toward the mercy seat and, as it were, through it to the contents of the Ark of the covenant: Aaron's rod, a pot of manna, and, most importantly, the Ten Commandments, inscribed on two tables of stone. The moral law of the people of Israel was thereby enshrined as a liturgical reminder of the ethical and political expectations of Israel's God: "You shall be holy, for I the Lord your God am holy."[24]

The various sacrifices and services that took place throughout the year in the sanctuary also emphasized the overriding importance of personal and social holiness. Burnt offerings, sin offerings, and peace offerings expressed gratitude and contrition to God; in addition, however, guilt offerings expressed repentance especially for offenses toward other humans, some of which may actually have been inadvertent. A burnt offering was presented every morning and every evening throughout the entire year, even on those days when other offerings were also presented. Additional burnt offerings were offered on the Sabbaths, on the "new moons," and on the three major festivals of the year: (1) the Feast of Unleavened Bread at the time of the barley harvest; (2) the Feast of Weeks, or Pentecost, at the wheat harvest; and (3) the Feast of Tabernacles at the olive and fruit harvest. The Feast of the Blowing of the Trumpets celebrated the inauguration of the civil year on the first day of the seventh month.

Nine days later, on the tenth day of the seventh month, the Day of Atonement, by far the most holy day of the year, was celebrated. The Day of Atonement was a time of "holy convocation" in which the people were instructed to offer themselves in intense repentance and moral resolve as they contemplated the year that had ended and the one that was beginning. On this, the holiest of all holy days, the priests offered special sacrifices and conducted special rituals, including that of slaying one goat before the Lord and releasing another in the wilderness after the sins of the people had been confessed over its head, as liturgical symbols that reminded all that "on this day atonement shall be made for you, to cleanse you; from all your sins you shall be clean before the Lord."[25] It is doubtful that in the entire history of religions there has been a holy day with rituals that articulated more clearly and profoundly the religious importance of personal and social holiness than the ancient Hebrew Day of Atonement.

Although they differ in their explanations of this analogy, Seventh-day Adventists think that the present age relates to the whole history of humankind as the Day of Atonement related to the entire year in ancient Israel. This era, like the Day of Atonement, is a time of momentous spiritual and ethical importance. It is an epoch in which those who have ears that hear and eyes that see will be especially aware of their own needs, as persons and as communities, for repentance and renewal.

This time, like the ancient Day of Atonement, is a joyous epoch to be sure, but not in a giddy way. Ours is an era of joyous solemnity, a time in which there should be a heightened sensitivity to the holiness of God and to the holiness God expects of individuals and societies. From this perspective, intense religious devotion does not smother the quest for personal and communal holiness. Instead, it enables and enriches this search as virtually nothing else can.

What does it mean to "cleanse" the sanctuary? It means today what it has meant for thousands of years: to rid oneself and one's community of injustice in every form. The greatest paradigm of this for Christians is the picture of Jesus banishing from the Jerusalem temple those who had gradually and unwittingly transformed it into a den of thieves who plundered the poor.[26] In such acts of moral and political courage, and only in such deeds among humans, is the sanctuary truly "cleansed."

"Without the Shedding of Blood…"

The sanctuary motifs of Scripture remind us that there is no reconciliation without sacrifice.

The sacrificial system in the ancient Hebrew sanctuary offends many modern readers, and rightly so. The Hebrew word for blood occurs more than three score and ten times in the book of Leviticus alone. Those of us who read this book today are not drawn to its detailed instructions regarding animal sacrifice. One need not be a convert to some form of "animal liberation" to feel disgust at the Bible's specific mandates as to how the animals should be carved and arranged on the altar; about where the head, liver, and kidneys should be placed; about what should be done with a sacrificed animal's fat and sinew; about what should be done with its skin, and worst of all, the suggestions that the smell of burning flesh pleased the One who created life in its myriad forms.

What can one say regarding the notion that the burning of dead animals can provide "a pleasing odor to the Lord"?[27] How can modern persons understand this language of sacrifice in ways that neither distort the past nor require us to return to it?

Despite its indisputable goriness, the sacrifice of animals in the ancient Hebrew sanctuary may have constituted genuine moral progress in its time and place because it entailed a firm rejection of the sacrifice of humans.[28] To sacrifice human blood to the Creator of all life was to pollute the sanctuary so profoundly that capital punishment for the offender was judged appropriate. The sacrifice of animals may well have been progressive then, though it would be atavistic now.

Also important is the evident linkage between the idea of restitution to an injured human and the notion of expiation to God. This connection meant that it was not enough merely to atone for one's sins by sacrificing to God, because the one who was injured by one's misdeeds deserved compensation, as is evident from passages such as Leviticus 6:4-7. Here, while sacrificial expiation by way of the death of a healthy ram is declared to be religiously necessary, it was viewed as insufficient unless accompanied on the very day of the sacrifice with a restitution replacing that which had been injured or confiscated plus an additional twenty percent.

In time among Hebrews and Christians the notion of sacrifice as expiation was overwhelmed by the notion of sacrifice as restitution and even this was eventually eclipsed by the notion of sacrifice as living from day to day so as to foster reconciliation. Isaiah's portrayal of God's attitudes are very refreshing when read in light of the suggestions of Leviticus that the smell of burning animals provides a pleasing odor to the Creator:

> What to me is the multitude of your
>   sacrifices? says the Lord;
> I have had enough of burnt offerings
>   of rams and the fat of fed beasts;
> I do not delight in the blood of bulls,
>   or of lambs, or of goats.
> Wash yourselves; make yourselves clean;
>   remove the evil of your doings
>   from before my eyes;
>   cease to do evil,
>   learn to do good;
>   seek justice,

rescue the oppressed,
defend the orphan,
plead for the widow.[29]

Many centuries after Isaiah, Paul of Tarsus could invite the Christians at Rome "by the mercies of God, to present your bodies as a living sacrifice, holy and acceptable to God, which is your spiritual worship."[30] He went on to specify the meaning of sacrificial living in terms that bristle with the challenges of reconciliation:

> Bless those who persecute you; bless and do not curse them. Rejoice with those who rejoice, weep with those who weep. Live in harmony with one another; do not be haughty, but associate with the lowly; do not claim to be wiser than you are. Do not repay anyone evil for evil, but take thought for what is noble in the sight of all.[31]

Such a sacrificial life, a life in which one loves God with one's whole being and one's neighbor as oneself,[32] can be a very costly, even bloody, endeavor, as evidenced by the cross upon which Jesus died. Anyone who attempts to "overcome evil with good"[33] will suffer, and sometimes profoundly so. Though—or perhaps precisely because—He was God incarnate, even Jesus was not spared the sacrifices that living so as to enable reconciliation inevitably requires in a world such as ours. There is, in fact, no reconciliation unless someone is willing to sacrifice, as everyone knows who has attempted to reconcile a family, church, institution, or nation. The ancient letter to the Hebrew Christians declares that "without the shedding of blood there is no forgiveness of sins."[34] We might put it this way: "no sacrifice equals no reconciliation."

Some Christians understand the death of Jesus as a substitutionary payment made to God for human waywardness, almost as if in this one instance God demanded the slaughter of an innocent human life as Moloch did so often. It is neither necessary nor helpful to understand sacrifice in general or the sacrifice of Jesus in particular as an expiation presented by humans to God, however. If one holds that God was truly incarnate in Jesus, then one can also contend that at the cross the Creator and Sustainer of all things did not *receive* a sacrifice but *embodied* one so as to effect reconciliation throughout the entire universe.

Few modern Christians understood as clearly as did Martin Luther King, Jr., that there can be no reconciliation without sacrifice. King did not relish the shedding of blood. He thought it inevitable, however, in every attempt to foster reconciliation by challenging unjust social systems. He therefore was not surprised when in the course of his leadership he and his family faced the reality of suffering. But for King, suffering was more than inevitable; it could be, and often was, redemptive in the course of human affairs. Only if the oppressed, without capitulation but without retaliation, absorbed the pain caused by injustice could evils be overcome and achieved. King knew that this was painful. He also knew how hard it was to be willing to pay this price. But he paid it with his own life. King's life and death revealed what the words and deeds of Jesus demonstrated more perfectly and more profoundly two thousand years earlier: there can be no reconciliation where there is no willingness to sacrifice.

Sacrifice and Theodicy

The sacrifice of Jesus on the cross was unique because it demonstrated once and for all how God always responds to evil.

Those who do not understand the death of Jesus as an expiation by which humanity satisfied divine wrath are sometimes accused of depreciating the meaning of the crucifixion as well as the events that preceded and succeeded it. Seventh-day Adventists have on occasion been accused by other Christians of making this error. Some within the denomination have also argued that its understanding of Christ's atonement has been insufficiently sensitive to the uniqueness of the sacrifice of Jesus on the cross. This argument sometimes turns upon whether one holds that the atonement was "completed" at Calvary.

Some Seventh-day Adventists, anxious to underline God's continuing endeavors on behalf of reconciliation, have denied that the atonement was complete at Golgotha. Other Adventists have taken the opposite view out of a desire to protect the decisiveness of that event. The matter has therefore been the occasion for controversy between Seventh-day Adventists and other Christians and among Adventists themselves.

One reason that this debate continues is that both points of view protect important insights. From the very first, Christians have held that something unrepeatable, something decisive, something unique in the strictest sense of the term took place at Calvary. Thinkers within the various Christian communities have explained this decisive event in different ways. But its uniqueness is for them "a given," as it should be for us. On the other hand, however, it seems, *prima facie*, odd to imply that God's reconciling activity was not initiated until the time of Jesus and that it ended on Easter morning, as if God is no longer actively reconciling humans to each other and to God. Even to express the matter that baldly rightly seems offensive. Furthermore, if one limits the discussion to the words of Scripture, one can find passages in the New Testament that support the idea that the sacrifice of Jesus was unique as well as the idea that Jesus' intercessory ministry did not end on Easter.[35] The task, therefore, is not to side with either group in the continuing debates as to how "complete" the work of Jesus was on the cross. The challenge is to find some way to do justice to the uniqueness of that event as well as to God's reconciling activities before and after the cross.

Those who authored the book *Seventh-day Adventists Answer Questions on Doctrine*, a "representative" if not "official" statement by the denomination in the 1950s, accepted this challenge. "Seventh-day Adventists have frequently been charged with teaching that the atonement was not completed on the cross. Is this charge true?" they asked.[36] Perhaps the most helpful feature of the volume's response declared that the "answer to this question depends upon the definition given to the term 'atonement.'"[37] The discussion then indicated that some Christians understand the term to apply solely to what Jesus accomplished on the cross and that others use the word more comprehensively to refer to other aspects of God's reconciling activity as well.

In addition to reviewing the various ways the relevant Hebrew terms are used in the Old Testament and pointing to the differences between the daily and annual sacrifices in the ancient tabernacle, the authors gave this interpretation:

> Some of our earlier Seventh-day Adventist writers, believing that the word "atonement" had a wider meaning than many of their fellow Christians attached to it, expressed themselves as indicating that the atonement was not made on the cross of Calvary, but was made rather by Christ after He entered upon His priestly ministry in heaven. They believed fully in the efficacy of the sacrifice of Christ for the salvation of

men, and they believed most assuredly that this sacrifice was made once for all and forever, but they preferred not to use the word "atonement" as relating only to the sacrificial work of Christ at Calvary....Their concept was that the sacrifice of Jesus *provided* the means of the atonement, and that the atonement itself was made only when the priests ministered the sacrificial offering on behalf of the sinner. Viewed in this light, it will be seen that the question after all is a matter of definition of terms. Today, not meeting the same issues that our earlier writers had to meet, we believe that the sacrificial atonement was made on the cross and was *provided* for all men, but that in the heavenly priestly ministry of Christ our Lord, this sacrificial atonement is *applied* to the seeking soul.[38]

Thus, it would seem, the authors of this statement held that the atonement was "complete" with the sacrifice of Jesus on the cross in the sense that this offering established the objective foundation for reconciliation but that the atonement was not "complete" on the cross in the sense that the subjective realization of reconciliation was not wholly achieved at Calvary.

This solution has received mixed reviews. Some have found it very helpful. Others have found it problematic, either because it yielded too much or because it yielded too little to the notion of a "completed" atonement at Calvary.

My own reactions are mixed. *Questions on Doctrine* rightly attempted to do justice to both legitimate concerns. Its interpretation therefore deserves careful consideration. In addition, the volume staked its proposal upon a "wider" meaning of the notion of atonement. In several ways, the authors of this volume rightly contend that the term "atonement" can refer to the complete scope of God's reconciling gestures toward humans and not solely (one should not say "merely" at this point!) to the events of Easter weekend.[39] These are genuine contributions.

In my view, however, the argument's effectiveness is hampered by its reluctance to expand the meaning of "atonement" dramatically enough to ring true to the witnesses of Scripture and human experience. The approach of *Questions on Doctrine* functions within the boundaries established by those who understand the sufferings of Jesus to be expiatory, substitutionary, and vicarious payments rendered to God. Many Christians, including many Seventh-day Adventists, will not quibble about this. I must demur.

One difficulty with understanding the sufferings of Jesus in this way is that it runs the risk of making God appear as bloodthirsty on a single occasion as Moloch always was. Another difficulty is that when the sufferings of Jesus are understood as substitutionary payments they can cease to become normative for contemporary Christians. The inner logic too easily becomes: "Jesus suffered to overcome our estrangements; therefore, we can experience and enable reconciliation without similar sacrifices."

We know, however, from human experience that every attempt to overcome evil with good entails sacrifice. We also know that the New Testament invites Christians to take up their crosses[40] and even to "rejoice insofar as you are sharing Christ's sufferings, so that you may also be glad and shout for joy when his glory is revealed."[41]

These are not the masochistic utterances of those who love to be hated. They are realistic reminders that one who decides as a disciple of Jesus to participate in His way of overcoming evil, by neither capitulating to it nor retaliating vengefully against it, may well suffer as Jesus did.

The problem, then, with the interpretation presented in *Questions on Doctrine* is at least twofold: (1) it accepts the hazard of misinterpreting divine love as a demand for human expiation, and (2) it fails to show how the sufferings of Christ can be linked to the sufferings of Christians in ways that are morally and politically relevant. In these respects, *Questions on Doctrine* is still not wholly satisfying. It lacks any means of assuring the continuing exhibition of undiluted divine love as well as the connections between the way Jesus conducted His affairs and the way Christians should conduct theirs. The first difficulty makes the idea of atonement almost irreverent; the second renders it morally and politically irrelevant.

We do well to consider the possibility that the term "atonement" needs to be understood even more broadly than *Questions on Doctrine* does. From a wider perspective it can be seen that God has always responded, is now responding, and will always respond to evil in the same way. The sacrifice of Jesus at Calvary was unique precisely because it demonstrated in unrepeatable ways how God reacts to evil in every time and place. The cross was not an exception to God's usual ways; it was the unsurpassable demonstration of God's unending acts of reconciliation.

That demonstration was "complete" and "sufficient" at Golgotha. God's reconciling endeavors continue, however, and these are symbolized in the New Testament by the figure of Jesus Christ as the Heavenly High Priest whose work of intercession continues.[42] Christians of all times and places are invited to participate in practical ways in this ongoing activity by being "built into a spiritual house, to be a holy priesthood, to offer spiritual sacrifices acceptable to God through Jesus Christ."[43]

The best way to honor the work of the High Priest in Heaven is to participate in activities that engender reconciliation on earth. It is therefore wholly appropriate to speak, as do John Howard Yoder and others, regarding the moral and political relevance of the cross of Jesus for life here and now.[44]

A Sanctuary for the Weak

The sanctuary motifs of Scripture remind us that how it treats its least fortunate citizens is the truest indicator of any political system's moral worth.

Christians have responded to the obligations and opportunities of political life in a variety of ways. Some have denounced all forms of civic involvement as detrimental to the kingdom of God. Others have thought of two realms, one symbolized by God's right hand and the other symbolized by God's left hand, that provide overlapping but distinct spiritual and secular obligations. Still others have perceived the institutional church as authorized by God to utilize coercive power in the pursuit of worldly goals.

Rarely, however, have Christians who have enjoyed a measure of political power found it easy to remember the Old Testament mandates that political power be used to benefit the weak rather than the strong. This theme is especially apparent in those portions of the Old Testament that portray the sanctuary and its services. Of particular concern in this material and elsewhere in the Bible is the plight of the widow, orphan, and alien:

> When an alien resides with you in your land, you shall not oppress the alien. The alien who resides with you shall be to you as the citizen among you; you shall love the alien as yourself, for you were aliens in the land of Egypt: I am the Lord your God.[45]

Provision was made for the economic support of those who were disadvantaged:

> When you reap the harvest of your land, you shall not reap to the very edges of your field, or gather the gleanings of your harvest; you shall leave them for the poor and for the alien: I am the Lord your God.[46]

These and other passages require the community to treat the alien as a citizen, as a brother or sister. Notice, however, that on occasion the argument is reversed so that the community is directed to treat a brother as well as it would an alien:

> If any of your kin fall into difficulty and become dependent on you, you shall support them; they shall live with you as though resident aliens. Do not take interest in advance or otherwise make a profit from them, but fear your God; let them live with you. You shall not lend them your money at interest taken in advance, or provide them food at a profit. I am the Lord your God, who brought you out of the land of Egypt, to give you the land of Ca'naan, to be your God.[47]

The modern impact of these and similar passages is that moral assessments of political systems should evaluate these options not by what they provide the most fortunate but by what they assure the least fortunate members of the community.

Paul Tillich used the terms "creative" or "transforming" justice to refer to canons of distribution that hinged more on need than upon the power, merit, or even the equal worth of potential recipients.[48] Paul Ramsey pointed to something similar when he wrote of "redemptive" justice.[49] More recent authors have repeatedly written of God's special regard for the poor, a regard that translates today into a political presumption on their behalf.

According to this presumption, ancient Egypt's moral worth should be judged not by the splendor of its pyramids and the treasures they contained but by the way this nation treated those who built these wonders of the world. The same can be said of the architectural and cultural wonders of ancient Greece as well as of the Great Wall of China. Most importantly for us, our own civilizations should be judged not by how much they provide those who are at the top but by what they guarantee those who are at the bottom through no choice of their own.

These words may haunt those of us who have prospered during the last half of the twentieth century. Never in the history of humanity have so many enjoyed so much. Democratic societies, whether slightly more socialist or somewhat more capitalist, have found it possible to combine the energies of free enterprise with the restraints of centralized control in ways that have been overwhelmingly beneficial for millions. The moral embarrassment is that even in nations where wealth is the greatest there are those who cannot locate housing, work, medical care, and educational opportunities for their children.

The so-called "misery index," which is calculated by combining the rate of inflation and the rate of unemployment, measures the extent of the plight of those who are drowning rather than floating in rising economic tides. We rightly feel that things are encouraging if this index can be reported in single figures, and this is a remarkable achievement. The moral danger, however, is that a nation's people may rest content without attempting to improve the lot of those who are floundering.

This is an unexpected warning from the ancient Hebrew sanctuary. It is a warning that carries political punch. This warning does not specify what mix of public and private policies should achieve the desired outcome. It simply but urgently contends that in politics and economics, as well as in the more private interactions of life, the final judgment may surprise us:

> Then he will say to those at his left hand, "you that are accursed, depart from me into the eternal fire prepared for the devil and his angels; for I was hungry and you gave me no food, I was thirsty and you gave me nothing to drink, I was a stranger and you did not welcome me, naked and you did not give me clothing, sick and in prison and you did not visit me....Truly I tell you, just as you did not do it to one of the least of these, you did not do it to me."[50]

This, too, is part of the sanctuary message for today.

Sanctuary and the Ordinary

The sanctuary motifs of Scripture remind us that God does dwell with ordinary humans in the mundane experiences of ordinary life.

There is a point at which the "sanctuary message" of the Bible and the various "sanctuary movements" of modern times cross paths and perhaps even pollinate each other. At first glance, few topics of reflection seem as unrelated as these two. The first focuses upon the establishment of a portable tabernacle for the ancient Hebrews who wandered in the deserts south of Palestine for decades as they made their way to the Promised Land. The second concentrates upon the various ways political refugees in our day are housed, fed, educated, and given work, sometimes illegally, by sympathizers in democratic nations.

Further reflection upon the biblical materials reveals, however, how similar is the plight of illegal aliens today to that of the wandering Hebrews of antiquity. There are biblical warrants, therefore, for seeing some connection between the "sanctuary message" of old and the "sanctuary movements" of our own era.

One might thus expect to find Christians who emphasize the "sanctuary message" among those who are active in the "sanctuary movements" around the world. And one would not be disappointed.

It would be too much to argue that Seventh-day Adventists explicitly justify their involvement in today's "sanctuary movements" by appealing to the Bible's "sanctuary message." For one thing, members of the denomination are usually very circumspect about what they say along these lines because they know that the safety of the modern sojourners they assist could be jeopardized by careless chatter. In addition, it is doubtful that those Adventists who are engaged in such activities consciously connect the "sanctuary message" and the "sanctuary movement."

The impact of biblical motifs upon such persons is more subtle and indirect, but it is, I suspect, nonetheless real. It would be difficult to identify with the ancient wandering Hebrews in word, song, and liturgy for generations without feeling some kinship for the wanderers of our own age.

Of course, it is possible that it is purely coincidental that a denomination that emphasizes the "sanctuary message" is also involved in "sanctuary movements." Such an accident is surely possible. There are two things that cannot be denied, however: (1) Although Seventh-day Adventists are not the most visible or audible participants in the "sanctuary movements" of modern life, they are among the most active and effective; and (2) even if no historical connection between the two can be established beyond the shadow of doubt, there is a moral link between the "sanctuary message" and the "sanctuary movements" that is worth pondering.

Some may wonder what such reflections have to do with those of nineteenth-century Adventists. If Uriah Smith, for instance, could consider these remarks, how would he react?

I don't know! Neither does anyone else. I doubt, however, that Smith would be shocked by the suggestion that an emphasis upon the "sanctuary message" should prompt a political presumption in favor of the widow, orphan, and alien. After all, nineteenth-century Adventists assisted the "underground railroad" in the United States in its illegal efforts to transport Negroes from slavery in the South to freedom in the North.

There is, however, a more subtle and significant link between the "sanctuary message" in previous generations and its meaning today. This connection is that the sanctuary motifs of Scripture remind us that God does dwell with ordinary humans in the mundane experiences of everyday life. This divine presence comforts. It also confronts. It soothes. It also searches. It accepts. It also empowers. Most importantly, it never forsakes.

This comes close to the meaning of the "sanctuary message" in every age. We recall, for instance, that on one occasion when the wandering Israelites ran out of water, they asked, "Is the Lord among us or not?"[51] Faced with an impending disaster, they asked a question that humans frequently voice when they are threatened by internal or external disappointments. That question was heavy on the minds of many who heard Jesus as well, oppressed as they were by a foreign government. "The kingdom of God is among you,"[52] he declared.

Uriah Smith reported that following the Great Disappointment of October 22, 1844, many Millerites wondered if God was still in their midst or if indeed the prayer of the psalmist that Jesus repeated on the cross should be theirs as well: "My God, my God, why have you forsaken me?"[53] But God had not forsaken the Millerites even though they felt abandoned. The "sanctuary message" reminded Uriah Smith and others like him that no matter what happens, no matter how profound or pervasive life's disappointments or disasters are, God continues to work in everything for good.

Ellen White saw a parallel between the sanctuary as God's visible presence in the midst of Israel and the Incarnation.

> God commanded Moses for Israel, "Let them make Me a sanctuary; that I may dwell among them" (Exodus 25:8), and He abode in the sanctuary, in the midst of the people. Through all their weary wandering in the desert, the symbol of His presence was with them. So Christ set up His tabernacle in the midst of our human encampment. He pitched His tent by the side of the tents of men, that He might dwell among us (and we beheld His glory, glory as of the Only Begotten from the Father), full of grace and truth....
> Since Jesus came to dwell with us, we know that God is acquainted with our trials, and sympathizes with our griefs. Every son and daughter of

Adam may understand that our Creator is the friend of sinners. For in every doctrine of grace, every promise of joy, every deed of love, every divine attraction presented in the Saviour's life on earth, we see "God with us."[54]

The sanctuary of ancient Israel and the temple that eventually replaced it were less significant than the Reality toward which they pointed and in which they invited the faithful to participate. This Reality is none other than God's continuing, invigorating presence, not merely in the unusual events of life but in the ordinary disappointments and joys of typical people. "And remember, I am with you always."[55]

Endnotes

[1] Ex 25:8.

[2] Jn 1:14.

[3] Rev 21:3-4.

[4] See Francis D. Nichol, *The Midnight Cry* (Washington, DC: Review and Herald, 1944).

[5] LeRoy Edwin Froom, *The Prophetic Faith of Our Fathers*, 4 vols. (Washington, DC: Review and Herald, 1954) 4: 855-905.

[6] See Roy Adams' helpful study *The Sanctuary Doctrine: Three Approaches in the Seventh-day Adventist Church* (Berrien Springs, MI: Andrews University Press, 1981).

[7] Ibid., 165.

[8] For a sympathetic account of Andreasen's life, see Virginia Duffie Steinweg, *Without Fear or Favor: The Life of M. L. Andreasen* (Washington, DC: Review and Herald, 1979).

[9] I am reminded here of Professor Ninian Smart's quip that opponents of orthodox Incarnational Christology could prove that the belief that "God is in Heaven, Jesus in Galilee, but Jesus is God incarnate" incoherent only if "Heaven and Galilee are both places in the same sense of 'place.'"

[10] Cp. [R. A. Anderson, L. E. Froom, W. E. Read, *et al.*,] *Seventh-day Adventists Answer Questions on Doctrine* (Washington, DC: Review and Herald, 1957) 365-68.

[11] Qtd. in Adams 1; Smith has recourse here to Heb 9:23, 24.

[12] Ex 25:9; 26:30; Ac 7:44; Heb 8:2.

[13] For a study of "Analogy in Theology," see Paul Edwards, *The Encyclopedia of Philosophy* (New York: Macmillan, 1967) 1: 94-97.

[14] See Paul Tillich, *The Dynamics of Faith* (New York: Harper & Row, 1958) 41-54.

[15] A good example is the work of Sallie McFague; see her *Metaphorical Theology* (Philadelphia: Fortress Press, 1982) and *Models of God* (Philadelphia: Fortress Press, 1987).

[16] Lev 17:1-9.

[17] Ex 20:3.

[18] 1Ki 18:21.

[19] Walter Rauschenbush, *A Theology for the Social Gospel* (New York: Abingdon Press, 1945); see esp. pages 48 and 49, where Rauschenbusch declares, with embarrassing glibness, "The worship of various gods and the use of idols is no longer one of our dangers."

[20] H. Richard Niebuhr, *Radical Monotheism and Western Culture* (New York: Harper & Row, 1943).

[21] Mt 23:23.

[22] Am 5:21-24.

[23] 2Ti 3:5.

[24] Lev 19:2.

[25] Lev 16:30.

[26] Mk 11:15-19.

[27] Lev 1:9.

[28] See 2Ki 23:10; Lev 18:21, 20:1-5; Jer 7:31, 19:4-5, 32:35.

[29] Isa 1:11, 16-17.

[30] Ro 12:1.

[31] Ro 12:14-17.

[32] Mt 22:37-40.

[33] Ro 12:21.

[34] Heb 9:22.

[35] Traces of both notions can be discerned in Hebrews 9 and 10, for instance.

[36] *Questions* 341.

[37] Ibid.

[38] Ibid., 348.

[39] Ibid., 341-48.

[40] Mk 8:34.

[41] 1Pe 4:13.

[42] Heb 7:25.

[43] 1Pe 2:5.

[44] John Howard Yoder, *The Politics of Jesus* (Grand Rapids: Eerdmans, 1972).

[45] Lev 19:33-34.

[46] Lev 23:22.

[47] Lev 25:35-38.

[48] Paul Tillich, *Love, Power and Justice: Ontological Analyses and Ethical Implications* (New York: Oxford University Press, 1954) 64-66.

[49] Paul Ramsey, *Basic Christian Ethics* (Chicago: University of Chicago Press, 1950) 2-24.

[50] Mt 25:41-43, 45.

[51] Ex 17:7.

[52] Lk 17:21.

[53] Mt 27:46.

[54] Ellen White, *The Desire of Ages* (Mountain View, CA: Pacific Press, 1898) 23, 24.

[55] Mt 28.20, NEB.

Chapter Five

SABBATH

Miroslav M. Kis

Remember the sabbath day, and keep it holy. Six days you shall labor and do all your work. But the seventh day is a sabbath to the Lord your God; you shall not do any work—you, your son or your daughter, your male or female slave, your livestock, or the alien resident in your towns. For in six days the Lord made heaven and earth, the sea, and all that is in them, but rested the seventh day; therefore the Lord blessed the sabbath day and consecrated it.[1]

Then he said to them, "The sabbath was made for humankind, and not humankind for the sabbath; so the Son of Man is lord even of the sabbath."[2]

Why should anyone observe the Sabbath? What difference does it make? Does Sabbath-keeping promote human happiness, friendship, citizenship, and love? Can it help our contemporary civilization face the threats of dehumanization and consumerism? These were the kinds of questions I had to face from fellow graduate students in an interdenominational school of religion at a Canadian university a few years ago.

Frankly, the questions caught me by surprise. Born and raised in an SDA family, passing through hardships to keep the Sabbath in grade school and the army, being trained in theology and exegesis, I felt confident about my beliefs. I would have had no difficulty with historical, theological, and exegetical questions, I was sure. But these were not the sorts of inquiries to which I was now being called upon to respond. Rather, I was being asked, *Is there any evidence that the Sabbath influences the moral life of the Christian? Is the Sabbath doctrine redemptive?* There are several possible answers to these questions. We will briefly evaluate three; the fourth we will develop in fuller form.

1. It must be admitted that Seventh-day Adventism places the seventh day *first*. The Sabbath has become a hallmark of this movement and an

integral component of its religious lifestyle. The seventh-day difference has been and is used as an identifying mark.[3] With this in mind one can naturally expect to find considerable effort centered on defining, refining, and clarifying this doctrine and relating it to a larger corpus of beliefs. To teach and learn relevant facts and dates, to be able to explain the fine points of one's religious belief system, is a responsibility for one who wants to take the religious life seriously.

Yet the Sabbath was not given only to serve as an identifying badge. The seventh-day difference alone is an insufficient and extremely narrow foundation for moral activity in the social or personal sphere. To be morally relevant the Sabbath must be more than just another cultural singularity.

2. As Sakae Kubo points out, "it has been and still is possible to 'keep' the Sabbath and yet live a life that denies any relationship to Jesus Christ."[4] Examples of such Sabbath-keeping come readily to mind; Pharisees and Puritans are often cited as classic examples. In practical terms, the upshot of their understanding of the Sabbath seemed to be that one keeps the Sabbath if—and only if—one refrains, abstains, withholds, curbs, and forbids. We are told that in Calvinist homes in the American south the

> Sunday/Sabbath was a most unpleasant day, especially for active little children. It was a day on which religious customs prevented children from being normal. Sunday/Sabbath meant special clothes—fancy, stiff, restrictive clothes that one dared not dirty or tear.[5]

Evidently, such Sabbath-keeping is far from being a delight.[6] Sabbath-keeping cannot be just rule-keeping if its impact is to be sensed on a moral level.

3. More often than not, however, such an attitude is evinced in the most devout and sincere Christian families. Many SDA parents view their strictness in Sabbath-keeping as an expression of love to God and faithfulness to the commandments. Many SDA children grow up to recognize positive values in a careful observance of the Sabbath. It might even be difficult to prove that all Pharisees and Puritans followed the rules out of impure motives or an immature mentality.[7]

If the legalistic observance of the Sabbath is off the mark, there is a danger of swinging to the other extreme in the course of reacting to formalism and casuistry. Here are some things to consider:

a. As we dismiss the harsh imposition of rules for Sabbath observance, we need perhaps to keep in mind that the Sabbath *is* enjoined as a divine command. The response to a command may be either obedient or disobedient. What is objectionable, I am convinced, is not obedience to the Sabbath command *per se*, but rather the presence of a negative, coercive, self-righteous spirit.

b. The impression is sometimes given that any rule-making is wrong. A justifiable rejection of coercive or self-righteous attitudes, when followed by some very general clichés about love, freedom, or maturity may be interpreted as in fact implying that one may do whatever one wishes on the Sabbath—a stance which Scripture, at least, does not appear to license.[8] The command to remember and to keep is accompanied with a series of guidelines on "how," "when," and "why." When a person adheres conscientiously to those ordinances, all that may be seen or observed outwardly is careful and strict compliance. Love-motivated obedience is an invisible category; but surely the presence of love validates the conduct.

> Such obedience will be seen by some people as an escape from the ambiguities and responsibilities of personal discernment, escape that perhaps reveals low ego strength and high need for security. These dimensions, of course, may be present. But it is important for us to realize that obedience also can be a voluntary and mature submission of a strong ego to a particular disciplined way that is sensed as true. Looked at ascetically, it is precisely that 'strong ego' that must be relativized if the deeper image of God is ever to emerge and order our lives. Obedience to a transcendent purpose—even one we do not fully understand—is a historic method of freeing us from obedience to the whims of surface ego.[9]

c. Obedience is not natural to either four-, forty-, or fourscore-and-ten-year-old humans. We must all learn it, and with difficulty at that.[10]

> The alternative to obedience as a motivation for sabbath observance is the fulfillment of human need. This is a widespread justification for the sabbath in church history. When this motivation is divorced from a sense of transcendent command, however, the sabbath inevitably loses some of its power; it is then, as Barth points out, subject to counterarguments of human need and becomes wobbly as a motivating force.[11]

If we observe the Sabbath only because we are SDAs, if we view Sabbath-keeping only as rule-keeping, if we think we can trust ourselves as mature, self-sufficient, and beyond the law—then we have some growing to do.[12] The first group wears Sabbath-keeping as a mask. The second is not sufficiently open to grasp or relate religious attitude to moral need. And the third group may soon lose the stamina required to retain identity in the midst of personal and social challenges, provocations, and threats.

What follows now is an endeavor to offer an understanding of the Sabbath which is likely to enable Sabbath observance to exert a greater influence on the personal and social moral life.

Identity and Duty: Sabbath and Personal Ethics

The relevance of the Sabbath doctrine and its observance for contemporary human beings has an impact on the very substance of their being, their sense of identity.

Parmenides defined identity as the sameness of thinking and being. Heidegger argues that identity should not be equated with sameness alone when we speak of a human being. As he understands it, identity is *"belonging together."* When the human person and Being[13] meet and share their essential dimensions with each other (the moment Heidegger calls "appropriation") in a sudden, spontaneous, and unpremeditated fraction of time, identity is born. This birth cannot happen if the sharing occurs between a human being and technology or any other human creation.[14] In this case there is no "challenge" which would elicit a genuine response of self-giving. "The name for the gathering of this challenge which places man and Being face to face in such a way that they challenge each other by turns is 'the framework.'"[15] This framework is the basis for relating to other beings without the fear of losing one's identity.

Another important factor in Heidegger's concept of identity is the mood of "apprehension." He points out that in this face-to-face encounter with Being, there cannot be pressure or coercion. The genuine "belonging together" must be *"letting* belonging together."[16] The human person and Being belong together freely.

When and where in the world of human time and space can the experience of the birth and nurture of identity happen? Where would its cradle be? In a traffic jam on busy streets of the cities where most of the earth's population lives? And when in our schedules of meetings, parties, appointments, achievements, stock markets, deadlines, TV shows, Walkman stereos, and cartoons, our mourning for the past and hope for the future, would we find the time to meet the Present? Our space is polluted and our time weary. We need rest, and God gave us the Sabbath.

Or perhaps God did not *give* it. It is repeatedly referred to as "my Sabbath."[17] Perhaps it would be more accurate to say that God kept it, hallowed it, and then, making of it something delightful, shared it with humanity.[18] Better yet, God shared it by freely belonging together with humanity.

The Sabbath is the day of presence,[19] a mirror which does not convey a message of *how one looks* but rather *who one is*. For six days we are tempted to be concerned with hairdos, fashions, wrinkles on our faces, color coordination, manners, and forms. We imitate our heroes of the screen. We are urged to *act* and *look* like them, and if possible *be* like them. The tragedy of the six-day identification is that it robs us of our self-identity. When we imitate others we are not challenged to disclose ourselves. Rather, we cover our identities with ones foreign to (yet admired by) us. We hide. Our modern heroes become modern fig leaves.

On the Sabbath I can cease fixing up[20] and hiding. I know I cannot hide. The Presence of who I am, the image, meets with me and challenges me to rest from my pursuits and limitations. The mask falls; the fig leaves vanish; the real me stands bare.

What happens on the Sabbath is reminiscent of the experience of the prophet Isaiah. Redemption is reenacted.[21] As human being and God meet, the challenge rises. This challenge is bilateral and, for human being, moral in nature.

First, as I stand in the Presence, I am compelled to confess: "Woe is me! I am lost, for I am a man of unclean lips, and I live among a people of unclean lips; yet my eyes have seen the King, the Lord of hosts!"[22] Such is the moral inventory of my identity as "fixed up" by the imitations of the six days. The real me—the sinner—stands out.

Faced with God's holiness, I stand exposed but not rejected. On the contrary, I feel drawn, like a homing pigeon to its nest, like a weary pilgrim homeward bound, to my rest—God's Sabbath. The holy divine presence is humbling, but not humiliating; it is sanctifying, not demoralizing.[23] It is hostile to falsehood and it condemns my sin, but not me necessarily. Only if I refuse to let myself belong to God, and prefer my sin, only then do I share the fate of that sin. The Sabbath is a new opportunity to lock in my destiny with God's and open myself to redemption.

Then "the seraph touched my mouth with it and said: 'Now that this has touched your lips, your guilt has departed and your sin is blotted out.'"[24] The Sabbath rest is the rest of forgiveness. It is the time away from Egypt, out of the house of bondage, a time to begin anew. I can stretch out, breathe easily, knowing that there is a sufficient supply of manna.[25] I am found in my gracious God. I know who I am.

When the hours of the Sabbath pass, the divine presence lingers. I dwell in God-context.

> If I ascend to heaven, you are there; if I make my bed in She'ol, you are there. If I take the wings of the morning and settle at the farthest limits of the sea, even there your hand shall lead me, and your right hand shall hold me fast. If I say, "Surely the darkness shall cover me, and the light around me become night," even the darkness is not dark to you....[26]

Even there God's hand is present not to punish but to lead, not to push away but to hold.

When the enticement to adultery or fornication comes and no one is in the house,[27] if then I still know that I am standing in a holy presence, I will sense how out of place such conduct would be, and I can say and act a NO to the sin.[28]

On the plain of Dura, surrounded by a contemptuous crowd, under threat of death or loss, if then God's presence lingers with me, divine grace will help me muster enough courage to stand tall and true.

In the lion's den, in the fiery furnace, in dungeons, in prisons, in exile, God's Sabbath presence can bring me rest.

But, of course, the Sabbath is not given to me only. Its impact is by no means limited to personal ethics. As Edwards reminds us:

> Put in theological terms, we have an *ontological* relationship—an essential end-in-itself relationship of being—with God that needs intentional cultivation, and we have a *moral* relationship with God that involves us in caring for life in particular called-for ways, which also requires intentional cultivation.[29]

96

A Time to Notice, Fellowship, and Care

Sabbath is given to individual human beings. They are enjoined to remember and keep it. Yet in most of the passages of Scripture, the impressive fact remains that the Sabbath is a public experience as well. If I search for my own identity through meditation, prayer, and study, if I meet with my Creator on that day, and—when the hours of holy day are gone— if the divine presence tarries, I will inevitably turn outward. Secure and confident, forgiven and free, I can reach out and notice others. "Here am I; send me."[30]

The Sabbath is a time when I notice my son, my daughter, my workers, my property, and the stranger within my gates. During six days I know of them, I know who they are, but I do not pay attention to them as I should. The fourth commandment tells me to rest with others.

1. My first duty is to notice my family on the Sabbath day. I have an opportunity and a privilege to recognize our common birthright in the image of God and to resist the temptation to see them as anything less than the embodiment of that image. "There is a disease rampant—a chronic, low-grade depression that never knows how to smack its lips and say, 'It's good to be alive!' It does not know the haven of a Shabbos in the bosom of an unhassling family."[31]

As I turn from my preoccupations, I allow others to *be* with me. The parent becomes a child with the children. Debts and unresolved tensions are set aside in a family truce. We belong together; we share responsibility and play. Finally, a daughter can tell her story without being hustled along to the breakfast table. A son has all the attention he needs to explain the origin of his latest bruise. In short, the Sabbath is a

> time for 'useless' poetry and other arts; a time to appreciate a tree, your neighbour, and yourself without doing something to them....These Sabbath ways check the greed of a controlling mind. They relax mental reins that would drive us to dominate our neighbour and the world.[32]

But if experience teaches us anything, it is that such a break and radical change of rhythm do not come naturally in our civilization. The "mind is always whirring a grasping, utilitarian tune, even in rest time. It enslaves its owners unless an intentional halt is called. Sabbath is such an intentional halt."[33]

Planning activities between the sunsets greatly determines how we remember and keep the Sabbath. In so doing I must notice the needs of the other members of the family, keep in mind their energy levels, and ensure that the Sabbath facilitates *their* rest as well as mine. Surely neither the moods of mid-life nor the metabolism of old age should be allowed to set the criteria for the selection of Sabbath activities.[34]

The Sabbath is a call for "belonging together" with my spouse, a time for special attention. I remember that the Sabbath was fit for the first honeymoon and that each subsequent one celebrates the marriage of togetherness. Laxity or neglect in Sabbath observance may have more to do with troubled marriages than one would think at first. What other way is there to rediscover each other, to become one in mind and spirit, than to spend restful hours together.

With my family and my spouse, I come to meet our gracious God. We all stand before our Creator and Redeemer equally dependent and equally loved. In the divine presence we see and feel each other through our Lord, who belongs together with us. Our house becomes God's house—for our God is not a transient guest, but one who belongs. This presence cannot but impact my conduct and my choice of activities. I cannot turn my back on my Maker to watch TV or bury my face in the newspaper during our special time together. God comes to walk with my family and talk with us because on the Sabbath we are free from the bustle of the week. To repair my roof or hunt for bargains on the day of rest means to ignore the stipulation that the "Sabbath of the Lord" is to be observed "in *all* your dwellings."[35]

There is hardly any need to spell out all the benefits which the Sabbath affords society through its sanctifying influence on marriage and the family. The stability of the home and the marital closeness fostered by the Sabbath can free the family for creative and concerned service to the community.

2. The Sabbath is a call to worship. On a social scale this event establishes the time and place for a rendezvous with God. At the divine call, women and men from various backgrounds come together. Their liturgy integrates words, hymns, and minds in one purpose: to commune with God. Human beings are united, tied together in the divine presence.

Separate families now become one big family under the covenant of grace. We who once were strangers are now fellow citizens; we who once had no hope and were without God in the world, now belong to God and together discover our identity. We were scattered, but now we are members of the household of God. [36]

> Gathering for worship, we celebrate a common covenant that reveals and affirms our shared double purpose in life: to rest in God joyfully, and to direct the holy energy of that rest into caring for the creation with whom we share community.[37]

With that creation we share the same Creator as well.

On the Sabbath, the community of the church receives its mission from God. It learns to see the world outside as an estranged portion of the family—just as God sees it. The church senses God's yearning to protect, attract, and save humanity. And as the presence of God attends its members during the following days of the week, the priorities of Heaven, the divine sensitivity to injustice and oppression urge them to extend the Sabbath rest to those around them.

3. The Sabbath is a call to afford rest for those who serve or labor under our leadership, the "manservants and maidservants."[38] All classes of persons enjoy in equal measure the right to rest. As Andreasen notes:

> The Sabbath, then, faithfully protects man from totalitarianism of all kinds, whatever the source.
> The armistice in the cruel struggle between man and his world, about which Heschel speaks, provides two benefits: freedom of the worker from his work, but also freedom of the work from man's exploitation.[39]

4. The Sabbath is also a call to service for those who stand on the fringes of our society, the strangers. Jesus is our example here. He rested to fellowship with others.[40] So our Sabbath rest must extend beyond the limits of the household.

> It should provide us with time to send more than a hastily scribbled postcard to those who have long awaited a word from us; it should give us time to have more than a superficial conversation with a person who is ill. The commandment to rest on the Sabbath gives us time for the modern slave, who lives on the periphery of our society, no matter in what form he may stand before us.[41]

Thus, Ludwig Koeler has written, "Before God's throne there will hardly be a greater testimony given on your behalf than the statement, 'he had time for me.'"[42]

The Sabbath's call challenges our comfortable lifestyle. It urges us to meet the challenge of caring for unpleasant people. The ill and the suffering are not the most cheerful and agreeable company. All too often those who are lonely "waste" our time telling us for the seventh time the same story with the same enthusiasm as if it were new to us. No visible benefits are evident. Moreover, there are others who are trained (and even paid) to deal and counsel with such cases.

But the Sabbath recognizes and allows no case-like treatment. It calls us to set aside the ever-present tyranny of efficiency and profit-making at least for that one day. We are assured that there is enough manna and that it will not spoil, so that we can afford to give our time to others.[43] We can playfully "waste" our time for those who need us.

It is amazing how different we are, how affirming our influence is when there is nothing we are trying to get or expect from one another. Strangely enough (to our clinging ego-consciousness) in these graced, simple, earthly, unselfish moments we do not disappear with self-giving. Rather, when I lose my soul for others I suddenly discover that I have found it.[44]

5. Finally, Sabbath observance and the Sabbath doctrine reveal the extreme urgency, need, and relevance of God for society at large. It illustrates the divine love and benevolence for human beings and it reveals the essential goodness of all of the divine will—even when it appears arbitrary. Even though rest and meditation have multiple benefits at any time, and attention to my family and respect for my subordinates and care for those on the fringes need not and should not wait for the Sabbath hours, still the consciousness that the Sabbath is God's day with us reminds our contemporaries that people cannot and should not feel free to modify and "improve" everything in the universe. The Sabbath is something that is holy because God made it so, and we are thus called to sanctify it in our turn. We may not be able to explain, color, or dissect this holy time, but we certainly can bear witness to it and taste its reality.

Endnotes

[1] Ex 20:8-11.

[2] Mk 2:27-8.

[3] In some European countries Seventh-day Adventists are called "Sabbatarians" or "those who keep Sunday on Saturday." Cf. F. D. Nichol, "Daniel 2:43," *Seventh-day Adventist Bible Commentary* (Washington, DC: Review and Herald, 1957) 4: 1168.

[4] "The Experience of Liberation," *Festival of the Sabbath*, ed. Roy Branson (Takoma Park, MD: Association of Adventist Forums, 1985) 46.

[5] J. S. Sprong and D. G. Haines, *Beyond Moralism* (New York: Harper & Row, 1986) 49.

[6] As Isa 58:13 suggests it ought to be.

[7] Harvey Cox, *Turning East* (New York: Simon, 1977) 69.

[8] Isa 58:13.

[9] Tilden Edwards, *Sabbath Time* (New York: Seabury, 1982) 46.

[10] See Heb 5:8.

[11] Edwards, 47.

[12] See John Brunt, "Jesus' Way With the Sabbath," Branson 107-16.

[13] Heidegger defines Being as "the presence"; see *Identity and Difference* (New York: Harper & Row, 1969) 31. His language also suggests the possibility of identifying Being with God, whom he very briefly identifies as the only entity which does not need sustenance—as a self-sufficient entity (*Being and Time* [New York: Harper & Row 1962] 30, 74, 125).

[14] Ibid., 29-36.

[15] Ibid., 35.

[16] Ibid., 39.

[17] Isa 58:13, 56:4.

[18] Herbert Saunders, *The Sabbath* (Plainfield: American Sabbath Tract Society, 1970) 93-95.

[19] Fritz Guy, "The Presence of Ultimacy," Branson 29. See also Kubo 45-46, and Samuele Bacchiocchi, "A Memorial of Redemption," Branson 56-57.

[20] Cox, 65.

[21] Kubo, 50.

[22] Isa 6:5.

[23] Eze 20:12.

[24] Isa 6:7.

[25] Niels-Erik Andreasen, "Jubilee of Freedom and Equality," Branson.

[26] Ps 139:7-12.

[27] Ge 39:11.

28 Ge 39:9.

29 Edwards, 40.

30 Isa 6:8.

31 See Edwards, 45.

32 Ibid., 77.

33 Ibid.

34 Cf. Ellen White, *Testimonies for the Church*, 9 vols. (Mountain View, CA: Pacific Press, 1871-1912) 6: 356, 359.

35 Lev 23:3; italics mine.

36 Eph 2:11-22.

37 Edwards, 69.

38 Ex 20:9.

39 Andreasen, 99. See also 97-105 for a helpful treatment of this subject.

40 Sakae Kubo, *God Meets Man* (Nashville: Southern Publishing Association, 1978) 29.

41 Ibid.

42 "The Day of Rest in the Old Testament," *Lexington Theological Quarterly* (July 1972): 71-72, qtd. in Kubo 29.

43 See John Brunt, *A Day for Healing* (Washington, DC: Review and Herald, 1981).

44 Cf. Edwards, 71.

Chapter Six

LAW

JAMES W. WALTERS

The law of the Lord is perfect, reviving the soul; the decrees of the Lord are
    sure, making wise the simple; the precepts of the Lord are right, rejoicing
    the heart; the commandment of the Lord is clear, enlightening the eyes.[1]

The Ten Commandments are very special to Adventists. I recall as a
child how I used to dread Fridays. Not that Friday itself was a bad day, but
it preceded the Decalogue's Sabbath; and the way my Adventist community interpreted Sabbath-keeping made it the most boring day in my week.
Later, in a more religious phase of development, I meticulously kept every
law, fearing that the slightest deviation would risk eternal loss. Still later the
law lost much of its mystery, but gained in preciousness.

In my upbringing, I clearly went through stages of what Lawrence
Kohlberg calls "moral development." The simplified version of Kohlberg's
thought posits three stages: preconventional thinking, in which punishments and rewards determine ethical choices; conventional thinking, characterized by deference to peer-group preferences; and post-conventional
thinking, grounded in a commitment to principles which foster the well-
being of all.[2]

One of Kohlberg's independent collaborators, James Fowler, has proposed a similar model of religious development—six stages of religious
faith. Fowler's first stage is that of Intuitive Faith, which finds its authority
in a "primal" other—typically a parent. His sixth and highest stage is that
of Universalizing Faith, in which one reflectively and confidently resolves
issues of authority by grappling directly with ultimate questions. Fowler's
stage one is typical of preschoolers; stage six—where it exists at all—is
generally found in those forty years of age or older.[3]

My point in referring to these studies on individual moral and religious
development is twofold. First, I wish to agree with Kohlberg and Fowler

103

that our individual views of moral and religious life are dynamic; they predictably change as we mature. Second, I want to argue that dynamic moral/religious development, which we accept as normal for an individual, is also perfectly normal for a religious group.

John Cobb's *The Structure of Christian Existence* offers a helpful perspective in this regard. Cobb argues for three consecutive "structures of existence" which have relevance for Judæo-Christian faith: the primitive, the prophetic, and the Christian structures of human existence. In the more primitive intellectual and cultural area of nomadic near-eastern existence, humankind was incapable of apprehending the spiritual insights of the later prophets. The rational insights of the prophets were part of a larger cultural advance which occurred in five parts of Eurasia around the sixth century BC—an era Cobb terms the "axial age."[4]

My enterprise in this essay is much more modest than Professor Kohlberg's, Fowler's, or Cobb's. I desire to build on their insights, contending that religious groups go through—but do not entirely leave behind—dynamic stages of development which are at least loosely analogous to the stages of individual religious maturation. My specific contention is that *three* stages of thinking in regard to the law are evident in biblical thought and in Adventist thinking: law as *blueprint*, law as *motive*, and law as *wisdom*. These are idealized stages, painted in broad brush strokes to depict an overall historical reality. The stages overlap; they are only loosely linear; and, of course, it would be easy to point out exceptions. All offer benefits as well as cautions for contemporary Adventist life.

Law as Blueprint

Those in this camp view the law as an absolutely accurate depiction of the way things are in and of themselves. The philosophical presupposition is that life has a certain, concrete and fixed character. God set up life to be lived in a particular manner, and the divine plan for life is found in religious law. God's will is that the human creation obey the law for in the law is the summation of divine expectation.

Bible. The structure of ancient Near-Eastern existence included the belief that tabernacles and temples were to be patterned after heavenly models.[5] Thus it is not surprising that Yahweh is quoted as giving Moses very specific instructions regarding the construction of the desert sanctuary: "In accordance with all that I show you concerning the pattern of the tabernacle and of all its furniture, so you shall make it."[6] The tabernacle and its sanctuary were a replica of cosmic reality. When Isaiah was called to the prophetic office, he was given a vision of the *real* sanctuary.

As the common Hebrew believers shared in praise and adoration of Yahweh in the sanctuary, they joined with the heavenly hosts and fulfilled the goal of existence. "To share in worship then, according to this perspective, was to participate to the fullest extent in reality and to live according to a divinely willed order," comments Jewish scholar Ze'ev Falk.[7] Similarly, correct performance according to cultic law mirrored the divine order of reality. The role of the most ancient Hebraic law was not primarily moral in the sense in which we use the term—serving laudable *human* ends. Rather, given the world view of the ancients, the law reflected a *heavenly ordering* of all existence which must be honored. Sin was the breaking of that order. The rituals of the sanctuary were designed in large part to maintain or restore this divine order. If a person inadvertently broke the divine order, the person could make atonement for the offence. An *intentional* breaking of the order—regardless of the motive—was fatally inexcusable.

The penalty for willful sin, e.g., Sabbath breaking, was death. The book of Numbers contains contrasting penalties for inadvertent and deliberate breaking of the law: there is one law for the person who sins unwittingly; but "whoever acts highhandedly, whether a native or an alien, affronts the Lord, and shall be cut off from among the people."[8] An illustration is then given of deliberate sin and its punishment: A man is found gathering sticks on the Sabbath, and with no questions asked, he is taken outside the camp and the congregation stones him to death at God's command.[9] There was no remission through the sacrificial system for obviously intentional sin.

Patriarchy was a part of the eternal order of life which was reflected in ancient Hebraic law. Although male superiority and privilege are today increasingly regarded as unjust, patriarchy was unchallenged in ancient cultures—including that of the Hebrews. The Hebrews were a nomadic people of extended families or tribes. Existence itself could not be taken for granted, and loyalty to the patriarch was of the highest order. Take the story of Judah and Tamar: Judah found that his daughter-in-law had become pregnant through prostitution, and he ruled "Bring her out, and let her be burned."[10] Only when Tamar produced evidence that Judah himself

105

had been intimately involved in her "prostitution" did her father-in-law reverse his decision. To rule or withhold the death penalty regarding his kin was the great discretionary power of a patriarch.

In sum, law in ancient Israel reflected early notions of existence which were not unique to Israel but which Israel shared. First, their view of law reflected a cosmic scheme of religious reality that must not be violated. Second, their view of law was conditioned by the nature of nomadic, tribal existence. This included provision for blood vengeance, corporate license, patriarchal license, and other features which are legitimately questionable today.

Adventism. Early Adventism, much like the early Hebrews, believed in a close affiliation between an earthly and heavenly reality and further, that it was privy to knowledge of such an interrelation. This is evident in Adventism's view of the sanctuary, particularly early "shut door" views. Simply put, the shut door theory held that on October 22, 1844 the destiny of every living person was forever fixed. The Millerite Adventists had done their work in preaching the cleansing of the sanctuary, and on the fateful twenty-second of October, God had shut the sanctuary's door. Hence the faithful saw no need to evangelize; their only role being, in the words of Miller, to "stir one another up to be patient; and be diligent to make our calling and election sure." Ellen White backed this interpretation of heavenly reality declaring in 1849 that the door was shut "and no man can open it." Yet White and other church leaders soon found their firmly held views untenable in light of the converts who began to sincerely adhere to fundamental Adventist beliefs.[11] Recognition that earlier views of the sanctuary were in error was difficult for Adventist pioneers[12] because of their concreteness and conceptual strictness—a good example of "blueprint" thinking.

However, a part of the genius of Adventism is the modesty of its claims regarding knowledge of God's will—even as revealed in Scripture. Ellen White was clear in distinguishing between the Bible writers as being God's "penmen" and God's "pen."[13] Siding with the "penmen" perspective, Mrs. White explicitly allowed for the human element in holy writ. This understanding of Ellen White was that of the mature prophetess, and it does not necessarily represent early Adventist thinking or even certain contemporary Adventist trends of thought.

Some Adventists today call for a return to the "blueprint" for how life ought now to be lived. With little regard to context or time, these advocates of the writings of Ellen White on education and other matters see Mrs. White having described an eternal, normative ordering of life.

Law as Motive

Law as motive represents a dramatic shift in the paradigm or framework within which law is seen. Whereas the blueprint typology focuses on universal structure, motive focuses on the individual person. Law as motive posits the absolute importance of an individual's reason for doing the right as the all-important requirement. Whether the right is actually done is not as important as one's motive in doing it. The shift in emphasis from blueprint to motive may not appear large to the casual observer because the explicit law itself may remain identical. However, the paradigm shift from cosmos to conscience is radical. Now the spirit of the law—not its letter—is all-important.

Bible. Nowhere in the Bible is the focus on law as motive more explicit than in the Pauline eulogy on love: "If I give away all my possessions, and if I hand over my body so that I may boast, but do not have love, I gain nothing."[14] Paul, of course, is not unique in the New Testament for uplifting love as the essence of Christian morality. He is merely following in Jesus' footsteps.[15] Jesus' strongest contrasting of motive and action is found in his Sermon on the Mount. An illustration is Matthew 5:27: "You have heard that it was said, 'You shall not commit adultery.' But I say to you that everyone who looks at a woman with lust has already committed adultery with her in his heart."

In explaining the relationship of motive to law, Jesus cites *agape* as the undergirding religious/ethical reality behind all the specific, concrete commandments. Asked by a Pharisaic lawyer about the essence of the Torah, Jesus refuses to cite any one of the Ten Commandments—as important as each is. Rather, he refers to the essence of all divine commandments as *agape*—the commitment to transcend oneself in genuine concern for other persons. The divine and human elements of the commitment are inseparable.

Jesus is not the first to recognize the importance of a parallel love for God

107

and fellow persons. Although a double commandment of love appears neither in the rabbinic writings, Qumran literature, nor contemporary apocalyptic writings, it does appear in several places in the Testaments of the Twelve Patriarchs, a second century BC pseudepigraphal book influenced by Greek thinking. The most direct statement in the Testaments is, "But love the Lord and your neighbor."[16] Neither was Jesus alone in his own Jewish tradition in stressing the central character of love. The great Hillel taught that behind the rabbis' distillation of the law into 613 commandments was the common fountain of the Golden Rule. Thus, following John Cobb's insight, we might say that several thought leaders around the time of Jesus exemplified a structure of existence that transcended an earlier epoch absorbed in an external ordering of life.

Although earliest Hebraic thought reflected an objectification of the universe, later Hebrew thinking exhibits greater similarity to that of Jesus and the best thinking of his contemporaries. In the classical prophets we see an outright dismissal of the cultic rituals which had so long provided religious security, and an underscoring of the more basic ethical norm of concern for the underprivileged.[17] This central prophetic theme is epitomized by Micah: "Will the Lord be pleased with thousands of rams, with ten thousands of rivers of oil?...He has told you, O mortal, what is good; and what does the Lord require of you but to do justice, and to love kindness, and to walk humbly with your God?"[18]

Even explicit reference to love for God and fellow persons is not unknown in the Hebrew Bible. Love of God was a part of the Hebrews' sacred creed, the Sh'ma.[19] Although love of God was not linked to neighbor love, the latter is also a commandment: "You shall not take vengeance or bear a grudge against any of your people, but you shall love your neighbor as yourself: I am the Lord."[20] However, the command of neighbor love is only one in a list of commandments. Jesus, in a preeminent manner, emphasized the inseparability of love of God and neighbor and proclaimed them as the *raison d'être* of all law. Love is the fulfilling of the law, as summarized the apostle Paul.

Adventism. Although early Adventism put an equal if not heavier stress on the letter of the law as compared to its spirit, later Adventism clearly recognized the centrality of good motive. In two of the books which came from the mature Ellen White we read:

> A man may be a law-breaker in heart; yet if he commits no outward act of transgression, he may be regarded by the world as possessing great integrity. But God's law looks into the secrets of the heart. Every act is judged by the motives that prompt it.[21]
>
> There are those who profess to serve God, while they rely upon their own efforts to obey His law, to form a right character, and secure salvation. Their hearts are not moved by any deep sense of the love of Christ, but they seek to perform the duties of the Christian life as that which God requires of them in order to gain heaven. Such religion is worth nothing.[22]

Such thinking was slow in permeating the ranks of the church. For instance, early Adventists engaged in heated debate with mainline Protestant clergymen. Coldly rational marshaling of texts and legalistic interchange were not uncommon. Within the denomination, particularly acrimonious debate at the 1888 General Conference session was held between those who tenaciously held to an emphasis on the unique Adventist doctrines and others (including Ellen White) who applauded two young Adventists who were preaching the all-sufficiency of Christ and his grace.[23]

Today in the denomination, the explicit doctrines of the church have undergone little change. However, a drastic alteration has occurred in the way many church members perceive those doctrines. The Sabbath is a case in point. No longer do North American Adventist preachers hurl proof texts at opposing ministers in an attempt to evangelize. More typically, a contemporary presentation on the Sabbath by a seminary-educated pastor emphasizes the concept of sacredness within time and the interpersonal, creative aspects of Sabbath celebration.[24]

Law as Wisdom

Law as blueprint can be faulted for its grandiose presupposition: that there is, and we can know, an unchanging structure for how the details of life are to be lived. Law as motive is a fundamental truth but can be faulted for its limited focus: persons can have the best of motives, but be sincerely wrong because of lack of knowledge or judgment. Law as wisdom encompasses insights from the blueprint and motive models of law, but itself emphasizes the value of careful reflection on life experience. It is analogous to Fowler's sixth stage of religious faith, which in part is defined as "unmediated participation in...the ultimate conditions of existence."

Bible. An important genre of Bible writing is known as the wisdom literature—Proverbs, Job, Ecclesiastes and just as importantly, many of the psalms and Jesus' parables—the latter largely unrecognized as coming from a wisdom background. I will briefly comment on the proverbs, a wisdom psalm, and Jesus' parables.

In contrast to the great prophets, the wisdom writers as personified in Proverbs do not directly attack pressing social problems such as unjust treatment of the poor. Rather, these writers approach life from the viewpoint of conundra of life which remain the same and point to truths that are generally valid regardless of social circumstances.[25]

The Proverbs are often thought to contain the essence of Hebraic morality.[26] A more adequate characterization would be that they encapsulate an important aspect of Hebraic ethical thinking. Whereas the major writing prophets particularly emphasize issues of social justice, the wisdom writers emphasize prudent behavior—thoughtful reflection on how to achieve what we would call both *the* good life and *a* good life. The Hebraic view of "the good" is very different from later Christian views (such as the expressed will of God) or the later philosophical idea of happiness. The Hebrews shared with their own contemporaries the view that the good was a social, public force or phenomenon that promotes the flourishing of both individual and community. "When it goes well with the righteous, the city rejoices."[27] The "righteous" person is the one who is "in order" and is thus successful and prosperous. The notion of an individual ethic at odds with the community was unheard of; and similarly there is a "complete lack of ethical exclusivism" in the Proverbs.[28]

Psalm 1 is a wisdom psalm: "Happy are those who do not follow the advice of the wicked, or take the path that sinners tread, or sit in the seat of scoffers; but their delight is in the law of the Lord, and on his law they meditate day and night."[29] Contrary to later Judaism, for which the law was a codified and objective standard of behavior, the Hebrews who wrote the Proverbs saw their law as "gracious instruction."[30] The law was "a source of life, wisdom, joy and enlightenment."[31] It was a divinely bestowed guideline for good living. This psalm was chosen as a prologue to the book of Psalms because of the central importance of its message: the superior way of life of the wise man who delights in the law as opposed to the fool who counsels with the wicked.

Jesus' parables originate in the world of wisdom.[32] Only because of Jesus' close scrutiny of human experience in the workaday world could he draw profound religious truths from his stories. Some of the parables are somewhat extrinsic to the lesson drawn (e.g., the unjust judge).[33] Others, however, make points which are evidently derived from Jesus' observation and study of human experience. For example, consider Jesus' parable of the contrasting prayers of the Pharisee and publican. After telling the story, Jesus concluded: "I tell you, this man went down to his home justified rather than the other; for all who exalt themselves will be humbled, but all who humble themselves will be exalted."[34]

Adventism. The wisdom literature, and indeed the Bible more generally, does not comment on the supposed conflict of human and divine truth—a longstanding concern of Adventism. Typically, common understandings of the world were encompassed by Bible writers within a divine framework of reality. For example, Isaiah writes that God will "gather the dispersed of Judah from the *four corners* of the earth."[35]

Traditionally the Adventist church has not held knowledge gained from human experience in high regard—especially knowledge which may raise difficult questions for faith. For example, the study of philosophy has not been favored. A conflict between divine and "human" truth is feared.

This supposed dichotomy poses a special dilemma for Adventism because of the church's fundamental position on the wholism of all truth—truth which its members pursue through a wide-ranging and increasingly sophisticated educational system. The church's educational emphasis has led hundreds of Adventists to pursue doctoral programs—often with denominational backing—in leading universities across the country. Adventist college faculties have advanced knowledge in diverse fields because of the denomination's commitment to pursuit of the whole truth. Such a conceptual commitment for largely rural, uneducated pioneers is one thing; the realization of that commitment by privileged descendants is quite another. However, there is little to fear if an undergirding appreciation for the biblical wisdom tradition can be nurtured and incorporated into the uniquely Adventist heritage.

The Vector of Law

The word "law" is an excellent motif for probing the Scriptures for their instruction on how we ought to live. As we have seen, the Bible does not speak with one voice here. However, it is possible to suggest a vector in regard to law, which emerges from biblical study. Such a vector moves from very concrete religio-cultural notions of right to thoughtful reflection on the good life and recognition of a mandatory inner spiritual commitment to others.

Internal biblical evidence suggests the inadequacy of any one of the models we have examined taken by itself. The cosmic blueprint model is challenged, for instance, in the later Deuteronomic rendition of the Decalogue,[36] which substitutes the exodus experience for the creation story as the rationale for the fourth commandment, and by Jesus who proclaims that the Sabbath—and by extension all law—is made for persons and not persons for the law.[37]

The motive model presents an imperative which we cannot ignore, but it is not sufficient because good intentions can be wholly misdirected. Hence the judgment serves for the weighing of both motives *and* deeds.[38]

The wisdom model cannot stand in isolation because of its tendency toward strictly personal if not prudent behavioral thinking; it particularly needs a corrective from the other two models discussed. However, the wisdom model is most helpful in its advocacy of careful, reflective thought on the breadth of human experience and knowledge. Job's reflection on astronomy, meteorology and a plethora of other natural phenomena and Jesus' keen scrutiny of and learning from everyday human experience is an important paradigm for us in our pursuit of the whole truth for our modern era.

Judæo-Christian law or instruction for our contemporary lives, in light of the above considerations, cannot be easily read off any single list or gained from any one story. In sum, the vector of law which God would have us refine as we face a new millennium is one which has at least four dimensions—

1. *substantive guidelines:* guidelines which are concrete and sure but not unassailable;

2. *human needs:* norms which are orientated toward genuine human need rather than toward humanly oppressive religio-cultural absolutes;

112

3. *general experience:* principles which comport with and are not alien to generally perceived human experience; and

4. *integrated action:* prescriptions which are proclaimed in recognition of the personal hollowness which results from adherence to letter without spirit.

Endnotes

[1] Ps 19:7-8.

[2] Lawrence Kohlberg, *The Philosophy of Moral Development: Moral Stages and the Idea of Justice* (San Francisco: Harper & Row, 1981) 17-23.

[3] James Fowler, "Stages in Faith: The Structural Developmental Approach," *Values and Moral Development*, ed. T. Hennessey (New York: Paulist, 1976) and "Mapping Faith's Structure: A Developmental View," *Life Maps: Conversations on the Journey of Faith*, ed. Fowler and Sam Keen (Waco, TX: Word, 1978).

[4] See his *The Structure of Christian Existence* (Philadelphia: Westminster, 1967). He cites evidence of a watershed of intellectual activity in the sixth century BC: Confucius and Lao-tzu were active in China, Gautama Buddha in India and Zoroaster in Persia. At the same time Thales and Pythagoras were founding Greek philosophy and the Hebrew prophetic movement was reaching its apex.

[5] Ze'ev W. Falk, *Hebrew Law in Biblical Times* (Jerusalem: Wahrmann, 1964) 108.

[6] Ex 25:9.

[7] *Hebrew Law in Biblical Times* (Jerusalem: Wahrmann, 1964) 108.

[8] Nu 15:30.

[9] Nu 15:32-36.

[10] Ge 38:24.

[11] See R. W. Schwarz, *Light Bearers to the Remnant* (Mountain View, CA: Pacific Press, 1979) 55, 69.

[12] See Wes Ringer, "From Shut Door to Investigative Judgment: Legacy of Guilt," *Adventist Currents* 1.4 (Jul 1984): 30-34.

[13] Ellen White, *Selected Messages*, 2 vols. (Washington, DC: Review and Herald, 1958) 1: 21.

[14] 1Co 13:3.

[15] Gal 5:14; Ro 13:9; see also Jas 2:8; Mt 19:19.

[16] *Testaments*, Issachar 5/2. See Reginald H. Fuller, "The Double Commandment of Love: A Test Case for the Criteria of Authenticity," *Essays on the Love Commandment*, by Luise Schttroff, *et al.* (Philadelphia: Fortress Press, 1978) 47-52. Fuller claims that "Hellenistic influences could have affected Jesus as well as the earliest Aramaic speaking church, even in Palestine."

[17] E.g.; Isa 1:10-17.

[18] Mic 6:7-8.

[19] Dt 6:4-9.

[20] Lev 19:18.

[21] Ellen White, *Christ's Object Lessons* (Mountain View, CA: Pacific Press, 1900) 316.

[22] Ellen White, *Steps to Christ* (Mountain View: CA: Pacific Press, 1907) 44-45.

[23] See LeRoy Edwin Froom, *Movement of Destiny* (Washington, DC: Review and Herald, 1971) for an excellent interpretive history of the 1888 General Conference session and the theme of righteousness by faith within the Adventist church.

[24] See Roy Branson, ed., *Festival of the Sabbath* (Takoma Park, MD: Association of Adventist Forums, 1985).

[25] Gerhard von Rad, *Wisdom in Israel* (Nashville: Abingdon Press, 1972) 76.

[26] Ibid., 74.

[27] Pr 11:10.

[28] von Rad, 81.

[29] Ps 1:1-2.

[30] Martin Buber's translation of *torah*.

[31] Joseph Blenkinsopp, *Wisdom and Law in the Old Testament: The Ordering of Life in Israel and Early Judaism* (Oxford: Oxford University Press, 1983) 76. Blenkinsopp adds that the sharp contrast which some Christians have drawn between law and gospel, with legalism being attributed to the Old Testament, is unfortunate; he particularly laments Julius Wellhausen's characterization of Jewish law as "a petty scheme of salvation."

[32] Walter Harrelson, "Ethics in Wisdom Literature," *The Westminster Dictionary of Christian Ethics*, ed. James F. Childress and John Macquarrie (Philadelphia: Westminster, 1986): 662-63.

[33] Lk 18:1-8.

[34] Lk 18:9-14.

[35] Isa 11:12; italics mine.

[36] Dt 5.

[37] Mk 2:27.

[38] See Mt 25.

Chapter Seven

SALVATION

CHARLES SCRIVEN

I am the Lord your God, who brought you out of the land of Egypt, out of the house of slavery.[1]

When thoughtful Seventh-day Adventists consider the doctrine of salvation, they focus, especially in periods of controversy, on the conditions that must be met in order for it to occur. What does God do in order to make salvation possible? What must we, in our turn, do in order to benefit from what God does?

This has been so, I believe, from the beginning. For Millerism, from which Seventh-day Adventism sprang, salvation depended upon the work of Christ and upon the correct human response to that work, including, Gerard Damsteegt tells us, "the necessity of accepting Millerite apocalyptic-eschatology."[2] Following the Great Disappointment, the tiny minority who became Seventh-day Adventists, reinterpreting the Millerite vision, argued that what had really happened on October 22, 1844, was the beginning of a new phase of Christ's work. This work was focused upon the sanctuary in heaven, they said, and testified to the last-day importance of obeying the Decalogue, including the Sabbath commandment, and having the faith of Jesus. Again, interest focused upon conditions that needed to be met in order for salvation to occur.[3]

In the years before the famous (and contentious) General Conference of 1888, Adventist preachers continued the emphasis upon obedience to the law, to the point of obscuring the message of Christ's grace. Although some church leaders gave evidence of belief in the message of grace, it was not until E. J. Waggoner advanced his view that the law in Galatians is the ten-commandment law, not just the ceremonial, that this message began moving toward center stage.[4] Once again the dominant concern was with what makes salvation possible. Little attention was devoted to the question of what salvation actually is.

Judging from such works as *Answers to Objections* and *Questions on Doctrine*, two works of Adventist apologetics dating from the 1930s to the 1950s,[5] this focus continued in our century. Certainly the Ford controversy of the late 1970s and early '80s suggests that it did; the debate included discussion of what salvation is, but interest converged as usual upon the conditions that make salvation possible.[6]

During the relatively uncontroversial commemoration of the 1888 centennial, substantial effort went into the elucidation of the salvation *experience*.[7] But the results mostly repeated (and amplified) what has always been taken for granted, namely that salvation gives individuals acceptance with God, empowerment for moral growth, and assurance of eternal life.[8] This preoccupation with the individual—with the individual's insecurity before God, struggle toward obedience, and hope of personal fulfillment— reflects the impact of Luther, Methodism, and the Enlightenment in general.[9] But whether it fully reflects the Biblical heritage is doubtful. That is why it is important for the church to consider anew what salvation *is* according to Scripture. In doing so we will also gain fresh insight into issues that have typically dominated our thinking in this area: what God does to make salvation possible and what we in turn must do to have a part in that salvation.

Healing the Life We Live Together

My initial claim is this: in Scripture salvation is the healing of persons *in society*; it is the healing of the life we live *together* in God's creation.

In both the Hebrew of the Old Testament and the Greek of the New, the word translated into English as "salvation" refers to healing. Throughout Scripture, moreover, the healing described and envisioned transforms society; though it touches individuals, it saves and enhances the *common life* these individuals share.

Let us begin with the Old Testament. Here as in the New Testament it is the story of a people, a community, that shows God's saving purpose in the world. The beginning of this people is the call of Abraham. God summons a man who has "settled" with his family in Haran to take up an adventure to a new land and mission to "all the families of the earth."[10] He is to be a "mediator of blessing" to others on the earth.[11]

116

The summons begins a relationship. A covenant, an agreement sealed by the oath of both parties, binds God and the family of Abraham together, guaranteeing the relationship. Later, when the family finds itself enslaved under the Pharaohs of Egypt, God, in partnership with Moses and in faithfulness to the covenant, effects a rescue. The exploited people are able to flee. With the destruction of pursuing Egyptian armies the Exodus is assured, and Moses leads the people in a song to the God who, precisely in virtue of this liberating deed, is said to be their "strength" and their "salvation."[12]

Here, then, salvation is the healing of shared life, the ending of oppression, the beginning of a march to a promised land. Soon afterward, when the people commit themselves to God at Mount Sinai, the basis of their commitment is that God has delivered them from the "house of slavery."[13] Individuals, according to the Old Testament, experience forgiveness.[14] Individuals receive empowerment for moral growth.[15] But the sense of sharing in redeemed life, of sharing in communal emancipation, remains central, not only in Genesis and Exodus but elsewhere as well.[16] When the classical prophets dream the future they envision a society where swords are plowshares and spears are pruning hooks, a society where people have what they need and live without fear.[17] For the Old Testament, indeed, the Exodus experience—the experience of being freed from oppression and injustice—is the paradigm of what salvation truly is.[18]

Moving to the New Testament, we may note first what J. M. Lochman declares, namely that the Jesus presented here "assimilates the Old Testament view of salvation."[19] In Luke's account, to take a Gospel example, Jesus is an agent of salvation[20]—and he explicitly invokes the Old Testament vision in portraying his mission. In the Nazareth inaugural sermon[21] he sounds the message of Isaiah 61: good news to the poor, release to the captives, sight for the blind, liberty for the oppressed. This is a picture, especially when considered in light of Isaiah ("they shall repair the ruined cities"[22]), of the healing of persons in society, a picture of the rejuvenation of common life through the establishment of justice.

The idea of the healing of the life we live together is central, too, in Paul's letter to the Galatians, a favorite (and typically misunderstood) book of those who interpret salvation individualistically. Under the impact of Luther, interpreters have affirmed for years that Paul's message of justification by faith in Christ was meant primarily to provide comfort to the guilt-ridden, to sinful individuals who need a sense of personal acceptance with God. Now, however, exegetes are agreeing more and more on the idea that the whole point of the book is to build community among Christians in the Galatian churches.

If through faith in Christ we find acceptance with God—this is what the message of justification declares to be possible—then we must in turn accept one another. All barriers that divide must come down, for once we have "clothed...[ourselves] with Christ," there is "no longer Jew or Greek, ...slave or free,...male and female": all of us "are one in Christ Jesus."[23] Again it is clear that salvation is the healing of social relations, the establishment of just and loving life together under God.[24]

My whole point thus far is to question the individualistic conception that, whether assumed or explicitly set forth, has always dominated Adventist thinking about salvation. This does not change for a moment the importance of such familiar metaphors of salvation as reconciliation, forgiveness, adoption, sanctification, and the like. Nor does it undermine the hope of victory over death through resurrection. The point is that whatever the healing God intends, it is a healing not of solitary persons but of persons in society, persons whose lives cohere with other lives in common life, in community.

"In Solidarity With Jesus Christ"

We come now to my second broad claim: salvation happens in solidarity with Jesus Christ. Healing takes place—the healing, that is, of persons linked together in common life—when we link our own destinies with the destiny of the crucified and resurrected one.

In the Gospels salvation happens through connection with Christ. The sick and guilty find healing and forgiveness in his presence;[25] personal renewal occurs in responding to his message.[26] As the Gospel of Mark declares, the Way of salvation consists in following Jesus, in uniting with his purpose.[27]

This idea is present, too, in the writings of Paul. According to E. P. Sanders, the idea of union with Christ is central for Paul; it, and not, for example, justification by faith, is the theme that explains all the other themes.[28] In Paul's thinking, of course, union with Christ is, in large part,

118

solidarity with Christ's body, the church. That is where believers find forgiveness, the acquittal of justification.[29] That is where they encounter community and shared life, gaining strength from one another.[30] That is where they experience moral growth, sanctification.[31] That is where they realize the breakdown of social barriers and hostilities.[32]

This idea of solidarity with Christ is reminiscent, of course, of the heritage of Anabaptism, a key movement of the Radical Reformation. I have elsewhere argued that this is Seventh-day Adventism's true Reformation heritage.[33] The phrase "solidarity with Christ" summarizes the movement's basic convictions. According to Anabaptism, Christ is the Jesus of the Bible story now exalted, now Lord and Liberator, now embodied in the church, soon to effect a final apocalyptic transformation. It is Christ, understood in this way, said the Anabaptists, with whom believers are to share their lives in trust, loyalty, and like-mindedness.

My claim is that just in the degree that we do this, we experience salvation. In this broken world each of us lives a life that is a broken story, a story of wrong turns and unhappy endings. But if we link our lives with the larger life of Christ, with the Great Story of the divine healing of our world, then we experience salvation, a salvation that, though fragmentary now, will one day come to complete fulfillment. As Stanley Hauerwas tells us, we are saved through sharing the work of the kingdom Christ came to establish. Finding our role in the Great Story of that kingdom, we place ourselves "within an adventure which we claim is nothing less than God's purpose for all of creation."[34] That adventure—shared in the community of faith, guided by the story of Jesus, nourished by the grace of the living Christ—*is* our salvation.

Salvation, then, is the healing of the life we live together in God's creation, the healing not of solitary individuals but of the politics and social structures within which individuals live; at the same time, salvation is solidarity with Christ, the adventure of participation in the Great Story of the Kingdom.

Granting this, we find insight into the questions that have always dominated Adventist thinking about these matters: what God does to make salvation possible and what we in turn must do to have a part in it. The truth here, put briefly, is that God achieves the healing of persons and societies *in the manner of Jesus Christ*, and that we experience this healing for ourselves *in solidarity with Jesus Christ*.

119

"The Grand Adventure of the Kingdom"

Let us now turn explicitly to ethics. I have just sketched a doctrine of salvation according to which the ethical life is not something we embrace in order to win salvation, but something we embrace because it belongs to our salvation, because it bears its own intrinsic satisfactions. Salvation is the personal and social healing that happens in solidarity with Christ, and part of what that experience involves is our own adventurous participation in that healing process. Salvation is not just in the present tense, of course; we must look forward to its completion in the future. But we still experience it precisely *in* the grand adventure of the Kingdom, the grand adventure of full union—moral as well as spiritual—with our Lord.

For Christian ethics this means discipleship, following Jesus, and following Jesus even off the beaten track of the dominant cultural life around us. Among the things H. Richard Niebuhr showed us, in ways both purposeful and inadvertent, was this: the temptation to accommodate ourselves unthinkingly to fashionable, surrounding cultural life is very strong.[35] That temptation must, however, be resisted. The risk of failure is the risk of forfeiting the full measure of the salvation God offers us today.

One could suggest many ethical implications of discipleship. Let me suggest one overarching virtue that certainly must be considered central—the virtue of compassion. Jesus inhabited a social world, Marcus Borg tells us, where faithfulness to God meant avoidance of defiling associations, separation, in other words, from those considered to be unfaithful. The dominant ethos called for distance between Jew and Gentile, between the pure and the impure. Economic reality kept many Jews from meeting all the requirements of holy separation and these Jews themselves tended to become sinners and outcasts in the eyes of the religious establishment. Jesus criticized this separationist mentality, saying that it subverted the full responsiveness to human need that God's call requires.

The virtue of compassion was his remedy for this. In the heritage of Jesus, the word for this virtue was the plural form of the word for womb. Compassion was "wombishness." In the making of another human being a mother gives generously of herself, focusing tender feelings upon the developing person and providing an environment suitable for growth toward full humanity. We ourselves must embody such motherly traits.

Compassion is the ability to feel the needs that others feel, and to be moved by them, moved to caring, constructive action. As interpreted by Jesus, it comes to expression in deeds of helping, in loyalty to all creation, in commitment to peace and justice.[36] When we show forth such compassion we imitate the God who made us.[37]

Seventh-day Adventists have long regarded evangelism as a key imperative of church mission. By now many thoughtful Adventists disapprove both the methods and theology that have dominated the church's evangelism, but the basic imperative surely remains intact. A compassionate people must enlarge the circle of compassion in order to enlarge the environment suitable for human growth toward full humanity. Evangelism is the recruitment of new disciples and the recruitment of new disciples is itself an expression of compassion.[38] We are therefore bound, and bound morally, to make evangelism a central practice of church life.

Another compassionate practice is equally imperative, though unequally acknowledged, at least within Adventism. Although we have accepted the challenge of inviting non-believers to join the grand adventure of the Kingdom, we have largely failed to regard political engagement as part of that adventure. But if Christ, the key to our salvation, called us to compassion, then we must accept political engagement as a basic Christian task. A compassionate people must, as I have suggested, enlarge the environment suitable for human growth toward full humanity. This demands a commitment to social transformation. The world's political structures determine to a large degree how people fare in life. The church must, in ways appropriate for disciples, engage these structures, shaping them, whether by direct involvement or by prophetic witness, toward the ideal of compassion which is central to God's Kingdom. Addressing private lives is simply not enough, not when salvation itself, far from being a private matter, is the healing of persons *in society*.

Failing to be engaged politically, we miss a large part of the adventure that *is* our salvation in the world. Once Jesus' critics complained that unlike John's disciples and those of the Pharisees, his own disciples did not fast. Jesus replied, "The wedding guests cannot fast while the bridegroom is with them, can they?"[39] His movement was, and was meant to be, a joyous one. The enlarging of compassion was no gritty, grudging duty but an intrinsically satisfying experience, a reason for celebration. If political engagement enlarges compassion, then it enlarges, too, the joy of those who practice it. Whether we Adventists can outgrow our individualism in these matters is hard to say; that our lives are blighted when we don't is certain.

I have argued that salvation is the healing of persons in society, not solitary individuals, and that we experience salvation today at just the point of solidarity with Christ. I have argued, too, that solidarity with Christ means discipleship and discipleship means compassion. Compassion expresses itself in many ways, of course. One of these, I have said, is evangelism, a practice prominent in the Adventist heritage but often questioned today. Another is political engagement, which to our own and to the world's impoverishment, we have typically refused.

The interpretation given here goes substantially against what most people would consider traditional Adventism. Let me consider finally two elements of our heritage that in fact point us in the direction I have been suggesting.

A Heritage of Concern

The first is this: though it has been largely suppressed, concern for the healing of society has played a small but significant role in the Adventist tradition. Jonathan Butler has shown how this was the case (ambiguously, to be sure) during the middle and later portions of the nineteenth century.[40] In 1921 the Autumn Council of the church's General Conference authorized the sending of a letter to United States President Warren Harding expressing, out of loyalty to "Him who is the Prince of Peace," the church's support for "a limitation of armaments." The letter affirmed the hope that "the vast sums spent for armaments of war may be devoted to the amelioration of human woe and to the advancement of peaceful pursuits."[41] The *Adventist Review* published a statement of the 1986 Annual Council, asking Seventh-day Adventists to help "remove underlying causes" of social discord, build respect for "human rights," advance "social, cultural, and economic justice," and urge nations to "beat their 'swords into plowshares.'"[42]

These examples, taken from widely different periods, suggest, certainly, that a social interpretation of the salvation experience is compatible with our church's heritage. A famous metaphor of Ellen White, the most influential of our founding leaders, underscores this point. According to her,

122

Christ's love knows no boundary, touching all of Adam's sons and daughters, and we who follow Christ must therefore feel a deep attachment to the perishing world around us. We belong, she declares, "to the great web of humanity."[43] And that, of course, is the point: the healing we need is not merely private but also public, a healing of the life we share with one another.

The second element in the Adventist heritage that points in this direction is the theme of the "Great Controversy," a theme which assumed a place of importance in Adventist consciousness as a result of the significance attached to it in the writings of Ellen White. This is, in part at least, an expression of what theologians call the "classic view" of the work of Christ, or the atonement.[44] Other dominant views—that Christ's work not only expressed but also *legitimated* God's grace, or that its primary point was to inspire us to be more loving—have often, at least in the modern period, been interpreted individualistically. The classic view asserts that through Christ God destroyed the works of the devil, defeating the powers, *both personal and socio-political*, that work against the Kingdom. The Great Controversy theme in Ellen White similarly declares that the whole world, not just private individuals, undergoes healing at God's hand. The lyrical ending of her last work on the "conflict of the ages" describes a universe, finally cleansed of sin, in which a single "pulse of harmony and gladness beats through the vast creation."[45]

This, according to Ellen White, is what salvation involves, a healing peace that touches the life we share and indeed the entire context of that life. Coming as it does from deep within our own heritage, it constitutes a second reason for thinking that the direction of this essay is the direction we ought to take as a church. To risk less, as I have suggested already, is to assure impoverishment.

Endnotes

[1] Ex 20:2.

[2] P. Gerard Damsteegt, *Foundations of the Seventh-day Adventist Message and Mission* (Grand Rapids: Eerdmans, 1977) 49.

3 Ibid., 143-45, 147-48, 189-92, 209-12.

4 On this see, for example, A. V. Olson, *Through Crisis to Victory* (Washington: Review and Herald, 1966) 1-49.

5 Francis D. Nichol, *Answers to Objections*, 3rd ed. (Washington: Review and Herald, 1952) and [R. A. Anderson, L. E. Froom, *et al.*,] *Seventh-day Adventists Answer Questions on Doctrine* (Washington: Review and Herald, 1957).

6 See, for instance, *Spectrum* 9.3 (Summer 1979) and *Spectrum* 11.2 (Spring 1981).

7 E.g. *Adventist Review* 134.1 (2 January 1988) and *Ministry* 41.4 (February 1988).

8 Cf. the discussion in *Questions on Doctrine* of the "three tenses" of salvation: "we *have been* saved—justification; we *are being* saved—sanctification; and we *shall be* saved—glorification" (118, 19).

9 On individualism in Luther see Krister Stendahl, *Paul Among Jews and Gentiles* (Philadelphia: Fortress, 1976) 78-96, and Alasdair MacIntyre, *A Short History of Ethics* (New York: Macmillan, 1966) 125, 126; on sanctification and individualism in Wesley, see John Dillenberger and Claude Welch, *Protestant Christianity* (New York: Scribner, 1954) 129-34 and H. Richard Niebuhr, *The Social Sources of American Denominationalism* (New York: World, 1972) 59-69; on Enlightenment "privatization" see Johann Baptist Metz, *Faith in History and Society* (New York: Seabury, 1980) 34-47.

10 Ge 11:31, 12:3.

11 Gerhard von Rad, *Genesis: A Commentary* (Philadelphia: Westminster, 1972) 160.

12 Ex 15.

13 Ex 20:2.

14 Ps 32.

15 Ps 119.

16 E.g., Dt 26:5-9; Ps 44:1-3; Ps 144:12-15.

17 See, for instance, Mic 4:1-4.

18 See, e.g., J. M. Lochman, *Reconciliation and Liberation* (Philadelphia: Fortress Press, 1980) 37.

19 Ibid., 38.

20 Lk 19:10.

21 Lk 4:16-21.

22 Isa 61:4.

23 Gal 3:11, 25-28.

24 On this interpretation of Galatians, see numerous recent treatments, including that of Hans Dieter Betz, *Galatians*, Hermeneia Commentary Series (Philadelphia: Fortress Press, 1979).

25 Mk 2:1-12.

26 Lk 19:1-10.

[27] See Mk 8:34-36; 10:52; 14:22-25. In Mark the "way in which salvation is appropriated by the believer is through discipleship," writes Hendrikus Boers in "Reflections on the Gospel of Mark: A Structural Investigation," *SBL 1987 Seminary Papers*, 259.

[28] E. P. Sanders, *Paul and Palestinian Judaism* (Philadelphia: Fortress Press, 1977) 431-520.

[29] Ro 8:1, 10.

[30] Ro 12:5; 1Co 12:13, 27.

[31] Ro 6:4-11; Php 3:12-14.

[32] Gal 3:27-28.

[33] Charles Scriven, "Radical Discipleship and the Renewal of Adventist Mission," *Spectrum* 14.4 (Winter 1983): 11-20.

[34] Stanley Hauerwas, *The Peaceable Kingdom* (Notre Dame: University of Notre Dame Press, 1983) 62.

[35] See Niebuhr's classic *Christ and Culture* (New York: Harper and Row, 1951). For a critical appreciation of this and other Niebuhr works, offered from a point of view rooted in Anabaptism, see my work, *The Transformation of Culture* (Scottdale, PA: Herald Press, 1988).

[36] Marcus J. Borg, *Jesus: A New Vision* (San Francisco: Harper & Row, 1987) 83, 87, 91, 93. See also Phyllis Trible, *God and the Rhetoric of Sexuality* (Philadelphia: Fortress Press, 1978) 31-33.

[37] Lk 6:36; see the New Jerusalem Bible's translation.

[38] I have considered objections to evangelism—what I call the "relativity," "autonomy," "hypocrisy," and "irrelevancy" objections—in "When the Jailhouse Rocks: A Defense of Evangelism," *Spectrum* 18.2 (Winter 1988): 22-29.

[39] Mk 2:19.

[40] "Adventism and the American Experience," *The Rise of Adventism*, ed. Edwin S. Gaustad (San Francisco: Harper & Row, 1974) 173-206.

[41] A copy of this letter may be obtained by writing to Bert Haloviak of the Department of Archives and Statistics at the church's world headquarters, 12501 Old Columbia Pike, Silver Spring, MD 20904-1608.

[42] *Adventist Review* (5 December 1985): 19.

[43] Ellen White, *The Desire of Ages* (Mountain View, CA: Pacific Press, 1898) 638.

[44] The term "classic view" was popularized through the influence of Gustaf Aulén, whose historical study *Christus Victor* (New York: Macmillan, 1969) has been widely read.

Chapter Eight

WHOLENESS

Ginger Hanks-Harwood

Man and woman were made in the image of God with individuality, the power
and freedom to think and to do. Though created free beings, each is an
indivisible unity of body, mind and spirit, dependent upon God for life
and breath and all else.[1]

Since 1863, Seventh-day Adventists have promulgated a wholistic view
of the human person. The view that the body, mind, and spirit are all
integrated and interrelated constituent elements that together form a single
being is the very cornerstone on which much of our work as a church has
been built. Believing that these three are interdependent and constantly
interacting, we have adopted a "systems" approach in our anthropology: the
whole person cannot be understood merely as the sum of separate, constituent parts. Each variable in the system is so enmeshed in its interaction with
the other parts as to make the relationship the key to understanding each
individual component.

The recognition of the internal triad is only the first step in the process
of deriving a wholistic approach. The next step involves appreciating the
total web of life in which these dimensions implicate us—the vast physical
world of material and sensate elements, the historical world of social
meanings and values through which an individual must negotiate to
accomplish personal goals and objectives, and the sphere of spiritual
intuition, insight, and awareness. In short, it necessitates the generation of
an "ecology of existence," in which the different components of the
individual's existence are consciously traced and recognized. The individual is seen, understood, and approached as a complex being simultaneously shaped by the internal and the external, historical and sociological
realities, conscious and unconscious needs and motivations, personal and
communal frameworks and experiences.

From this vantage point, the spiritual enterprise addresses a sentient being with the capacity to monitor the universe and respond to it (both consciously and unconsciously) on the basis of information gleaned from physical, rational-emotive, and spiritual radar. Thus, each of these spheres provides the total person with methods of learning and wisdom distinctly its own, and may be the appropriate starting point for spiritual education or discernment, just as distortion or distress in any one of these spheres will serve to undermine the survival or well-being of the person.

Wholeness not only recognizes the ecology of the individual, but emphasizes the absolute significance of adequately addressing the human needs derived from each dimension of the person. Responsibility for adequately nurturing these aspects of one's being falls to the individual, who is credited with both the power and the authority to know, to will, and to do that which is in his or her best interests.

Origin of "Wholeness" in Adventist Theology and Culture

While the actual beginning of the importance of wholeness as a theme is generally traced to Ellen White's 1863 health vision, its roots extend into earlier ground. Wholeness, as it was developed in Adventist theology, represented the nexus of conditionalism, transcendentalism, and the health reform movement. A brief review of these three movements will serve to highlight some of their contribution to the theme of wholeness as it was developed in the nineteenth century.

Conditionalism, which can itself be traced back through the ages of Christianity, had emerged on the American continent as a response to Calvinist preachers like Jonathan Edwards. Edwards, along with many of his contemporaries during the First Great Awakening, had laid out the terrors of eternal damnation in such strong and vivid fashion that he evoked a negative reaction among his hearers. The God depicted in his theology appeared merciless and arbitrary—merciless and arbitrary enough to provoke a revolt in some circles. Conditionalism, the view that life is only in Christ and immortality the privilege solely of the regenerate, was promulgated as an alternative to the doctrine of eternal hell for sinners. As humanity is by nature mortal, a new condition was needed in order to procure life—

spiritual rebirth. Salvation was the gift given to the righteous, and without that gift one met extinction at death. Christ had come to redeem humanity, and the ultimate goal of redemption was to renew the image of God in humanity.

In the early 1800s this view was promoted by such well-known ministers as Henry Ward Beecher, Lyman Abbot, and Leonard Woolsey Bacon. In the 1840s, some Advent Christians (including the Whites and Joseph Bates) embraced conditionalism; others were too absorbed in eschatology to consider the question of humanity's nature and destiny. Although William Miller's group disclaimed sympathy for conditionalism, and the issue was avoided in the 1845 meeting to bind the Advent group back together after the Great Disappointment, the view grew. By 1858, the Sabbatarian Advent group was placing major emphasis on the issue, and it became one of about seven coordinated fundamentals of belief.

It is significant to note that the very heart of the conditionalist argument centered around the doctrine of redemption of the free moral agent (as opposed to Calvinist notions of predestination). Adventists placed this notion beside the view of the "last days," and generated a picture of humanity standing before the Great Judge. Preparation to stand on that awful day necessitated a reformed life and rectification of belief—salvation was the result of the free choice of a morally accountable agent. Failure to meet the mark resulted in the death sentence (God's promise to Adam, "You shall surely die" [Ge 2:17]), and nothing short of the death of the whole person would validate this promise. Thus, it would be the whole person who either perished or received eternal life.

A second philosophical current to impact the New England population at this time was transcendentalism. A widespread grass roots movement throughout America before the Civil War, transcendentalism emphasized the importance of inner reform as a prerequisite for social reform. The urge to usher in a new kingdom was strong in this era, and transcendentalists underscored the role individual conscience, choice, and values played in determining the social order. Further, transcendentalists frequently developed themes of mystical connection between the individual and the universe, living in harmony and balance with nature, and the significance of the inner search for meaning. Each of these strands of thought would find its way into the doctrine of wholeness.

Finally, a third major reform movement of the early eighteen-hundreds focused on natural healing techniques. A reaction to practices of drugging and bleeding patients, natural medicine emphasized the significance of understanding the body and working with it to help it heal itself. The significance of fresh air, proper diet, water applied internally and externally, sunshine, and exercise were extolled at such institutions as Caleb Jackson's "Our Home on the Hill," eventually frequented by many of the leaders of the Adventist flock.

There can be no doubt but that the dialogue concerning these issues contributed to the shape of our early understanding of the significance of the concept of wholeness. Our pioneers were, as we all are, in dialogue over the issues of their day. These were the burning theological questions that captured the imagination and interest of the theologically minded of the mid-nineteenth century. The exploration of the nature and destiny of humankind has always invited lively debate, but its significance was more clearly outlined when it was set against the dogmatic harangues of the Calvinists.

Impact on Adventist Culture and Doctrine

Ellen White's vision of June 6, 1863 was to have immediate as well as long-term ramifications for the Adventist movement. From the vision she derived not only the connection between physical welfare and spiritual health, but also the mission to educate all who were preparing for eternal life about the reforms needed in their daily living. "I saw," she asserted, that "it was a sacred duty to attend to our health....The more perfect our health, the more perfect will be our labor."[2] On this basis, health reform and temperance were placed next to other "saving truths" and became an integral part of the message designed to prepare the world for Christ's return. It was, in the words of E. J. Waggoner, the "means whereby a weak people may be made strong to overcome, and our diseased bodies cleansed and fitted for translation....It comes to us as an essential part of present truth."[3] The year before, Uriah Smith had commented in the *Review and Herald* on a meeting at which Ellen White had underlined the connection between the physical, mental, and moral. He had summarized by reflecting upon "the important bearing of the subject upon the present truth," which he assumed would "be seen at once by all who realize how necessary is reform in our physical habits to that high state of spirituality involved in the preparation needful for us to be partakers of the latter rain."

The early vision of 1863, along with subsequent visions which reinforced and amplified the initial exposure to wholism, was to become the energizing principle behind much of the work accomplished for the rest of the nineteenth century. When Ellen White perceived the connection between the physical condition of the individual and accessibility to the proddings of the Holy Spirit, she became involved in a critical paradigm shift. Breaking with earlier models that exalted the spiritual aspect of a human at the expense of the physical, she began to articulate the significance of viewing and responding to humans as "embodied" beings. She states this principle in her book, *Education:*

> Since the mind and the soul find expression through the body, both mental and spiritual vigor are in great degree dependent upon physical strength and activity; whatever promotes physical health, promotes the development of a strong mind and a well-balanced character. Without health, no one can as distinctly understand or as completely fulfill his obligations to himself, to his fellow beings, or to his Creator. Therefore, the health should be as faithfully guarded as the character.[4]

This paradigm shift engendered a fresh release of spiritual energies as the pioneers began to conceptualize ways in which they could legitimately care for their own needs as human beings while devoting themselves to the Gospel. The central insight derived from the ethic of wholeness was that the medium was indeed the message. The good news was to be lived out and enfleshed on a daily basis as the young flock shepherded themselves as well as the larger world. The Gospel was more attractive both to themselves and others when they included themselves in the circle of care.

As the tension between discipleship and personal stewardship lessened, more energy was available for the development and promulgation of the Advent mission. The first and probably most significant impact the doctrine of wholeness had on the church was the beginning of the healing process for those founders who were suffering from burn-out and physical depletion as a result of their attempts to propagate the kingdom.

The combination of the vibrant vision provided through Ellen White and subsequent attention to personal physical needs became the vehicle for transformation of the foundling church. They began to see themselves as the artists and designers of their own lives; participating in the establishment of a new model for human existence, one as old as Creation but as revolutionary as anything proposed by the Transcendentalists. From the groanings of a worn-out and flawed culture a new awareness of eternal values and principles was being born, and the leaders of the little church were to be the midwives. At that point, the church gave up its basic passivity (waiting for the return of Christ to rescue it from the fallen world) and began to transform individual minds, lives, and the environment on the basis of their new understanding of the ecology of existence.

The new model pictured a wholistic human being embedded in a living universe. As Ellen White observed, "Mysterious life pervades all of nature....In everything upon the earth, from the tree of the forest to the lichen that clings to the rock, from the boundless ocean to the tiniest shell on the shore,...[observers] may behold the image and superscription of God."[5] Humans had been designated as stewards over the spiritual and material resources of this fragment of creation. As stewards, as co-administrators with God, they retained the ability to increase their spiritual discernment and select life commitments and habits on the basis of respect for the natural ecology of existence. In the hands of the leaders of the little flock, the nature and destiny of not only humanity (corporately and individually) was probed, but the very structure of accepted roles and relationships was subjected to scrutiny. In their movement toward the establishment of a new value-based culture, they went beyond the "given" of society to see the patterns, relationships, and contextual setting of their social milieu that provided the warp and woof of their existence. As the latent functions of the structures were made manifest, they lost their mystique and began to appear as one way out of many to organize society. The pioneers had determined to reclaim their power from cultural customs and authority.

Established institutions and ideas were mercilessly scrutinized for congruence with the new paradigm, and where they were perceived to have failed the examination they were redesigned and reformulated. The quality and breadth of their critique is evidenced in the wide range and types of questions asked of accepted institutions and customs:

What end have our cultural institutions served?
What is the nature of wellness?

What role should reason and logic play in moral discourse?
What educational curriculum is appropriate for children?
What in our environment is conducive to wholeness?
What role is dress playing in the subjugation of women?
What forms of recreation serve to revitalize and restore?
What is the meaning of the marriage institution?
Where may God be seen in this docudrama?

And the recurring question, *Does the current practice renew in the human being the image of God, or does it need to be replaced?*

In sum, the doctrine of wholeness has had a significant impact on the Adventist church. Its presence can be demonstrated in our theology, anthropology, ecclesiology, and ethics. It has provided the church with a central part of its identity and sense of mission. It would be hard to envision the history of the church without the doctrine of wholeness, since this theme is woven into almost every recurrent theme and doctrine of the church. The law of God, which we are to obey, is not only the transcript of God's character, but the law of our own nature or being; the remnant people are those who prepare themselves to enter God's kingdom by aligning their whole selves with the will of God; the Sabbath is celebrated as a gift for human renewal and restoration; and so forth.

In every attempt to renew in humanity the divine image, Seventh-day Adventists have applied the ecological paradigm of being and asked how God could be glorified in our present social milieu.

Early Applications to Personal Ethics

After her 1863 vision Ellen White began focusing the attention of theologically inclined members on the significance of the character. Since the individual was viewed as the locus of decision-making, great concern arose as to the factors likely to influence him or her. In this light, ethics could be viewed as a matter of virtue, as appropriate decisions could most probably be generated from an informed and virtuous character.

The self, as the decision-maker, prepared to meet quandaries by the cultivation of proper habits as well as thoughts. As it would be the self which would be required to decide and accept the responsibility or consequences of the decisions, negotiating between biblical principles and the situation, the proper formation of the self was of critical importance. As such, anything which informed, educated or stimulated the self took on new importance. Beliefs, dispositions, affections, and intentions were all affected by the milieu and in turn shaped the character. All of the social setting became material for predisposing the character of the individual either toward or away from clarity and moral insight, as either facilitating or detracting from the goal of bringing an individual into the "full stature of Christ."

Thus, several of the early workers spent anywhere from a few days to several months at "Our Home," a health reform institute founded by Caleb Jackson, in order to regain their strength and acquire more complete knowledge concerning the relationship between their lifestyle and their physical and spiritual health. The message was clear: to give glory to God, to faithfully steward the body temple, the mind must be alert and prepared to discern the presence of either heavenly or hellish devises.

The primary principles derived from the wholistic paradigm of being centered around doing only that which brought the self and others closer to a state prepared for redemption. Honor God by honoring God's handiwork. Where there is brokenness, work for healing. Educate yourself and others as to the nature of your being and how to care for it. Exhibit God's love and caring by ministering to the physical as well as the emotional and spiritual needs of others. Invest your time, energy, and resources in that which will promote wholeness and happiness for both the present and eternity. Guard against practices or habits that might deaden the sensitivities.

As a result of these guidelines, the little flock took an inventory of personal diet, dress, and hygiene to see where their moral sensibilities could be improved by eliminating counterproductive health habits. They re-examined their efforts to spread the Gospel, looking for ways to minister more effectively to the whole person. Many began to prepare themselves to be public lecturers on hygiene and temperance. But most significant of all, they began to view themselves as stewards of creation with the right and obligation to speak and act on behalf of God's redemptive plan for their world.

Early Applications to Social Ethics

Almost from the very moment of its introduction, the doctrine of wholeness began to shape Adventist social ethics. Understanding the link between the soul and the body, and between the person and society, led early Adventist leaders to appreciate the necessity of the struggle for piety; and that the redemption of humanity must take place in the public arena as well as in the church or prayer closet. Ellen White was very clear on the path that opened up before those who would take up the way of the cross:

> We need not go to Nazareth, to Capernaum, or to Bethany, in order to walk in the steps of Jesus. We shall find His footprints beside the sickbed, in the hovels of poverty, in the crowded alleys of the great cities, and in every place where there are human hearts in need of consolation. We are to feed the hungry, clothe the naked, and comfort the suffering and afflicted. We are to minister to the despairing, and to inspire hope in the hopeless....With all who are seeking to minister in His name,...[Christ] waits to cooperate.[6]

The entire denomination was enlisted in the battle against the forces identified as obliterating the image of God in humanity by clouding the sensibilities and flawing the character. The campaign for diet and hygiene reform was begun immediately. A series of pamphlets was prepared for distribution, with James White setting forth the close relationship between physical and spiritual well-being in the first one, entitled "Sanctification." Women from the Battle Creek church (especially sisters Lockwood, Loughborough, Cornell, Smith, Amadon, Driscoll, and Patten) furnished some twenty pages of recipes for hygienic cooking for that first pamphlet. The *Review and Herald* carried advertisements for the gem irons required for the whole wheat "gems" intended to replace biscuits, thus ensuring the availability of the irons for those who wished to reform their diet in this manner.

Meanwhile, Ellen White had monitored the results of the Annual Dress Reform Convention held in Rochester, New York, and created a dress—modeled after the famous "bloomers" of Emily Bloomer—incorporating health principles that suited her taste more precisely than did the so-called "American Costume." She and at least a portion of the church continued to wear the reform dress for several years. The dress was offered as an alternative to the fashion health leaders viewed as crippling to women and dangerous to the public health—since the long dresses were seen as tending to spread disease. This revision of dress standards was seen as promoting not only individual but public health.

By 1868, John Harvey Kellogg was serving as a roaming health lecturer, and the publication of a regular health journal, *The Health Reformer*, had begun. While temperance had taken a back burner during the Civil War, the post-war years saw a resurgence of interest in the issue. Seventh-day Adventists joined the ranks of reform clubs such as the Women's Christian Temperance Union. The goal was to abolish the liquor trade and thereby put an end to the misery and chaos created by the free use of alcohol. James and Ellen White both led out in this campaign, with Ellen White pressing the rank and file of the temperance movement to scrutinize the problem more closely, to also consider the diet which stimulated the appetite for tobacco and liquor. In so doing, she used the stage set by the liquor reform movement to promote a larger view of healthful and temperate living.

In 1878, the American Health and Temperance Association was formed, with Kellogg as president. The Association called for abstinence from liquor, tea, coffee, opium, and all other narcotics and stimulants. They called this the Teetotal Pledge, and circulated it for public support. Great influence on general sentiment regarding alcohol was gained through the literature, lectures, and pledges provided to the public.

In that same year, Adventists, along with other members of the WCTU, organized a restaurant in conjunction with the arrival of Barnum's Menagerie and Circus at Battle Creek. The food and beverage served there were intended as alternatives to the fare provided by the saloons organized around the event. The Battle Creek Sanitarium supplied fresh fruits and vegetables for the center.

By 1877, the church had begun its initial efforts on behalf of freed slaves in the South. Mrs. H. M. Van Slyke engaged in teaching a school for blacks in Ray, Colorado, while Mr. and and Mrs. Joseph Clarke taught and organized the construction of a similar institution in Texas. R. M. Kilgore was sent to Texas to assist in the work, and during his administration became caught in the rising tension concerning racially mixed congregations. Edmund Killen, a black preacher from Georgia, accepted the Adventist message in 1878 and began to work with blacks in that area, and a school was established near Huntsville, Alabama. Despite strong urging from Ellen

White that the "Negro People" be given priority in the work since they had a "right to receive the benefits of the last gospel message, in health, in social betterment, in education, in the hope and joy of the Advent message,"[7] the field was generally neglected. Perhaps the most dramatic work undertaken specifically for the Southern black population was that of James Edson White on his Mississippi riverboat, *The Morning Star*. On the boat, a combination schoolroom, chapel, and house, Edson undertook a literacy campaign, the teaching of health principles, and the preparation of workers to teach branch schools to raise the level of education among the freed slaves. Within ten years of starting, there were over fifty schools in some six Southern states, and more advanced schools were being created. The campaign to spread to the Afro-American population of the South the benefits of health, literacy, and education had made an impact on the lives of many who would in turn spread these benefits to others.

This period also showed major activity among the faithful involved in medical work. By 1890 the denomination boasted three medical institutions: the Battle Creek Sanitarium, the Rural Health Retreat in Saint Helena, California, and the Mount Vernon (Ohio) Sanitarium. These were soon to be joined by another twenty-four sanitaria. Further, the medical missionary work had been outlined and firmly implanted. Emily Schramm had organized a ministry of mercy to alleviate the misery of the destitute in Chicago under the auspices of the Visiting Nurses Association. The sanitarium eventually gave financial support to a number of nurses who enlisted in this endeavor.

In 1893 Kellogg donated forty thousand dollars to medical missionary work in Chicago. This made possible the opening of a dispensary at the Pacific Garden Mission, which offered a nursing bureau, providing home visits, as well as an evening school for the Chinese, baths, and a laundry. It grew until it boasted four doctors and twenty-five Bible workers in addition to the nursing staff. Missionary nurses cared for the poor in their homes, and eventually another dispensary opened. Through the two dispensaries, some twenty thousand persons were seen annually. The work in Chicago increased to include a branch sanitarium and several missions as well as a Workingman's Home.

The work was being extended to other areas of concern as well as other populations. Dr. Lillis Wood went to Guadalajara, Mexico, to begin medical work, James White began work on a home for the aged, and the Haskell

Memorial Home, a large orphanage, was established and filled to capacity.

More than four hundred city missions were begun to "educate and uplift" fallen humanity, while centers of Christian education were rapidly expanding for the training of dedicated missionaries to take hold of the work opened by these outreaches. Ellen White spoke clearly as to the reason, purpose, and design of these institutions; they were to be founded so as to facilitate the development of Christian character by the students. "In the highest sense, the work of education and redemption are one," observed White; "they are the principles of the character of God, and to aid the student in comprehending these principles."[8] Thus, Adventist methods and curriculum would be distinctive in their reflection of the wholeness of human beings. The students gathered to be educated at Adventist institutions were not simply individuals to be provided with systems of information and the skills necessary for gainful employment, but Christians desiring to mold characters in conformity with divine principles. "Education," explained White, "has to do with the whole being." Not just an intellectual endeavor, it "is the harmonious development of the physical, the mental, and the spiritual powers." The goal of this process was to prepare the student for "the joy of service in this world and for the higher joy of wider service in the world to come." Thus, their methods and curriculum would be distinct from those of secular institutions lacking the vision of the fullness of humanity into which we have been called.[9] Arthur Spalding reflected these sentiments in his account of the church when he described the motivation of Christian education with these words: "It is to receive and exercise the love of God, which heals, soothes, builds, gives life and service to men."[10]

Much of this work on the character was to be accomplished through training in biblical lessons on moral courage, stringent lessons on health and hygiene, and the example set by precept and practice, but another portion was to be accomplished by suiting the students with various sorts of practical training:

> The outlay provided for manual training would prove the truest economy. Multitudes of our boys would thus be kept from the street corner and the groggery. The expenditure...would be more than met by the savings on hospitals and reformatories. And the youth themselves, trained to habits of industry, and skilled in lines of useful and productive labor...who can estimate their value to society and the nation?[11]

The school, as one arm of the church, was to provide a matrix in which the character of students could be nourished and shaped into congruence with divine principles. Schools were vital in providing formative personal encounters which would facilitate the foundational moral experience of the value of the self, of others, and the interrelation of all things in God.

While Martha Byington and Eliza Morton had pioneered the area of church-related Adventist schools in the 1850s, the strong impetus for church schools came after the White visions concerning the wholistic approach to character. Educational work took off in 1867 at Battle Creek, when the need for "an army of rightly prepared workers" emerged into the consciousness of the leaders. In 1874, the Seminary had been started at Battle Creek, in 1882 Healdsburg College was opened in California, and Lancaster Academy (later to become Atlantic Union College) opened in Massachussets. Union College opened in Lincoln, Nebraska in 1891, and Walla Walla and Southern Missionary Academy in 1892. Keene Academy (later Southwestern Adventist College) began operating in 1894, and plans were soon concretized to establish the College of Medical Evangelists in Loma Linda.

At the turn of the century, with hostility against big business on the rise, the liquor industry—responsible for evident social ills and allied with machine politics—was easy prey for progressive attacks. Thus, by 1917 twenty-six states had voted for prohibition. When the Prohibition amendment went into effect, Adventists celebrated "one of the greatest days in history." Religious Liberty Secretary Charles Longacre assured the International Dry Confederation that Seventh-day Adventists would cooperate with the Confederation in working for the inclusion of the entire world within the scope of Prohibition.

Just as Adventists had labored long and hard for the enactment of Prohibition, they mobilized their resources to prevent its repeal. The *Review and Herald* published discussions of the polls that had been taken favoring repeal and urged each reader to "stand in your neighborhood as a sentinel" to ensure that the "footsteps of growing youth [are] diverted from...the downward path."[12] The 1932 Spring Council formed a Temperance Commission in the General Conference designed to educate the public through public speaking, evangelistic services, rallies, radio, and the press. Francis Nichol published *Wet or Dry?* and copies were sent to members of Congress. And the active support of the denomination was solicited, for as Ellen White had noted in 1881, "Every individual exerts an influence on our society." Speaking of the ruinous effect of the liquor license, she had said, "In our favored land, every voter has some voice in determining the laws that control the nation. Should not that influence and vote," she queried, "be cast on the side of temperance and reform?" She had reminded her cohorts rather firmly that "We need not expect that God will work a miracle to bring about this reform and thus remove the necessity for our expertise."[13] Thus, it is clear that the church's view of the significance of environmental factors in shaping human conduct inspired Adventists to utilize all their resources, to exercise all their privileges, in the service of the kingdom of God. Evangelism, education, literature, crusades, rallies, and the ballot box were all pressed into the service of social reform. It seemed clear to many within the church that evil needed to be restrained, that society needed to be Christianized through laws prohibiting the promotion and use of products injurious to human well-being, and that it was the solemn duty of every Christian to fight against the tools Satan used to erase the image of God from humankind.

Today, the effect on Adventist ethics of the wholistic approach is seen in the continuation of major educational and health-care facilities, in the mobile health units that circulate to bring medical care to the disenfranchised, the temperance departments of the various conferences, the ministries of the community service centers, Pathfinder clubs, and the corporate and individual acts of benevolent service to "educate and uplift" our neighbors. The work of Adventist Development and Relief Agency (ADRA) stands as a monument to the vision of service to humanity, with its international efforts to reduce infant mortality, distribute clothing, seed agricultural programs, provide usable water by financing wells, run emergency relief food-for-work programs, and respond to natural disasters.

Significance of Wholeness
for the Present Cultural Context

As far as Christian social ethics is concerned, the major theological questions focus on our vision of the world, the nature of the hope that shapes our lives, and the possibilities for the community that evolves from the living-out of our commitments. How that vision of the world and our place within it may be embodied most fully is the ethical challenge faced by every Christian community and each Christian individual in every age. With Paul, every generation must confront the Gospel and then ask, How then shall we live?"

Reflection on the doctrine of wholeness will provide many of the clues necessary to approach this question. In order to find the fullness of our being we must be willing to live in harmony with the ecology of our existence. In a practical sense, this means acknowledging that spiritual needs are as real and as pressing as physical needs for shelter and food. Our need to be aesthetically nurtured and emotionally connected with other people and the earth is as immediate as the physical necessity of protection from extremes of weather. Acting upon this wholistic understanding cannot help but be transformative in our age of material excess and spiritual famine. Re-comprehending what it means to be human will mean enduring the tremendous shock of discovering the price for material surplus. We will begin to see that the luxury afforded to our class in Western culture has been paid by the narrowing of our field of consciousness, the deadening of our conscience, the atrophy of our senses, and the diminishing of our being. Realigning our lives and loyalties to reflect the nature of the universe and our being will eventuate personal and social transformation.

Re-visioned, the ethical task is to discern in our respective circumstances the possibilities for morally responsible action. As we investigate the possible openings in the present that can lead to a transformed future we must act in accordance with our vision of the world, struggle with whatever is necessary in order to witness to and effect this alternative pattern. We must seek to discover and create a range of responses in our social context which will render the vision realizable.

The doctrine of wholeness, of the integration and interrelatedness of the mind to the body and the person to the rest of spiritual and material society and earth, if it is applied consistently and conscientiously, has the potential of aiding ethical discernment by clarifying that behavior which is fitting to persons. As the principles we apply largely determine the outcome of our project, we can appreciate the significance a wholistic understanding will have on the final shape of our visioning.

When the interconnectedness of all life on this planet is considered as part of the equation, we will experience a new sense of urgency and clarity with regard to our responsibility as Christians. Any event, institution, or convention which denies or undermines the sacredness of life or the wellness of the person is a matter of concern to a Christian community that would prepare humanity for redemption.

At this point in time, the social issues facing Adventists as individuals, patriots, and citizens of the world community are pressing. They include such diverse yet interrelated problems as hunger, homelessness, poverty, war, race and gender discrimination, the extinction of wildlife, the destruction of biomes, pollution, the farm crisis, the population explosion, illiteracy, drug abuse, lack of medical care, the plight of the aged, child care, AIDS, crime and punishment, unjust governments, marital instability, nuclear waste and armaments, mental illness, the stresses of the cities, domestic violence, and child abuse. The doctrine of wholeness provides a basis for disciplined reflection on these issues and moral action in response to them. It alerts the Christian to conventions which dehumanize and deface the image of God from the individual and society.

While the doctrine of wholeness stresses our agency, our power to form ourselves and our environment as we envision and choose courses of action, it proposes more than band-aid solutions or stop-gap measures. In addition to addressing these problems or wounds directly and alleviating the suffering of those caught within them—employing (in the words of Ellen White) "pen and voice and vote"[14]—the principle of ecological personhood gravitates toward the root or source of the issue. It prescribes a proactive rather than reactive stance: mobilize and organize around that which is conducive to well-being. It assumes that the ultimate (not the intermediate) cure for social dis-ease lies in promoting the wellness of the society and the individual components within it. This necessitates abandoning passivity in the face of forces which work to destroy the image of God and instead pursuing the stance of "advocacy ethics": speaking and acting on behalf of wholeness and healing wherever and whenever humanity or the creation is threatened. Reapplying the vision of wholeness to our present situation will undoubtedly move us to intervene in areas unforeseen in Ellen White's time: the shipment and storage of toxic wastes, the pollution of the oceans, the destruction of the rain forests, the fate of whales and dolphins, the use of animals in the testing of cosmetics, nuclear weaponry, and a myriad of other issues which pose threats to health and life on this planet.

Again, the healing of the individual and the nation begins with the foundational moral experience of the value of the self and others and the connectedness of the two. From this base the seeds of conscience take root and are nurtured by our decisions, temperament, and experience. The church community provides a matrix in which our moral awareness is cultivated through introduction to a world of meaning and value contained in the communal narrative. As we incorporate the worldview of the church into our experience, we find ways of acting which express the underlying values, understandings, and interpretations we have adopted. Our moral vision is enlarged as we utilize the paths to spiritual insight provided by the community: group experience, authority, principles, tradition. But most significantly, our character is subtly and effectively brought into harmony with our place in the universe, and we more fully reflect the image of God. We become part of the solution rather than part of the problem.

As Seventh-day Adventists, we have a heritage that promotes the wholistic understanding of our nature and role in the universe. The pioneers of our church applied this doctrine to their lives, and it provided the basis for their personal and social ethics. They learned to live out a worldview that was divergent from that promulgated by the larger culture, to do things for their own reasons, measure themselves by their own standards, act out of a set of ethics and values emerging from the process of experiencing a healing self. While we have adhered to paths they blazed in temperance, in educational and medical expertise, and in charity, faithfulness requires more of us. It requires that we apply the principles involved to our present setting, measure our own institutions and conventions against the ecological paradigm and discern where voices and pens and votes need to be mobilized to uplift and redeem humanity from oppression and corruption. We need to dream the dream, see the vision of the human in the web of life so that we know what end we are working toward and find the means to accomplish the goal. It has been said that "without a vision the people perish."[15] If that is the case, it is the vision which gives life to the people. The vision engendered by the doctrine of wholeness remains to be dreamed in its fullness. Perhaps it will be dreaming that dream that will energize and reinspire Seventh-day Adventists to become leaders in interpreting and applying Christian ethics to our ever-changing social milieu.

Endnotes

[1] *Seventh-day Adventist Church Manual* (Washington, DC: Review and Herald, 1986) 24.
[2] Ellen G. White, Letter 4, 1863.

[3] J. H. Waggoner, "Present Truth," *Review and Herald*, (7 August 1866).

[4] Ellen White, *Education* (Mountain View, CA: Pacific Press, 1907) 195.

[5] Ibid., 99-100.

[6] Ellen White, *Ministry of Healing* (Mountain View, CA: Pacific Press, 1905) 105.

[7] Arthur F. Spalding, *Captains of the Host* (Washington, DC: Review and Herald 1949) 636. For a more in-depth view of White's views on the question of the work that needed to be performed on behalf of the Afro-American population, see *The Southern Work* (Washington, DC: Review and Herald, 1966).

[8] White, *Education*, 30.

[9] Ibid., 13.

[10] Arthur F. Spalding, *Origin and History of Seventh-day Adventists* (Washington, DC: Review and Herald, 1931) 93.

[11] White, *Education*, 218.

[12] Ellen G. White, "Temperance and the License Law," *Advent Review and Sabbath Herald* 58 (8 November 1881): 289.

[13] The Adventist discussion of prohibition and the moral necessity of preventing its repeal was featured in the *Review and Herald* throughout 1932. For an overview of this discussion, see Larry White, "The Return of the Thief," *Adventist Heritage* 5.2 (Winter 1978): 36-7.

[14] White, "Temperance," 290.

[15] Pr 29:18.

Chapter Nine

SECOND ADVENT

Roy Branson

For this reason they are before the throne of God,
    and worship him day and night within his temple,
    and the one who is seated on the throne will shelter them.
They will hunger no more, and thirst no more;
    the sun will not strike them,
    nor any scorching heat;
for the Lamb at the center of the throne will be their shepherd,
    and he will guide them to springs of the water of life,
    and God will wipe away every tear from their eyes.[1]

Our family of missionaries, just home on furlough from Egypt, was driving across the United States on Highway 66. We had reached one of the midwestern states when an electric thunderstorm suddenly engulfed us. I was six years old. Except for my first few months I had lived all my life in the parched suburbs of Cairo. I was terrified as rain poured down, lightning split the sky, and thunder simultaneously cracked over our heads.

I was terrified, not because I didn't know what was happening, but because I did: the Lord was returning. I began to wail. I had already heard countless Adventist sermons. I knew this was how it all ended. First, a cloud the size of a man's hand, then lightening and thunder; next, in front of everybody—the whole world—would come the separating of the wheat from the tares, the sheep from the goats. And I was a goat. I was naughty, disobedient, wicked, and was going to be condemned in front of all those thousands and thousands of people—those who had never died and others who had been resurrected with their own bodies.

The storm was so intense my dad soon had to pull over to the side of the road. I remember my mother trying to calm me by quoting Psalms. "The Angel of the Lord encampeth round about them that worship him" (Ps 34:7). The Lord loved me, she assured me. He wouldn't want anything terrible to happen to me. Without realizing it, my parents were face to face with their youngest child's "apocalyptic consciousness."

Many other Adventists have had similar experiences. Clouds the size of a man's hand have been carefully watched by thousands of Seventh-day Adventist youngsters to see if they grow into the cataclysm of the last day. Dreams of the final judgment haunt Adventist teenagers. In mine I was always in a large field with a raised platform on which a kingly judge, surrounded by dignitaries, started calling the final roll. Those who were saved went to one side and those who were lost went to the other. Tom Dybdahl chronicles my own experience as well as his—and, I suspect, that of thousands of others—when he notes that we always wake up from such dreams just before learning whether or not we're saved.[2]

Extending The Time

Despite all this concern with the evaluation of our behavior in the final judgment, people question whether the Second Advent has anything to do with morality. They wonder if the apocalyptic books and passages of the Bible—Daniel, the Apocalypse, Matthew 24 and 25, to name a few—are not inherently escapist. They question whether an apocalyptic consciousness is a moral consciousness. Of course it is. *The Drama of the Ages, The Great Controversy between Christ and Satan*, in which Adventist youngsters—and adults—place themselves is a morality play: good vs. evil, the oppressor vs. the oppressed, the powerful vs. the weak.[3]

Consider what's going on in the minds of youngsters when storms and dreams fill them with not only awe, but dread and fear. On that midwestern road I was convinced that every aspect of my life was under constant scrutiny. I dreaded an evaluation, an assessment of whether my motives and character were good and my actions right or wrong. I thought a judgment had probably already been rendered on whether or not I would be saved. In moments, I would learn in front of all humans, angels, and unfallen beings what that verdict would be. I was not trembling before an avalanche or an earthquake, but before a judging will. I was not frightened of nature; I was terrified of God.

There are theological problems with *this sort* of apocalyptic consciousness. At the very least, it is incomplete. But whatever its faults, such

146

a consciousness makes some assumptions crucial to any attempt to begin the moral enterprise. Such a consciousness assumes that our destinies are not predetermined; they depend on the actions of free wills. Not only actions but the persons performing them can be morally evaluated. There will be a day when we as individuals, with our distinctive, unique bodies, will be judged. And to believe that I, as an individual, am being judged by God before the entire universe is certainly to believe that my actions are important. On that road in the Midwest I thought it mattered a great deal what I did and what sort of a person I ought to be. Such a consciousness forms individuals who are highly motivated—an entire universe is waiting for them to act. People who live in the shadow of God's great, final act of the great controversy between good and evil are a people anxious to respond with their own dramatic actions on behalf of goodness and against evil.

Some have said that while an apocalyptic consciousness may be concerned with personal morality, it robs Christians of the sense that they can do much of anything to affect the world and history. God is so powerful, so active, so immediate for people steeped in the visions of Daniel and Revelation, of the end of the world and the Second Advent, say these critics, that Adventists understandably don't want to take the time to become involved in complex moral decisions about how they ought to live with others in a highly urban, technological society. Certainly, these critics say, a vivid apocalyptic consciousness ignores social reform, a concern to change the moral behavior of institutions.

To be fair, that *has* happened. If the Lord is returning momentarily, there is scarcely time to worry about shaping or reforming social institutions. Many Millerites in the days before October 22, 1844, stopped worrying about some of their long-standing obligations. As early as the spring of 1844 farmers in northern New England left their crops in their fields. In New York City "Brother Abraham Riker, a well-known shoe dealer in Division Street, who was for many years a class leader in the MEC, closed his store and spent considerable time distributing papers, attending meetings and warning others."[4] If one believes the Second Advent of the Lord is to happen momentarily, if it is a part of the present (not the future), then it doesn't make sense to establish an Adventist Ethics Center—or, for that matter, of course, to establish an Adventist college, hospital, food factory or church bureaucracy.

For a while, even after the Great Disappointment, some Adventists continued to believe that the Lord would return within days. A year later, in October, 1845, James White, in the pages of *The Day Star*, condemned an Adventist couple who had announced wedding plans. They had "denied their faith in being published for marriage, and we all look upon this as a wile of the Devil. The firm brethren in Maine who are waiting for Christ to come have no fellowship with such a move."[5]

Of course, a year later, James and Ellen Harmon themselves got married and began confronting all the questions of right and wrong surrounding the family, that fundamental human institution prolonging the existence of life in this world. By 1859 (fifteen years after the Great Disappointment) Ellen White made it clear that in her mind the Second Advent was not a present reality, but a future event. "I saw that this message would not accomplish its work in a few short months." Invoking the second epistle of Peter, she underscored her point: "I saw that God would prove his people. Patiently Jesus bears with them and does not spew them out of his mouth in a moment." With the Second Advent clearly in the future, Ellen was clear that Adventists must become involved in organizing institutions. "God is well pleased with the efforts of his people in trying to move with system and order in his work."[6] Within a year, James and Ellen White had convinced an often reluctant group of Adventists to create a publishing association and adopt the name "Seventh-day Adventist." Ellen wanted them to go further and create a denominational structure. "Unless the churches are so organized that they can carry out and enforce order, *they have nothing to hope for in the future.*"[7] Ellen White was no longer a Millerite; the Millerites had had no future, only a present. With Ellen restoring the future, a denomination could come into existence—and it did, in 1863, nineteen years after the Great Disappointment.

Avoiding Temptations

Ever since Seventh-day Adventists, under the leadership of Ellen and James White, finally stopped being Millerites and became convinced that there was a period between the present moment and the Second Advent during which they needed to act in a morally responsible way, they have struggled to know how to relate the Second Advent to moral action. Several temptations have plagued Adventist theology and history. Interestingly,

these are not temptations to be passive and inactive. They are the temptations of activists.

One temptation has been to fill the void of Christ's non-appearance with
our own presence. The invisibility of divinity in 1844 is answered by the
visibility of the Adventist church. For many Adventists the answer to the
Great Disappointment is the Great Achievement: creating a world-wide
Seventh-day Adventist denomination. The anxiety caused by the delay of
Christ's Second Advent in time is answered by the assurance of a tangible
Seventh-day Adventist church in space. In response to a universal event
that has not yet happened, Adventists will create a ubiquitous church with
institutions that are reassuringly concrete and tangible. Both defenders of
the *status quo* and critics of church structure sometimes become more
consumed with expanding or improving the church than with anticipating
the Second Advent. In the lives of many Adventists—not just denominational employees—the doctrine of the church has actually superseded the
doctrine of the Second Advent.

Another temptation has been to expand the strong commitment of
Adventists to sanctification of individual Christians to encompass the
sanctification of all history. Some of the nineteenth-century Methodist
forebears and contemporaries of Adventism proclaimed the moral responsibility of believers to reach perfection. Building on this foundation, some
Adventists have called, in effect, for their church to perfect history. It is the
responsibility, they say, of Adventists to act in such a morally praiseworthy
fashion that the Second Advent can take place. Practically speaking, on this
view, the perfection of Adventists causes the Second Advent. Such a
commitment to the doctrine of sanctification, then, determines for some the
relationship between the Second Advent and morality.[8]

A third temptation has been to allow our commitment to God's created
order and laws to overwhelm our apocalyptic sense of the ongoing struggle
between good and evil. Some Adventists are so conscious that God is creator
and sustainer of the world they forget the divine judgment of rebellious
powers. Some Adventists seem to read Romans 13 and its admonition to be
subject to "the higher powers" to the exclusion of Apocalypse 13, with its
condemnation of the beast to whom "power was given over all kindreds, and
tongues, and nations," that "makes wars with the saints." They ignore the
fact that in Apocalypse 13, this political power is warned that "he that killeth
with the sword must be killed with the sword." Some Adventists have

expanded their concern to observe God's laws and created order in their own living habits—temperance, diet, abstention from tobacco and alcohol, exercise—to include a commitment to respect all human institutions. Just as Adventists—indeed all people—should energetically align themselves with God's natural order, they believe Adventists should not just conform to but actively support the established political and social order.[9]

At perhaps the nadir of Adventist social responsibility, German Adventist leaders from 1933 through the end of the war, in official church publications, fulsomely supported Hitler and his policies, including international aggression, anti-Semitism, and the sterilization of the mentally weak, schizophrenics, epileptics, the blind, the deaf, crippled alcoholics, drug addicts, and the chronically ill. Why? Because, as the president of the East German Conference wrote in the German equivalent of the *Adventist Review* after Hitler's ascendancy in 1933, the Christian welcomes Hitler, a "nondrinker, nonsmoker and vegetarian," for his defense of "morality and order, incorruptibility and justice in government." Long after Hitler had invaded Austria, Poland, and Czechoslovakia, the *Morning Watch Calendar* for April 20, 1940, celebrated Hitler's fifty-first birthday with a long encomium to the Führer as a moral exemplar:

> The unshakable faith of Adolf Hitler allowed him to do great deeds.... In Christian humility, at important times when he could celebrate with his people, he gave God in Heaven honor and recognized his dependence upon God's blessings. This humility has made him great, and this greatness was the source of blessing, from which he always gave for his people."[10]

How might the Second Advent more appropriately be related to moral action? This question has recently become more acute as Adventists, somewhat to their surprise, have become more prominent and powerful. When Loma Linda University performs unprecedented heart transplants, the media asks physicians and ethicists, "What is the relationship between these operations and your religion—the fact that you are Adventists?" As Adventists assume more political power in third-world countries, the public wonders if Adventists have a social ethic. "Does your view of the Second Advent affect how you think institutions in society, including government, ought to relate to one another?" is a relevant question to ask such people as the Adventist prime minister of Uganda, the Adventist cabinet ministers in the government of Jamaica, the twenty Adventists who are elected members of parliaments in independent countries of the South Pacific, and the Adventists who recently organized in the country of Vanuatu (formerly the New Hebrides) the opposition New People's Party.[11]

Can an apocalyptic consciousness possibly be relevant to upwardly mobile Seventh-day Adventists—in both this country and the third world—who are gaining influence and power? These Adventists, after all, are clearly not Millerites. The Second Advent is for them decidedly *not* in the present but in the future. These Adventists are not oppressed. Every day they see the providence of God pouring out blessings on their work and lives. What does Patmos have to do with Loma Linda or Kingston, Jamaica, or Papua-New Guinea?

The fact is that many scholars now believe that the congregations to whom the Apocalypse of John was first directed were not enduring physical persecution but experiencing relative deprivation. Members were not always able to join Jewish synagogue communities or Roman social and commercial guilds. Early Christians may have felt themselves marginal, but few were actually enduring pain. Some scholars go further and believe that the Apocalypse was written to arouse wealthy congregations, such as Laodicea, who may have been too ready to accommodate to their immediate social and political environment. Far from inviting his readers into a moral quietism, John saved his most severe scorn for the moral torpor of social-climbers, ready to prostitute themselves with corrupt groups rather than challenge institutional evil. John, then, wanted not simply to comfort the fragile, but to confront the upwardly mobile, to expand the moral perceptions of the Christians of Asia Minor, to take Christians preoccupied with exclusion from guilds and thrust them into a universal controversy between good and evil.[12]

An Adventist social ethic can draw on the theological resources available to all Christians. But what would happen if we did not subordinate the importance of the Second Advent to other Christian affirmations, such as the doctrines of the church, sanctification, or creation? What are the implications of constructing an ethic from the perspective of the Second Advent, specifically a Second Advent experienced within an apocalyptic consciousness?

Judging Institutions

First, it is not an ethic simply for individuals. It is also an ethic concerned about the behavior of institutions—a social ethic. It is true that the picture of last-day events in the apocalyptic portions of scripture includes a resurrection of persons with their bodies, emphasizing their individuality, and the relevance of their actions now, as individuals, to their ultimate destiny. But John's reference to Babylon and the kings who are judged at the last day suggests that in the apocalyptic consciousness corporate powers are held morally responsible for their present actions. Adela Yarbro Collins is certain that the symbols of the Apocalypse play distinctly *moral* roles. "Any reader in the Mediterranean world in John's time, when reading the words, 'and authority was given it over every tribe and people and tongue and nation, and all who dwell on earth will worship it'...would think of Rome."[13]

The founders of the Seventh-day Adventist movement also believed that the symbols of Revelation referred to oppressive corporate powers, both private and public. Ellen White cast the abolitionist attack on slavery in apocalyptic terms:

> God will restrain His anger but a little longer. His anger burns against this nation, and especially against the religious bodies who have sanctioned, and have themselves engaged in this terrible merchandise.
> ...God's anger will not cease until He has caused the land of light to drink the dregs of the cup of His fury, and until He has rewarded unto Babylon double....All the sins of the slave will be visited upon the master.[14]

While Ellen White identified a slave-owning United States with Babylon, James condemned pre-emancipation America as having the heart and voice of the dragon of Revelation. The nation's

> outward appearance and profession is the most pure, peaceful, and harmless possible. It professes to guarantee to every man liberty and the pursuit of happiness in temporal things, and freedom in matters of religion; yet about four millions of human beings are held by the Southern States of this nation in the most abject and cruel bondage and servitude, and the theological bodies of the land have adopted a creed-power, which is as inexorable and tyrannical as is possible to bring to

bear upon the consciences of men. Verily with all its lamblike appearance and profession, it has the heart and voice of a dragon; for out of the abundance of the heart the mouth speaketh.[15]

Uriah Smith, James White's successor as editor of the *Review*, kept up the condemnation of corporate powers in apocalyptic terms, pointing to "the pulpits supporting slavery" as evidence that "the dragonic spirit of this nation has of late years developed itself in accordance with the prophecy" of Apocalypse 13.[16]

Adventist professionals and office-holders today should realize that they are not only responsible for their actions as individuals. If they are faithful to the the apocalyptic consciousness of scripture and their Seventh-day Adventist forebears, they will regard the actions of the institutions of which they are a part as having great moral import. It is not just a question of whether individuals stop smoking—and thereby stop harming those around them. It is also a question of confronting powerful multinational corporations and governments friendly to them (such as that of the United States), institutions working together to dramatically increase worldwide smoking among women and children, thus contributing to soaring deathrates—a projected 12 million a year by 2020. It is important that a person avoid conflicts of interest in managing medical centers in Adventist Health Systems/US; but it is also important that the system itself act responsibly in society to provide health care—a responsibility that includes working to make sure that those who have the least resources can somehow obtain a decent minimum level of care.

Transforming Society

Secondly, any ethic from the perspective of an apocalyptic consciousness is comfortable with change, radical change, in the institutions of society, including government. The Great Day of the Lord will overturn all society. An ethic in anticipation of that event would not be surprised to see institutions transformed. From the standpoint of an apocalyptic conscious-ness the creation is in turmoil and dramatic divine action is required if the oppressive, wicked powers that disrupt God's reign of justice and goodness are to be overturned.

Throughout the history of Christianity apocalyptic groups have been in the forefront of change. During the Middle Ages, in what is now the Netherlands and Belgium, millenarian visionaries led mass movements for change in society. During the English Civil War apocalyptic sects, such as the "Fifth Monarch Men," proposed the most radical transformations of politics. In nineteenth century America those who set out to overthrow slavery, intemperance, and prostitution were often those who lived in expectation of the Second Advent. According to Ernest Sandeen, "when the millenarian argued that the perfect society of the millennium would be created only by the cataclysmic return of Christ, he was suggesting different means, not different ends."[17]

Many of the early Seventh-day Adventist leaders had been part of the religiously motivated social reform movements to which Sandeen refers. During the time they were establishing the new denomination they remained impatient with the slowness of change in the nineteenth-century American political system, particularly its reluctance to officially outlaw slavery. After Abraham Lincoln declared in his first inaugural speech, "I have no purpose, directly or indirectly, to interfere with the institution of slavery in the states where it exists," Uriah Smith, as editor of the *Review*, seemed to threaten the sitting president with death if he did not immediately change the American legal order regarding slavery:

> He has to stand up against the 'enthusiasm for freedom' which reigns in nearly twenty millions of hearts in the free North, and against the prayers of four millions of oppressed and suffering slaves. If he continues to resist all these, in refusing to take those steps which a sound policy, the principles of humanity, and the salvation of the country, demand, it must be from an infatuation akin to that which of old brought Pharaoh to an untimely end.[18]

As Seventh-day Adventists spread around the world, they, like other Protestant missionary groups, deliberately set out to transform not only religious ritual but social practice. For better or worse, Adventists, through their schools, hospitals, and dietary programs, were even more ambitious and successful than other denominations in revolutionizing every aspect of their converts' culture. And for Adventists the more sweeping and rapid the changes the better.

If Adventists were to take seriously a social ethic drawn from the apocalyptic consciousness seen in scripture and their own heritage, they would have a hard time simply supporting the *status quo* in their societies. In totalitarian societies of either the left or the right they would work, however possible, for fundamental transformation.

That is what the True and Free Adventists, Sabbath-keepers unrecognized by the government, did in the Soviet Union during the regimes of Stalin, Khrushchev, and Brezhnev. They were repeatedly imprisoned by Soviet authorities for not bearing arms, for refusing to work or attend school on Saturdays, and for insisting on speaking out in defense of human rights. State power, the True and Free Adventists said, should not dictate faith and religion. When state power establishes either a state religion or state atheism it has become the beast of Revelation.

These Sabbath-keeping Adventists persistently demanded that the Soviets at least live up to their own constitutional provisions protecting some religious liberty. Their underground printing presses published materials for Alexander Solzhenitsyn, as well as publishing their own ringing defenses of such well-known human rights activists as Alexander Ginzburg, Yuri Orlov, and Anatoly Sharansky. They assisted these activists in establishing the initial Helsinki Watch human rights committee.[19]

In relatively more open countries, Adventists with a social ethic based on an apocalyptic consciousness will work for reform, as early Adventists did in the United States, Australia, and New Zealand.[20] In no country will Adventists be able to give their ultimate loyalty to any institution.

Confronting the Oppressor

Thirdly, a social ethic drawing on apocalyptic consciousness would decide what changes to pursue in society, particularly on the basis of justice and freedom from oppression. Throughout the Apocalypse we read condemnations against unjust and oppressive political, commercial and military powers. In addition to the beast/Rome of chapters 13, 17 and 18, the whore/Babylon/Rome will be burned and her flesh eaten as punishment for her present, physical oppression. The "kings of the earth" who have been seduced by her power are doomed. So also are "the merchants of the earth;" those "great men of the earth" who have "grown rich from the power of her luxury,"[21] and the ship owners, who "grew rich by her wealth."[22] These doomed merchants and ship owners are so perverse they weep that "no one buys their cargo any more"—including slaves.[23]

It is no wonder that Allan Boesak, head of the colored Reformed Church in South Africa and one of the leaders of the United Democratic Front, wrote a commentary on the Apocalypse, *Comfort and Protest*. It is no wonder that in this book, Boesak describes John the Revelator as "this banned pastor of the church," and characterizes the Apocalypse as "protest literature," filled with "explicit political criticism."[24] Boesak sees the new Jerusalem as a city "where our children shall live to bear children and not die untimely, where we shall build homes and live in them without fear of being driven out by war or influx control or the Group Areas Act, where there shall be peace so that no one will 'hurt or destroy.'"[25] When one reads chapter after chapter filled with condemnations of injustice and oppression one is not surprised to read in Gustavo Gutierrez' landmark *Theology of Liberation* that "eschatology is not just one more element of Christianity, but the very key to understanding the Christian faith."[26]

Far from providing an escape from moral engagement, John's apocalypse is a call to arms; not physical warfare, but a fundamental revolt nevertheless. Those immersed in the Apocalypse are drawn into a condemnation of the evil empire, its oppression, its ostentatious wealth, its blasphemous pretension to ultimate authority. The taunts and threats of the Apocalypse carry out surprise attacks, execute frontal assaults; its metaphors strip Rome of its glamor, attraction and legitimacy, enlisting the reader in a revolution of the imagination against the oppressor.

Some contemporary Adventists, like Dr. Samson Kisekka, the leading Adventist layman who kept the Adventist church alive in Uganda during the time of Idi Amin, have even understood their religious and moral commitments to demand that they participate in political revolts against oppression. At a time when innocents were being slaughtered, Dr. Kisekka helped lead the successful revolution that put the present government in power. After the revolution, he became Uganda's first prime minister.[27]

Adventists in positions of power, acting according to an apocalyptically formed social ethic, would not work to increase the power of the economically and politically powerful, but that of the economically and politically deprived. Sometimes the economically and politically powerful are capitalists or colonels in the military; sometimes they are party members in one-

156

party socialist states. Specific economic and political policies will vary according to time and place. But whether in East or West, whether in the first- and second-world countries of the North or third- and fourth-world countries of the South, Adventists faithful to the apocalyptic consciousness will exercise a preference for the weak, the vulnerable and the destitute.

Embodying the Future

Finally, a social ethic from the perspective of the Second Advent is an ethic of expanding vision and imagination. It is a vision that begins with an ending, a special kind of ending; an ending that is also a beginning. The Second Advent is an ending, but not like some black hole of history—after the Second Coming—nothing at all. The Second Advent inaugurates a time *beyond* the end. The Second Coming is not an ending like the dropping of the stage curtain; it is more like the climax of the play. The Second Coming is a commencement—a passage from one era to the next. Just as the special, final day of the week, the Sabbath, is an ending that does not destroy the week that follows, so the Second Advent is the culmination of history, not its annihilation.

Scripture portrays the risen Christ Himself, following the resurrection, maintaining his human identity in heaven. With the Second Advent there is not only crisis but continuity. Adventist views of the body and health have always assumed that there will be some concrete continuity between this time and that which follows the Second Advent. In their earliest days Adventists abstained from tea, coffee and especially tobacco because they expected to step directly from this world into heaven, and could not conceive of polluting it with their filthy habits. Today, Adventist young people are taught that they must treat their bodies as temples of God and their talents as divine gifts, partly because they must be ready to enter, after the Second Advent, directly into heaven.

Consequently, a social ethic fueled by an apocalyptic consciousness will not simply work to end oppression and injustice. A social ethic expanded by the apocalyptic vision will not just rupture society—condemning injustice and fighting to throw off the shackles of oppression. The most powerful word of apocalyptic is not denunciation, but annunciation.[28] Even more than proclaiming the end of evil, apocalyptic evokes the good. The Apocalypse of John does not simply cast evil into the bottomless pit, into the lake of fire. The dazzling color and music of goodness allures us, alienating our affections from the horrifying images of evil. Apocalyptic not only expands moral perceptions; it ignites the passions. We do not merely identify and evaluate; we love goodness and hate evil.[29]

The social ethic emerging from an apocalyptic consciousness glimpses a time beyond the end. Apocalyptic fulfills what Walter Brueggemann calls the "ministry of imagination," whose vocation is "to keep on conjuring and proposing alternative futures."[30] Here we find the ultimate mission of the remnant. The work of the remnant is not to be the cause, and the Second Advent obediently to be the effect. The relation of the remnant to the Second Advent is not cause and effect, but part to whole, microcosm to macrocosm. The remnant is not to bring about the Second Advent, it is to envision the Second Advent in both words and deeds. The remnant is to embody in present moments of protest and joy the Great Day of the Lord.

When we oppose tyranny we point to that final liberation. When we act on behalf of the weak and destitute we signal the coming of that new, just society. When we create communities of freedom and fellowship we invite others to experience that city at whose coming all tears are wiped away. Social reform does not coerce the arrival of the city of God; moments of social reform are enactments of that future, ideal civilization. Apocalyptic evokes a vision of a social ideal—a holy city filled with gold and precious jewels, a city of justice and harmony, where death "will be no more; mourning and crying and pain will be no more."[31] In apocalyptic, we step from the prosaic order of tyranny into surprising, liberating poetry; we experience the kingdom of God. Social reform is a sacrament of the Second Advent.

Endnotes

[1] Rev 7:15-17.

[2] Tom Dybdahl, "How to Wait for the Second Coming," *Pilgrimage of Hope*, ed. Roy Branson (Takoma Park, MD: Association of Adventist Forums, 1986) 19-26.

[3] W. H. Branson, *Drama of the Ages* (Washington, DC: Review and Herald, 1950); Ellen G. White, *The Great Controversy Between Christ and Satan* (Mountain View, CA: Pacific Press, 1888).

[4] Francis D. Nichol, *The Midnight Cry* (Washington, DC: Review and Herald, 1944) 354.

[5] James White, *Day Star* Oct. 11, 1845: 47, qtd. in Ron Graybill, "The Courtship of Ellen Harmon," *Insight* Jan. 23, 1973: 6,7.

[6] Ellen G. White, *Spiritual Gifts*, 2 vols. (Washington, DC: Review and Herald, 1945) 2: 224, 225, 231.

[7] Ellen G. White, *Review and Herald* August 27, 1861: 101, 102, qtd. in A. V. Olson, *Through Crisis to Victory, 1888-1901* (Washington, DC: Review and Herald, 1966) 154 (italics mine).

For a fuller discussion of the difference between Millerite and Seventh-day Adventist eschatology, see Roy Branson, "Adventists Between The Times: The Shift in the Church's Eschatology," *Spectrum* 8.1 (September, 1976): 15-26, repr. *Pilgrimage of Hope*, ed. Roy Branson (Takoma Park, MD: Association of Adventist Forums, 1986) 41-63. For a thought-provoking expansion of this distinction see Jonathan Butler, "The Making of a New Order: Millerism and the Origins of Seventh-day Adventism," *The Disappointed: Millerism and Millenarianism in the Nineteenth Century*, ed. Ronald L. Numbers and Jonathan M. Butler (Bloomington, IN: Indiana University Press, 1987) 189-207.

[8] For more discussion of this position in the works of Adventist writers such as Graham Maxwell and Herbert Douglass, see Roy Branson, "Responding to the Delay," *Pilgrimage*, 8-17.

[9] Romans 13 is the most important proof text defending Adventist's courtship of such diverse political leaders as Marcos in the Philippines, Pinochet in Chile, and whoever headed the former Soviet Union.

[10] Qtd. in Erwin Sicher, "Seventh-day Adventist Publications and the Nazi Temptation," *Spectrum* 8.3 (March, 1977) 14, 21.

[11] See Raymond L. Coombe, "Adventists Lead South Pacific Governments," *Spectrum* 18.5 (June, 1988): 60-61. See also Dionne E. Phillips and Glen O. Phillips, "Preacher-Politician in the Caribbean," *Spectrum* 16.2 (June, 1985): 14-18, for a profile of the former leader of the Barbados Labor Party and a minister in the ruling cabinet.

[12] For a more extensive argument in favor of this reading of the Apocalypse and further references to the scholarly literature on which it is based, see Roy Branson, "The Demand for New Ethical Vision," *Bioethics Today—A New Ethical Vision*, ed. James Walters (Loma Linda/Riverside, CA: Loma Linda University Press, 1988).

[13] Adela Yarbro Collins, *Crisis and Catharsis: The Power of the Apocalypse* (Philadelphia: Westminster, 1984) 124.

[14] White, *Gifts*, 1: 192-3.

[15] James White, "Thoughts on Revelation," *Adventist Review* 23 (Nov. 11, 1862): 188.

[16] Uriah Smith, note preceding "The Degeneracy of the United States," *Adventist Review* 23 (June 17, 1862): 22; cf. note preceding "The Cause and Cure of the Present Civil War,"*Adventist Review* 23 (Aug. 19, 1862): 89.

[17] Ernest R. Sandeen, "Millennialism," *The Rise of Adventism*, ed. Edwin S. Gaustad, (New York: Harper & Row, 1974) 115. On the involvement of apocalyptic groups in revolutionary movements in the history of Christianity in Europe, see Norman R. C. Cohn, *The Pursuit of the Millennium* (New York: Harper & Row, 1961).

[18] Uriah Smith, editorial comment before "Letter to the President," *Adventist Review* 23 (Sept. 23, 1862): 130.

[19] See *Spectrum* 11.4 (June 1981)—Marite Sapiets, "Shelkov and the True and Free Adventists" (24-28); "Adventists and the Madrid Conference," "Shelkov's Daughter Protests: An Open Letter to Brezhnev," and "Amnesty International and Adventists" (28-36); Tom Dybdahl, "An Interview with Alexander Ginzburg" (37-41). See also the chapter on Adventists in Ludmilla Alexyeva, *Soviet Dissent* (n.p.: Wesleyan University Press, 1985). The author is an exiled founder of the Moscow Helsinki Watch Committee.

[20] See Peter H. Ballis, "Seventh-day Adventists and New Zealand Politics, 1886-1918," *In and Out of the World: Seventh-day Adventists in New Zealand*, ed. Peter H. Ballis (Palmerston North, New Zealand: Dunmore, 1985); reprinted in slightly edited form as "Early Adventists Plunged Into New Zealand Politics," *Spectrum* 18.5 (June 1988): 40-56.

[21] Rev 18:3, 23.

[22] Rev 18:17-19.

[23] Rev 18:11, 13.

[24] Allan Boesak, *Comfort and Protest: The Apocalypse from a South African Perspective* (Philadelphia: Westminster, 1987) 122.

[25] Ibid.,129.

[26] Gustavo Gutierrez, *A Theology of Liberation: History, Politics and Salvation* (Maryknoll, NY: Orbis, 1973) 162.

[27] D. D. N. Nsereko, "Adventist Revolutionary Leads Uganda" *Spectrum* 17.4 (May, 1987): 5-13.

[28] See Gutierrez 233 on utopia's significance as both "a denunciation of existing order," and "also an annunciation of what is not yet, but will be."

[29] See Branson, "Demand."

[30] Walter Brueggemann, *The Prophetic Imagination* (Philadelphia: Fortress Press, 1978) 45.

[31] Rev 21:4.

Chapter Ten

MILLENNIUM

Gerald R. Winslow

Then I saw an angel coming down from heaven,
   holding in his hand the key to the bottomless pit and a great chain.
   He seized the dragon, that ancient serpent, who is the Devil and Satan,
   and bound him for a thousand years,
   and threw him into the pit, and locked and sealed it over him,
   that he would deceive the nations no more,
   until the thousand years were ended.
   After that he must be let out for a little while.
Then I saw thrones,
   and those seated on them were given authority to judge.
   I also saw the souls of those who had been beheaded
   for their testimony to Jesus and for the word of God,
   and who had not worshipped the beast or its image
   and had not received its mark on their foreheads or their hands.
   They came to life and reigned with Christ a thousand years.
   The rest of the dead did not come to life until the thousand years were
   ended. This is the first resurrection.
   Blessed and holy are those who share in the first resurrection!
   Over these the second death has no power,
   but they will be priests of God and of Christ,
   and they will reign with him a thousand years.[1]

   How will the world as we know it end? What happens after that? And what difference does it make?

   No treatment of Adventist ethics could avoid such questions and still claim to represent the Adventist heritage faithfully. They are questions that are intriguing and troublesome, and not just for Adventists.

   "How Will It All End?" asks theoretical physicist Freeman Dyson in a chapter of his currently popular book *Infinite in All Directions*. Dyson says he is "hoping to hasten the arrival of the day when eschatology, the study of the end of the universe, will be a respectable scientific discipline and not merely a branch of theology."[2]

He applauds the fact that it is now common for scientists to discuss the first few minutes, or even the first few microseconds, after the birth of the universe—the moment of the so-called "Big Bang." But where, he wonders, is comparable work on the end of the universe? Why are the few scientific articles on the universe's destiny written in timid, apologetic, or jocular terms? Dyson wants to correct this imbalance.

Such scientific projections as do exist, Dyson observes, are not happy ones. Does the universe finally reach the end of its expansion and then implode in a "Big Crunch"—a fiery collision of galaxies that would make biblical images of fire and brimstone seem tame by comparison? Such a collapse into a space-time singularity would, of course, mean the death of all humanly imaginable life. Or does the universe continue to expand and to cool indefinitely until all matter is unimaginably scattered, uniformly and absolutely cold and static—an endless night in an infinitely large deep freeze?

There is sadness and anxiety in these scenarios. They portray a universe that is apparently devoid of meaning. Something in most of us rebels against such threats of meaninglessness. Pierre Teilhard de Chardin once surmised that if most people imagined that their lives were not productive of any lasting good, then most of the human race would simply go on strike.[3] Our life-long efforts would make less sense than the sand castles that my daughter and I like to build at Huntington Beach.

But Dyson rejects such gloominess. Without apology, he mixes philosophy, ethics, theology, and science to offer what he thinks is a scientifically possible and humanly preferable vision. The universe, he contends, is infinite in all directions. Life that has given rise to mind will continue to reach into all corners of the expanding universe. As the universe continues to expand and cool, increasingly clever minds will find ever new ways to draw heat and energy from matter. Such minds may also find perfectly efficient ways to communicate with each other across ever-widening distances, thus continually expanding the network of friendships and acquaintances. In other words, Dyson hopes for a universe, including intelligent life, without end. He calls on his contemporaries to let their imaginations wander among the stars so that they too "may hear whispers of immortality."[4]

When I let my own mind wander through the universe and contemplate the destiny of my world, I, too, hear promises of immortality. They are, to be sure, fed by sources different from Dyson's. But they satisfy, I suspect, much the same longing—a desire to have grounds for hope.

I first became aware of those promises as a child. They are linked in my memory with small metal cannisters containing filmstrips. My father bought these as aids in giving Bible studies to neighbors or acquaintances—anyone, actually, who admitted the slightest interest. Each cannister had a small round label disclosing the topic of the filmstrip inside: the Sabbath, the Battle of Armageddon, the seven last plagues, the state of the dead, the investigative judgment, the Second Advent of Jesus, the Millennium. Inserted properly into a cumbersome projector with an enormous bulb which produced near-blinding light and no small amount of heat, the filmstrips came alive.

Through these filmstrips, with their fantastic pictures and key texts from the Bible, and through a few family books, Sabbath sermons, and occasional evangelistic meetings, a country boy learned the Adventist vision of the end of the world: Soon Jesus will come again. If our names have been cleared in the judgment, we will be translated (or, if we have died, resurrected) to meet Jesus in the air. Then we will ascend to heaven where, for a thousand years, we will learn the truth of God's judgments. Finally, we will return to a world that will be cleansed from sin and death, there to spend eternity in the presence of Jesus. The sensational pictures of those filmstrips could not have shone more brightly. Nor could they have produced in a young boy any greater certainty of belief.

Even if the intervening years have dimmed some features of those wonderful images, I believe the Adventist vision of the future may still bless us. It may, that is, if the vision establishes in us firmer belief in a gracious God. And it may if it leads us to a more mature understanding of the relationship between our hopes for a heavenly future and our responsibilities in the present.

To illustrate what I mean, I will explore a component of Adventist eschatology that might seem an unlikely topic for consideration in this volume: the millennium. I take it as representative of the Adventist heritage of apocalyptic vision that fueled this movement at its beginning. Even now, while those Adventists I know best are are less likely than their predecessors to dream millennial dreams, the vision of a heavenly future hovers over contemporary Adventist thought like a residue of stardust. What, if anything, might this most heavenly of Adventist doctrines have to do with ethics?

Alternative Interpretations

The doctrine of the millennium (a non-biblical expression for the biblical idea of a thousand-year reign with Christ) is based on the passage from the Apocalypse with which I opened this essay. It is difficult to think of a few sentences that have produced more strident debate among Christians than these cryptic expressions. They have been the wellspring of continual speculation about the details of human destiny. St. Augustine summed up the frustration many Christians have had with such speculation when he complained that the Revelator's millennial teaching "has been misunderstood by some of our people and...has even been turned into ridiculous fables."[5] He was especially disgusted by those who imagined the millennium to be a time of "the most unrestrained material feasts."

I suspect that a number of Augustine's readers found his own view of the millennium something of a "ridiculous fable." He believed that the millennium had begun at the First Advent of Jesus and would continue until His return. During this time Satan is spiritually "bound" in the sense that he is prevented from entering the lives of true believers. Those who are described in the passage as reigning with Christ, according to Augustine, are the ones who exercise authority over the church until the Second Advent.

I mention Augustine's view of the millennium partly to illustrate the diversity of interpretations to which this passage from the Apocalypse has been subjected. However, for my present purpose, the relationship between Augustine's conception of the millennium and his ethics is more interesting than his creative thinking about its time and place. His offense at the millenarian teachings of some of his fellow Christians clearly has a moralistic tone. To him, the thought of a thousand year "sabbath" of lusty feasting is repulsive. (One need know only a little about Augustine's lusty early biography to understand some of his disgust.) His own understanding of the millennium as the time between the First and Second Advents of Jesus also has significant implications for behavior. The binding of Satan means that he could no longer lead the church astray. True believers are now

164

liberated from Satan's power and can keep the commandments of Jesus. And if those who sit on thrones and reign with Christ are the ecclesiastical authorities, imagine the extent of their legitimate power.[6]

Over the centuries, millennial dreams multiplied, as did the interpretive schemes for understanding the twentieth chapter of the Apocalypse. Most of these views can be grouped loosely under three headings: premillennialism, postmillennialism, and amillennialism. It may be useful at this juncture to describe briefly some examples of each.[7]

Premillennialism lives on today among large numbers of conservative Christians. In their view, Jesus' Second Advent occurs prior to the millennium. (Hence the "pre" in "premillennialism.") Just before the *parousia* there are wars, famines, earthquakes, and a "great tribulation"(Mt 24:6-8). After Jesus arrives, a thousand-year period of peace begins, it is generally believed, on the earth. During this period the Jews are converted and play an important role in ruling the world with Christ. The earth, including its wildest beasts, is subdued and brought under the power of Christ. At the end of the millennium Satan foments a rebellion, but this uprising is crushed, the wicked are consigned to hell, and the everlasting reign of the righteous with Christ in Heaven begins.

In addition to charges of naive, literalistic biblicism, premillennialists have often been accused of morbid pessimism about achieving much good in the world. They are imagined to be preoccupied with the imminent destruction of this world and thus inclined to neglect present social responsibilities.

Postmillennialism commonly designates the belief that Christ's kingdom is already being established through the work of the gospel. As the world is gradually brought under the influence of the Christian faith, a long period of peace and justice will emerge. More and more people will be converted to Christianity. Evil will be more and more subdued. Finally—in more conservative versions of the postmillennial position—Jesus will come again, the dead will be raised, and heaven will begin.

Postmillennialists are supposed to be more willing to work to make the world a better place. They are often accused, however, of excessive optimism about the human potential for moral and spiritual progress. Critics have argued that good biblical exegesis is sufficient to refute postmillennialism. But if not, then, the twentieth century—with its two world wars (the second including the Nazi holocaust) and now the threat of

165

nuclear holocaust—has served to demolish permanently the credibility of the notion that the world is progressively improving. By the middle of the twentieth century, liberal optimism had come under the withering attack of leading theologians. Reinhold Niebuhr, for instance, wrote: "The history of mankind exhibits no more ironic experience than the contrast between the sanguine hopes of recent centuries and the bitter experience of contemporary man."[8] This view is now widely considered, as one sourcebook on Adventist thought puts it, "bankrupt today."[9]

Amillennialists believe that there is no specific period of one thousand years either prior to or following the Second Advent of Jesus. Rather, they believe that the verses in the Apocalypse are a symbolic reference to the entire story of the church, from Jesus' First Advent to His return. The details of the Apocalypse are spiritualized or allegorized so that they apply to the present life of the Church. In the church, Christ's kingdom has already begun. Already the souls of deceased Christians, including those martyred for their faith, are enthroned and reigning with Christ in heaven. The present kingdom of grace will finally become the kingdom of glory when Jesus comes again.

Amillennialists are often criticized for their erosion of belief in the literal promises of the Bible. For example, the first resurrection mentioned in the twentieth chapter of the Apocalypse must be reinterpreted as referring, say, to the rise of faith in the church. Where then, critics ask, is the firm hope in the promised resurrection?

Adventist Interpretation

Early Adventists took root in the type of literalistic biblical interpretation that felt no tug toward the allegorizing methods of the amillennialists. Even more offensive to the pioneers of Adventism were the postmillennialist promises of a gradually improving world. William Miller, for example, scoffed at what he and his associates called the doctrine of a "temporal millennium" which envisioned the spiritual reign of Jesus becoming worldwide through the work of the church. "Can any man, with a sound mind," Miller asked, "believe in a doctrine so full of absurdities?" His own conviction, at least, was clear: "I, for myself, can never believe it."[10]

What Miller and his cohorts *did* believe was a fervent brand of premillennialism. Their doctrine was given a measure of scholarly respectability when Harvard-educated Episcopal clergyman Dr. Henry Dana Ward chaired the first "General Conference of the Second Coming of Christ," which met in Boston in Joshua Himes' Chardon Street Chapel in October of 1840.

The major address of the conference was Ward's own lengthy disquisition on the history and basis of the Millerite perspective on the millennium. He canvassed the history of millennial interpretation, concluding with a militant affirmation of apocalyptic premillennialism: Jesus is coming in the clouds of heaven, Babylon will be defeated, the righteous will be resurrected, and the glorious millennium will begin. The conference ended with Ward's ringing declaration: "This is our millennium. Our faith sees no other, our hope anchors in no other, our heart embraces no other, for ourselves, for faithful Abraham, or any of his seed, or any of the seed of Adam."[11]

Miller's own exposition of the millennium is surprisingly simple when compared to his elaborate schemes for arriving at the time of the Second Advent. For example, in commenting on the passage that describes Satan as being bound for a thousand years, Miller says flatly: "I suppose this verse needs no explanation."[12] Later, referring specifically to the thousand years, he adds that since the Bible nowhere instructs us to place a figurative meaning on the duration, we "are to place upon it the most simple construction, and I shall therefore understand it literally."[13] His comments on Satan being "loosed a little season" at the end of the millennium are limited to one sentence: "This passage must be understood in its simple, plain meaning, no mystery in this."[14]

No mystery, indeed. With his generally literalistic approach to biblical interpretation, Miller was able to construct a relatively simple doctrine of the millennium: Jesus will come very soon. The saints, both the living and the resurrected dead, will be gathered to Jesus on this earth in the New Jerusalem where they will live for one thousand literal years. At the end of this time, the wicked will be resurrected and, with Satan as their leader, they will attempt to mount an attack on the Holy City. But they will be defeated quickly by the overwhelming power of God. They will be called before the final judgment, found guilty, and cast into everlasting torment. The earth finally will be cleansed and made available for the eternal habitation of the saints.

Miller appears to have been concerned mainly to refute the optimistic postmillennialism that was just then growing in popularity among America's mainline denominations. He simply could not find in Scripture the teaching that the world would progress through many more centuries to a state of bliss. Judging from the large numbers who accepted his message, Miller found audiences whose skepticism about human progress matched his own.

Among those who resonated positively with Miller's message were many of the early leaders of Seventh-day Adventism. The founders of Sabbatarian Adventism appear to have adopted most of Miller's premillennialism without much debate. His literal interpretations of the Second Advent and the millennium became foundational.

One interesting change, however, was made. The millennium, according to these Adventist pioneers, would occur in heaven, not on the earth.[15] This change gave Adventists an unusual (if not unique) view of the millennium. Other than this, the doctrine has remained almost entirely the way Miller delivered it.

Nor has there been much debate about the matter. The millennial view that became standard in Adventism was incorporated in the writings of Ellen White and thereby received the prophetic confirmation important to so many Adventists.[16] And in his massive *Daniel and the Revelation* Uriah Smith gave comprehensive expression to the orthodox Adventist interpretation of biblical prophecies, including the now-standard view of the heavenly millennium.[17] The first Adventist statement of fundamental beliefs (penned by Smith and offered cautiously because of concern about creedalism) included a straightforward affirmation of premillennialism and an abrupt dismissal of postmillennialism, calling it a "fable."[18] In countless "prophetic charts," Adventists diagrammed the millennium, usually with a pillar at both ends of the thousand years and fine print listing all the events supposed to occur at each end.[19]

From the middle of the 1840s to the middle of the 1980s not much has changed in Adventism's official teachings about what happens after the Second Coming. People like James White and Uriah Smith would probably be pleased to preach the lines from Richard Rice's currently popular text on Adventist doctrine:

With other pre-millenialists [sic], Adventists believe that the thousand-year reign of Christ begins with his return to earth,… but they are unique

168

in locating this reign, not on earth, but in heaven. After rescuing his people from the earth, Christ returns with them to heaven, where they enter the glorious places he has prepared for them....[20]

Rice goes on, step by step, to complete the picture of the final judgment and the earth made new.

The fact that the doctrine of the millennium has occasioned little debate within Adventism does not mean that contemporary Adventist thinkers are unfamiliar with the biblical and theological objections to the doctrine. For example, New Testament scholar and theologian Sakae Kubo admits that the "Seventh-day Adventist interpretation has its difficulties...." Still, Kubo goes on to say, the Adventist model "seems more in harmony with the Scriptures, more consistent, and less confusing than the other views."[21]

Millennium and Morality

This is neither the time nor place, and I am not the person, to settle the exegetical debates about Apocalypse 20. Such resolution, if it is ever possible, must take seriously the historical and literary background of Jewish apocalyptic sources. It must also consider what these verses meant to their original author and audience. (Adventists need to be reminded from time to time that the Apocalypse was not a "closed book"—the word *apocalypse* comes from the Greek for "unveiling" or "revealing"—to its original readers or auditors.[22]) Throughout, there will be need to make room for honest differences of opinion.

Rather than attempt once more to prove the biblical rightness of a premillennialist position, I simply want to ask what difference it makes. Understood in the Adventist way, does the millennium matter? What difference *should* millennial dreams make?

I believe it is best to begin by acknowledging that the millennium may be a morally dangerous doctrine. There are at least three reasons this might be so:

1. Millenarian enthusiasm carries with it the danger of pride in being right about the details of the future. The history of useless and divisive speculation about the precise times and locations of future events is a

scandal to the Christian faith. (Such speculations are likely to increase as we approach the end of the present millennium.) There is a distressing irony in the fact that those whose eyes are supposedly fixed on heavenly peace have so often fought viciously with their fellow Christians about that heavenly vision.

Arrogant certainty about specific future events is biblically unfounded. Jesus' words of reassurance to His disciples as He anticipated the time when He must leave them are words for all disciples: "And now I have told you this before it occurs, so that when it does occur, you may believe."[23] The disciples' comfort in these words does not depend on detailed knowledge about the future. The comfort is in knowing Jesus upon whom that future depends. The Bible is not a *TV Guide* listing program details for *As the World Ends*.

The antidote for such misconceptions is the humility that faith produces in those who know the grace of God. We study eschatology to learn about the character of God, not to amaze (or terrorize) our friends and neighbors. As John Brunt writes: "Eschatology tells us what kind of God we serve by revealing what He values and wants to make part of the future world."[24]

2. Strong convictions about an imminent heavenly millennium may lead to attitudes of earthly irresponsibility. I wish that this were not so. And, in fact, I often think that such charges represent unfair typecasting. Ruth Alden Doan describes the common stereotype:

> Premillennialists, as most students of American culture could recite, are so taken with visions of impending doom that they have neither time nor motivation to do anything in this world. Pessimists to their very core, premillennialists remain passive, accept no individual responsibility for present and future needs, and deny that man can do anything for himself or for his miserable, fallen world.[25]

Doan quickly adds that the stereotype badly misrepresents reality. For example, William Miller and many of his closest associates were heavily involved in social reform movements both prior to and after coming to faith in an imminent Second Advent. Indeed, they were sometimes criticized for being too involved in making plans for a future on this earth!

Still the danger of irresponsibility exists. I remember, for example, the chapel talk an esteemed colleague once gave. After describing in fascinating detail the rapid depletion of many of this earth's most valuable, non-renewable resources, the professor reassured his audience that they need not be concerned: as Adventists, they knew that such depletion coincided with the final days of earth's history. Thus, the millennial dream provides this small spaceship of a planet with a heavenly escape hatch.

For any who would take such a position, it is tempting to remember another apocalyptic passage:

> We give you thanks, Lord God Almighty, who are and who were, for you have taken your great power and begun to reign. The nations raged, but your wrath has come, and the time for judging the dead, for rewarding your servants, the prophets and saints and all who fear your name, both small and great, *and for destroying those who destroy the earth.*[26]

The apocalyptic picture of judgment is one that should sober those who would show wanton disrespect for God's creation.

3. The millennial emphasis on future reward may rob the present of its joy. This problem was stated clearly by Pascal:

> We scarcely ever think of the present; and if we think of it, it is only to take light from it to arrange the future. The present is never our end....[T]he future alone is our end. So we never live, but we hope to live; and as we are always preparing to be happy, it is inevitable we should never be so.[27]

Focusing on future rewards may diminish present joys in several ways. A particularly dismal way is through fear that the reward will be denied. The combination of apocalyptic vision and moral perfectionism can turn millennial dreams into present nightmares. Too many Adventists have suffered from a kind of "Santa Syndrome"—Someone in Heaven is making a list and checking carefully to find who has been nice. The trouble is, as we all know deep down, none of us is nice enough.

The solution, of course, is the good news that the millennial dreams are secure for all who trust that the gift has already been given in Jesus Christ. No other gift is needed than the one a gracious God has already awarded.

This Gospel is also the foundation for a positive relationship between our millennial dreams and our moral responsibilities. Understood in light of the ministry of Jesus, the doctrine of the millennium may enhance our present sense of moral responsibility and empower our present moral actions. I mention only three examples.

1. According to the Apocalypse, "Blessed and holy are those who share in the first resurrection."[28] Resurrection hope, central to the millennial vision, revolutionizes our understanding of human history and human destiny.[29] That hope is based on the reality of Jesus' resurrection, which is foundational for genuine Christian faith. Paul writes: "[I]f you confess with your lips that Jesus is Lord and believe in your heart that God raised him from the dead, you will be saved."[30] And again from Paul: "If there is no resurrection of the dead, then Christ has not been raised; and if Christ has not been raised, then our proclamation has been in vain and your faith has been in vain."[31]

Jesus Christ *was* raised by God from the dead. Our faith is *not* useless. This is the New Testament faith: In the resurrection of Jesus the *eschaton* has already begun. With this faith, Christians are empowered already to begin living by the principles of God's kingdom.[32]

Perhaps the most radical example of this empowerment is the capacity of believers to choose death rather than forsake God's kingdom. It is not by chance that the millennial text attends to the reward of martyrs. These are they who courageously refuse to have their lives dominated by the beastly powers of evil—they who are liberated from the tyranny of the fear of eternal death. Certain of their faith in the resurrection of Jesus Christ, they know that history is not a closed deterministic system but is open to the transforming power of God. The martyrs of the apocalypse are representative of all who share the resurrection hope that enables believers to speak and live the truth, regardless of what the mighty "beasts" of this world may do.

I know of no more powerful source for living a morally courageous life than the belief that God in His love raised Jesus Christ from the dead and will do the same for all who believe.

2. As understood by Adventists, the millennium is a time for reigning and judging with Christ. The saved will be "priests of God and of Christ, and...will reign with him a thousand years."[33] This image of divine and human cooperation can have a potent impact on ethics.

This impact is perhaps best illustrated by referring to a passage from Paul that Adventists have often quoted in conjunction with the doctrine of the millennium.[34]

Do you not know that the saints will judge the world? And if the world is to be judged by you, are you incompetent to try trivial cases? Do you not know that we are to judge angels—to say nothing of ordinary matters?[35]

Whatever this may mean for a heavenly future, the point of the passage is clearly a practical one. Paul makes use of the eschatological prospect of cooperation in judgment to make a point about present moral responsibility. If we are to join in judgment then, how ought we to resolve our disputes with fellow believers now? If we are really preparing for that time, Paul states boldly, then Christians ought to stop cheating people now and find ways within the community of faith to resolve their differences. Indeed Paul implies that a Christian ought rather to be cheated than to seek redress through lawsuits against fellow believers.

The image of partnership with Christ in millennial judgment may have a further and more general implication for ethics now. This vision brings into sharp focus the character of a God who does not mind explaining at length the basis for proper judgment. If the saints are supposed to join in reigning and judging, they must understand the principles upon which the kingdom of God is founded. I like to think that the millennium symbolizes the willingness of God to take a very long time, from our present perspective, to make those principles clear.

As I imagine it, then, we imitate God whenever we take time to explain to one another the principled bases on which we make our own moral decisions.

3. The millennial text promises that the powers of evil will be contained for a time and then finally and decisively defeated. This happens not through human efforts but through the awesome power of God. This promise of ultimate victory encourages our present efforts by assuring us that any apparent defeat of the kingdom is only temporary.

In this world, the justice we seek to establish always turns out to be imperfect. The health we seek to restore is always threatened again by disease and death. The peace we long for is always transient. Without the promise of an eschatological confirmation of our efforts, temporary defeats could be overwhelmingly discouraging. Millennial dreams are no escape from our present efforts. Rather, the dreams continually renew our courage to make the principles of the Kingdom as clear and real as possible now. Our present efforts for the Kingdom are a preview of eternity. Ellen White said it well: When "we love the world as...[Jesus] has loved it, then for us His mission is accomplished. We are fitted for Heaven: for we have Heaven in our hearts."[36]

It can be no coincidence that Jesus' most apocalyptic sermon, as recalled by the church, begins with predictions of cataclysmic signs (earthquakes, wars, and pestilence) and ends with words such as "I was naked and you gave me clothing."[37] It is not by chance that a sermon which opens with a prediction of famine ends with "I was hungry and you gave me food."[38] The message to all Christians is clear: the Christ in whom we have faith and hope is met personally, mystically now in each person who suffers great need. We wait best for Him and for His millennium when we seek now, however imperfectly, to meet such needs.

The Coming Kingdom

It is unlikely that people will ever outgrow the need for a vision of human destiny. If Freeman Dyson's effort to find a scientific eschatology is not sufficient evidence, consider the present spate of "star-wars" films with their "great controversies" between good and evil forces. Clearly the Adventist vision is on a competitive footing with many others in modern culture.

I do not expect, nor do I desire, a return to the millenarian enthusiasm exhibited by many of our spiritual forebears. What I *do* hope is that we may retain the essence of their millennial dreams in ways that are presently and joyously responsible. This is a vision worth the trouble.

To be Adventist is to believe that the Christ of the resurrection is in charge of our ultimate destiny. The magnet of our millennial dreams draws us into action now on the side of Heaven's principles. If we understand this, we will be better able to join in the prayer of Jesus, "Your kingdom come. Your will be done, on earth as it is in heaven."[39]

Endnotes

[1] Rev 20:1-6.

[2] Freeman J. Dyson, *Infinite in All Directions* (New York: Harper & Row, 1988) 99.

[3] Pierre Teilhard de Chardin, *How I Believe* (New York: Harper & Row, 1969) 43.

[4] Dyson, 121.

[5] *The City of God*, 20.7.

[6] In this regard Augustine invokes the words from Matthew: "Whatever you bind on earth will be bound in heaven; and whatever you loose on earth will be loosed in heaven" (Mt 18:18).

[7] A useful exposition of these alternatives is found in Robert G. Clouse, ed., *The Meaning of the Millennium: Four Views* (Downers Grove, IL: IVP, 1977). The summaries in this paper are based to a large extent on the discussions in this volume.

[8] Reinhold Niebuhr, *Faith and History* (New York: Scribner, 1949) 1.

[9] [Roy A. Anderson, LeRoy E. Froom, W. E. Read, *et al.*,] *Seventh-day Adventists Answer Questions on Doctrine* (Washington, DC: Review and Herald, 1957) 475.

[10] *Miller's Works*, ed. Joshua V. Himes (Boston: Himes, 1842) 240.

[11] This account is taken from LeRoy E. Froom, *The Prophetic Faith of Our Fathers*, 4 vols. (Washington, DC: Review and Herald, 1954) 4: 567-76. A version of Ward's paper, "History and Doctrine of the Millennium," was subsequently printed as *The Hope of the Church: A History of the Doctrine of the Millennium* (Buchanan, MI: Western Advent Christian, 1869), which is available on microfilm at the Loma Linda University Library Heritage Room.

[12] William Miller, *Evidence from Scripture and History of the Second Coming of Christ about the Year 1843* (Sandy Hill, NY: Howland) 31.

[13] Ibid.

[14] Ibid., 32.

[15] I am uncertain about precisely how this change took place. Writing in 1855, and attempting to refute the idea that his and other Adventist pioneers' beliefs came more from his wife than from the Bible, James White claims that, since 1845, he has taught that the saints would be in heaven during the millennium. He also claims that E. R. Pinney taught this view as early as 1844 ("A Test," *Adventist Review* 7.8 [16 October 1855]: 61). LeRoy Froom suggests that the doctrine of a heavenly millennium was "consolidated" during the so-called "Sabbath Conferences" held throughout New England in 1848 (*Faith* 4: 1039-41). The change from an earthly to a heavenly millennium does not appear to have occasioned much debate.

[16] See, for example, Ellen White, *The Great Controversy* (Mountain View, CA: Pacific Press, 1911) 653-61.

[17] Uriah Smith, *Daniel and the Revelation* (Mountain View, CA: Pacific Press, 1892) 732-47.

[18] Uriah Smith, *A Declaration of the Fundamental Principles Taught and Practiced by the Seventh-day Adventists* (Battle Creek, MI: n.p., 1872).

[19] See, for example, *Bible Readings for the Home Circle* (Mountain View, CA: Pacific Press, 1916) 356; W. A. Spicer, *Our Day in the Light of Prophecy* (Mountain View, CA: Pacific Press, 1917) 350; T. Housel Jemison, *Christian Beliefs: Fundamental Teachings for Seventh-day Adventist College Classes* (Mountain View, CA: Pacific Press, 1959) 378.

[20] Richard Rice, *The Reign of God: An Introduction to Christian Theology from a Seventh-day Adventist Perspective* (Berrien Springs, MI: Andrews University Press, 1985) 332.

[21] Sakae Kubo, *God Meets Man: A Theology of the Sabbath and the Second Advent* (Nashville: Southern Publishing Association, 1978) 123.

[22] John Brunt makes this point nicely in *Now and Not Yet* (Washington, DC: Review and Herald, 1987) 39-41, 63-71.

[23] Jn 14:29.

[24] Brunt, 49.

[25] Ruth Alden Doan, "Millerism and Evangelical Culture," *The Disappointed: Millerism and Millenarianism in the Nineteenth Century*, ed. Ronald L. Numbers and Jonathan M. Butler (Bloomington, IN: Indiana University Press, 1987) 132-33.

[26] Rev 11:17-18; italics mine.

[27] Blaise Pascal, *Penseés* 172.

[28] Rev 2:6.

[29] I borrow some insights from Jürgen Moltmann, *Theology of Hope* (New York: Harper & Row, 1967), though many of our theological conclusions are vastly different.

[30] Ro 10:9.

[31] 1Co 15:13-14.

[32] The best single recent statement of this truth by an Adventist for Adventists is Brunt, *Now*, 29.

[33] Rev 20:6.

[34] Rice continues this tradition (333).

[35] 1Co 6:2-3.

[36] Ellen White, *The Desire of Ages* (Mountain View, CA: Pacific Press, 1909) 641.

[37] Mt 25:36.

[38] Mt 25:35.

[39] Mt 6:10.

Contributors

ROY BRANSON is Senior Research Fellow at the Kennedy Institute of Ethics, Georgetown University. After earning a BA in 1959 from Atlantic Union College, he earned an MA in English at the University of Chicago and an MA in Religion at the SDA Theological Seminary at Andrews University in 1961. He received a PhD in religious ethics at Harvard University in 1968, with a dissertation on the theories of religious pluralism of the American founding fathers. He is the editor of *Spectrum, the Journal of the Association of Adventist Forums,* and of three books—*Pilgrimage of Hope, Festival of the Sabbath*, and *Ethics and Health Policy.*

GINGER HANKS-HARWOOD is a theologian and liturgist currently residing in Southern California. She earned a PhD (1991) in religion and society in a joint degree program offered by the Iliff School of Theology and the University of Denver. Her research focused on peace activist women of the 1980s. She received the BA (1972) and MA (1974) in sociology from the California State University at Chico, in addition to non-degree graduate study in religion at Andrews University, and training in clinical pastoral education at Bethesda Hospital. She has worked as an assistant professor of religion at Pacific Union College, a hospital chaplain, an adjunct professor at Summit School of Theology, an instructor in Andrews University's Department of Behavioral Sciences, and a secondary school teacher. She is currently an adjunct professor of religion at La Sierra University and an adjunct Professor of Christian ethics at Loma Linda University.

MIROSLAV M. KIS is Professor of Ethics at Andrews University, where he also serves as chair of the department of Theology and Christian Philosophy. Born in Yugoslavia, he served as a medic in the Yugoslav army (1961-63) before pursuing post-secondary education at the Seminaire Adventiste, Collonges-sous-Saleve (1968-73) where he earned the LTh for a thesis on adolescent spirituality supervised by Paul Tournier. The Quebec Conference of Seventh-day Adventists sponsored his study for the MDiv at Andrews University (1976). He received a PhD in philosophical ethics from McGill University in 1983, with a dissertation addressing the relationship between revelation and ethics.

DAVID R. LARSON is Professor of Ethical Studies and Co-Director of the Center for Christian Bioethics at Loma Linda University. After graduating from Pacific Union College (1968), he earned the DMin at the School of Theology at Claremont (1973) and a PhD at Claremont Graduate School (1982), where his work focused on a Whiteheadian approach to bioethical decision-making. Subsequent study and research involved him in addressing a variety of bioethical dilemmas as a consultant to the Loma Linda University Medical Center and other health system corporations. He has published a number of articles in Adventist publications and is the editor of *Abortion: Ethical Issues and Options* as well as a forthcoming anthology of classic and contemporary Christian discussions of sexual ethics.

MARTIN E. MARTY is Fairfax M. Cone Professor of the History of Modern Christianity at the University of Chicago Divinity School. A graduate of the University (PhD, 1956), he is distinguished as a historian, churchman, and social commentator. Among his more than forty books are *A Cry of Absence: Reflections for the Winter of the Heart; Religion and Republic: The American Circumstance; The Irony of It All;* and *A Short History of Christianity.* He also serves as senior editor of the weekly, *The Christian Century.* He has served as president, and is now George B. Caldwell Scholar-in-Residence, of the Park Ridge Center, an institute for the study of health, faith, and ethics, where he edits the journal *Second Opinion.* He is past president of the American Academy of Religion, the American Society of Church History, and the American Catholic Historical Association. He is an elected Fellow of the American Academy of Arts and Sciences, holds over fifty honorary doctorates, and won the National Book Award for *Righteous Empire* in 1972.

MICHAEL PEARSON is Principal Lecturer in Philosophy and Ethics at Newbold College, England. He took the BEd in French and philosophy from the University of London (1970); he received an MTh in philosophical theology from the same institution in 1976 and the DPhil in religion and society from the University of Oxford in 1986. His study of Seventh-day

Adventist responses to selective issues in sexual ethics, *Millennial Dreams and Moral Dilemmas*, was published by Cambridge University Press in 1990.

JACK W. PROVONSHA is Professor Emeritus of Philosophy of Religion and Christian Ethics at Loma Linda University. After receiving a Bachelor of Arts of Pacific Union College (1943), he engaged in pastoral and evangelistic ministry before earning an MD from Loma Linda University (1953). Continuing his studies at Harvard University (MA, 1963) and Claremont Graduate School (PhD, 1967), Dr. Provonsha has drawn upon his background in religion and medicine to explore a variety of ethical and philosophical issues—ranging from the ethical status of hallucinogenic drug use to the implications of modern medicine for Biblical notions of human wholeness. He is a former consultant to the Committee on Bioethics of the American College of Obstetrics and Gynecology. In addition to various articles, he has written *God Is With Us; Is Death For Real?; You* Can *Go Home Again; Ethics in a Situation of Change;* and *A Remnant in Crisis.*

CHARLES SCRIVEN is President of Columbia Union College in Takoma Park, Maryland. His career has combined pastoral ministry (Upper Columbia Conference of Seventh-day Adventists, 1968-69, 1974-75; Potomac Conference, 1985-92), magazine editing (associate editor, *Insight: A Magazine of Christian Understanding*, 1969-73; co-editor, *Spectrum*, 1975-78) and college teaching (Walla Walla College, 1973-74, 1981-85). He earned a BA from Walla Walla College (1966) in theology and biblical languages; an MDiv from Andrews University (1968) in systematic theology; and a PhD from the Graduate Theological Union (1984) in theological ethics. In numerous articles he has expressed his interest in human rights, Christian responses to war, and the radical reformation roots of Adventist ecclesiological identity. He is the author of *Jubilee of the World; The Demons Have Had It;* and *The Transformation of Culture: Christian Social Ethics After H. Richard Niebuhr,* as well as the editor of *Into the Arena.*

CHARLES W. TEEL, JR. is Professor of Religion and Society and Founding Director of the Stahl Center for World Service at La Sierra University. After completing a BA at Pacific Union College (1962), he worked as a pastor and secondary school religion instructor and completed an MA in systematic theology at Andrews University; graduate study at Boston University (PhD, 1972) and Harvard Divinity School (ThM, 1970) followed. Interested in social change since his involvement in the civil rights movement during the 1960s, Dr. Teel's research has included a study in the sociology of religion focusing on pastors arrested during the civil rights years and a book—currently in progress—exploring the relationship between Seventh-day Adventist mission and social change in Peru's Lake Titicaca basin.

JAMES W. WALTERS pastored in Georgia and Southern California following his graduation from Southern College of Seventh-day Adventists (1968). He earned the MDiv from Andrews University (1970) and a PhD from Claremont Graduate School (1979) with a dissertation centering on the ethics of the Jewish philosopher Martin Buber. He is presently Professor of Ethical Studies at Loma Linda University and has served as Associate Director of the University's Center for Christian Bioethics. He is co-editor of the *Theological Bibliography of the SDA Theological Seminary;* author of *Living is Loving: Relationships Matter Most;* and a forthcoming book on Buber. He is also editor of *Bioethics Today—A New Ethical Vision; Christian Faith and Nuclear Peace;* and founding editor of *Adventist Today.* He served as General Chair of the Society of Christian Ethics, Pacific Section, in 1987.

GERALD WINSLOW is Dean of the Faculty of Religion at Loma Linda University. A graduate (BA, 1967) of Walla Walla College—where he also taught for fifteen years—and Andrews University (MA, 1968), he received a PhD at the Graduate Theological Union. Postdoctoral fellowships afforded opportunity for subsequent research at the Universities of Cambridge and Tübingen. In addition to teaching at Walla Walla, he has served as a chaplain in the Portland area (1967), as adjunct professor at Andrews University (1982) and San Francisco School of Theology (1980-present), as professor of religion and chair of the Religion Department at Pacific Union College (1989-1994), and as visiting professor at Newbold College, England. Since the publication of *Triage and Justice,* he has been recognized as a significant contributor to ethical discussions related to the problem of scarce resource allocation.

Index of Scriptural References

183

Index

C

F

G

H

M

N

O

P

Q

R

S

T

U

V

W